JOURNALISM AS PRACTICE

Winner of the 2008 Clifford G. Christians Ethics Research Award by the Carl Couch Center for Social and Internet Research

Winner of the 2008 Award for Top Book in Applied Ethics from the National Communication Association's Communication Ethics Division

Top Three Finalist for t̶   ̶tion
for Education in J̶

Technologica̶l ̶ has been accelerating the commo̶dification of the news into just another product. The emphasis on the bottom line has resulted in newsroom budget cuts and other business strategies that seriously endanger good journalism. Meanwhile, the growing influence of the Internet and partisan commentary has led even journalists themselves to question their role.

In *Journalism as Practice*, Sandra L. Borden shows that applying philosopher Alasdair MacIntyre's ideas of a "practice" to journalism can help us to understand what is at stake for society and for those who have made journalism their vocation. As traditional business and delivery models in journalism become transformed by new technologies and globalization, what has the potential to endure is a moral identity that transcends how journalism gets done and focuses on why it's worth doing in the first place. With an understanding of journalism as a practice, journalists can better organize themselves and their potential allies to promote and support virtuous work in journalism in today's rapidly changing media environment. Throughout, the book examines key U.S. journalism ethics cases since 2000. Some of these cases, such as Dan Rather's "Memogate" scandal, are explored in detail in *Practically Speaking* sections that discuss relevant cases at length.

This book is essential reading for students and practicing journalists interested in preserving the ethical role of journalism in promoting the common good.

Sandra L. Borden is Professor of Communication and Co-Director of the Center for the Study of Ethics in Society at Western Michigan University. She is also co-author of *Making Hard Choices in Journalism Ethics*, forthcoming from Routledge.

D0322115

Journalism as Practice
MacIntyre, Virtue Ethics and the Press

SANDRA L. BORDEN

Western Michigan University, USA

Routledge
Taylor & Francis Group
New York   London

Paperback edition published in 2010
by Routledge
270 Madison Ave
New York, NY 10016

Simultaneously published in the UK
by Routledge
2 Park Square, Milton Park, Abingdon, Oxon OX14 4RN

First published by Ashgate Publishing Limited in 2007.

Routledge is an imprint of the Taylor & Francis Group, an informa business

Library of Congress Cataloging-in-Publication Data
Borden, Sandra L., 1963–
Journalism as practice : MacIntyre, virtue ethics and the press / Sandra L. Borden.
p. cm. -- (Ashgate studies in applied ethics)
Includes bibliographical references and index.
1. Journalistic ethics. I. Title.
PN4756.B66 2007
174'.9097--dc22
2007013123

ISBN 10: 0-754-66060-5 (hbk)
ISBN 10: 0-415-87767-9 (pbk)

ISBN 13: 978-0-754-66060-6 (hbk)
ISBN 13: 978-0-415-87767-1 (pbk)

Contents

List of Tables

(2007) concept of a practice to journalism. It seems to me that MacIntyre's ideas can help us to understand what is at stake for society and for those in newsrooms everywhere who have made journalism their vocation. The release of a third edition of *After Virtue* makes such an examination especially timely.

I limit my argument to American journalism, since that is what I know, but I think the idea of a practice can be useful for analyzing other journalistic traditions as well. The book:

- Includes key U.S. journalism ethics cases since 2000. Some of these, including the Dan Rather "Memogate" scandal, are highlighted in *Practically Speaking* sections that discuss relevant examples at length.
- Applies Lorraine Code's (1987) concept of *epistemic responsibility* to characterize journalism as primarily an intellectual practice, which puts increased focus on the so-called intellectual virtues.
- Draws attention to the function of virtues at the level of the *practice*, not just at the level of *individual* practitioners.
- Critically analyzes professionalism as a form of collective organization that might boost the power of journalists relative to news organizations.
- Considers the possibility of an expanded role for non-profits, citizens groups, and other non-practitioners in organizing and supporting journalists in their commitment to preserve the integrity of their practice.

Sandra Borden

Acknowledgments

Journalism as Practice fits into a continuing program of research into the ethical problems posed by the commodification of journalism, beginning with my doctoral work at Indiana University. I thank David Boeyink, my adviser at Indiana, who has provided a model of the journalist-philosopher that inspires my work. I would be remiss if I did not also acknowledge Kevin Stoner, who first pointed me in the direction of philosophy at The Ohio State University, where I went after the *Sun* to do my master's degree.

I am also grateful, as always, for the wise counsel of my philosophical mentor, Michael Pritchard, who has offered helpful comments on the manuscript. I also have benefited from the work and suggestions of Michael Davis, who recommended that this book be published in his capacity as an editor of the Ashgate Studies in Applied Ethics series.

I also appreciate comments from reviewers and audiences who previewed several chapters from this book at conference presentations:

- I presented a version of Chapter 4 in August 2006 to the Association for Education in Journalism and Mass Communication in San Francisco.
- I presented a paper based on Chapter 5 in March 2006 at the 15th annual meeting of the Association for Practical and Professional Ethics held in Jacksonville, Florida.
- I presented a slightly different version of Chapter 7 in August 2005 at the annual convention of the Association for Education in Journalism and Mass Communication held in San Antonio, Texas.

Some of the ideas in this book appeared first in journal articles:

- I first presented my ethical resistance model in Borden, S.L. (2000). A model for evaluating journalist resistance to business constraints. *Journal of Mass Media Ethics, 15* (3), 149-166. That article and an accompanying figure are reprinted in Chapter 6, slightly revised, with permission from Lawrence Erlbaum Associates.
- The analysis presented in the *Practically Speaking* feature for Chapter 6 was first published in: Borden, S.L. (2002). Janet Cooke in hindsight: Reclassifying a paradigmatic case in journalism ethics. *Journal of Communication Inquiry, 26* (2), 155-170. That article is reprinted in Chapter 6 in condensed form with permission from Sage Publications.

All quotations of MacIntyre's theory come from Alasdair MacIntyre, *After Virtue*, Third Edition (© 1981, 1984, 2007 by Alasdair MacIntyre. Published by the University of Notre Dame Press). They are reproduced here with permission. My thanks to Barbara Hanrahan of the University of Notre Dame Press for kindly letting me preview the new prologue MacIntyre wrote for the third edition of his seminal book.

I would not have been able to write this book without the benefit of a sabbatical leave in 2004-05, for which I thank my institution, Western Michigan University. I also appreciate the strong support that WMU's School of Communication has always given to my work in journalism ethics. My thanks also to all those at Ashgate who were instrumental in improving my manuscript and getting this book to press, especially Managing Director Rachel Lynch, Editorial Manager Nikki Dines, and copy editor Wendy Pillar.

And, of course, I thank my husband, Randy, for his love and support before, during, and after my days as a journalist.

Chapter 1

Ethics and the Commodification of Journalism[1]

Carol, a co-anchor of a respected local news broadcast, had begun to have serious doubts about the direction in which her station was headed. Then, one day, the station hired a talk-show host known for his raunchiness and shocking behavior to appear on the 10 p.m. newscast as an occasional commentator. The co-anchor's doubts mushroomed into full-fledged disgust, and she resigned her job. The move, although not totally unexpected, nevertheless shocked the staff. That would be the last night that this journalist would sit at the anchor desk after more than a decade. Colleagues from news organizations all over town gathered at the station for a vigil over pizza and pop (Samuels, 1998). Earlier, the co-anchor had written in one of the city's daily newspapers: "Many of us in the trenches of this battle believe that television news is already overwhelmed with too many transient fires, random acts of mayhem and network programming plugs. And now we see ... the poster child for the worst television has to offer, being added to the 10 p.m. news menu." The talk-show host's response? "What the hell? It's only reading a prompter. I mean, they make it seem like it's journalism" (as cited in Futrelle, 1997).

The controversy generated intense criticism, leading both the talk-show host and the remaining co-anchor at the station to quit. Eventually, the station's president acknowledged that he had erred in hiring the talk-show host, and the station ran ads in all the local newspapers attempting to reassure viewers of its trustworthiness. The co-anchor, for her part, went on to bigger and better things, receiving recognition from a journalism association and eventually landing a spot as a correspondent for one of the American television networks (Mitchard, 1997; Samuels, 1998).

The journalist was Carol Marin, a respected investigative reporter for NBC affiliate WMAQ-TV in Chicago, as well as co-anchor of its 10 p.m. newscast. WMAQ-TV hired Jerry Springer as a commentator in 1997. As of this writing, Marin was back in Chicago as a special contributor to the local NBC station and a political columnist for the *Chicago Sun-Times*. As the Society of Professional Journalists award suggests, she has come to be regarded as something of a "paradigm person" (Pellegrino, 1995, p. 257) within the narrative tradition of virtue in American journalism. In a word, her story is a parable for journalists.[2] The purpose of this book is to develop

---

1   Portions of this chapter were originally published in Borden (2000).

2   Although the lessons we drew from this story are different, I owe the idea of thinking about it as a parable to syndicated columnist Jacquelyn Mitchard (1997) of Tribune Media Services Inc., who referred to the Marin–Springer stink as a "kind of parable" (¶2) about journalism in one of her columns.

cutbacks, 2004). Later, Carroll cited budgetary pressures from the Tribune Company as a reason for his departure (Folkenflik, 2005). A year later, Caroll's successor was crossing swords with Tribune higher-ups over the same issue. Dean Baquet, with the support of publisher Jeffrey M. Johnson, publicly refused to make the staffing cuts demanded by corporate headquarters in Chicago. Baquet explained:

> This newspaper does so many things. It is one of only three or four papers in the country with really robust foreign bureaus and that cover the war in Iraq in depth … We have a D.C. bureau that competes on every big story. We cover the most complicated urban and suburban region in America. We do a lot of other things. You can't continue to do that if [staff reductions] keep up. (Rainey, 2006a, ¶30)

Nearly half of the *Times*'s newsroom staff signed a letter backing Baquet and Johnson. Even the community got into the act, with a handful of wealthy residents making plans to buy the paper and operate it at a much smaller profit than the paper's 20 percent margin at the time. In a separate action, a local coalition of business people, including former US Secretary of State Warren Christopher, wrote to Tribune asking the company to stop making staff cuts at the *Times* (Seelye & Steinhauer, 2006). Employees at other Tribune properties jumped into the fray, citing budgetary concerns at their own newspapers. Almost 100 Newspaper Guild members at the *Baltimore Sun* signed a letter addressed to Tribune CEO Dennis FitzSimons stating that "sometimes you have to make the tough decisions and forgo short-term returns for long-term gains" (*Baltimore Sun* Newspaper Guild unit, 2006, ¶4). In an open letter to his publisher, a staff writer for the *Hartford Courant* wrote, "You can't make money at newspapering—and there is still plenty of money to be made in newspapers—by positioning the brand as a money-losing operation whose future depends on perpetual budget cutting and the concomitant erosion of quality" (Buck, 2006, ¶4). Unfortunately, the *Los Angeles Times* showdown did not end as well as the Marin incident. The Tribune company asked both Baquet and Johnson to resign and replaced them with executives who planned to move forward with the company's downsizing plans.

The *Los Angeles Times* was not alone in facing cuts. Several other newspapers took similar measures, including the *New York Times*, the *Boston Globe*, and the *Philadelphia Inquirer* (Seelye, 2005c). *Newsday*'s top editor, Howard Schneider, resigned in fall of 2004 in part because of the severity of the staff cuts imposed on his newsroom—50 out of about 570 newsroom staff (Madore, 2004). The job cuts followed the disclosure that *Newsday* and several other papers had inflated weekday circulation figures to boost advertising rates. It is not just large metropolitan dailies that are making cuts. Deb Flemming quit as editor of *The Free Press* in Mankato (MN) in April 2005 when owner Community Newspaper Holdings Inc. announced new budget targets. The cuts were not necessary because revenues were down or expenses ran higher than expected; they simply were intended to bring the budget into line with industry standards. The paper's editorial staff of 30 was considered excessive for a daily circulation of 22,500. With Flemming's resignation, a few more editorial staffers could keep their jobs. "You need people to do the job," Flemming told the Associated Press (2005b). "Without people, it will impact the quality of the product you give readers" (¶3).

In its comprehensive 2004 report of both new and aggregated data on American journalism in eight different media, the Project for Excellence in Journalism concluded that the touchstones of so-called mainstream journalism—newspapers, network television, local television, and the three big newsweekly magazines—had all suffered audience declines in the previous decade and that many traditional news outlets were making up for these losses by cutting staff, increasing workload, reducing newshole, and "in various ways that are measurable, thinning product" (p. 6). The organization's 2005 and 2006 updates found the trend in downsizing continuing, with prominent losses at large metropolitan newspapers, news magazines, and radio news departments. Some pockets of reinvestment surfaced in 2004, but they tended to focus on "repackaging and presenting information, not in gathering it" (Project for Excellence in Journalism, 2005, Overview: news investment, ¶8).

Underlying this financial instability are recent changes in technologies, laws, marketing strategies, and political ideologies that are transforming the media market. Perhaps most influential has been the transformation of capitalism itself. Ohmann (2003) argues that we are experiencing a shift from the large stable corporations that developed beginning in the nineteenth century to a new form of capitalism he calls "agile capitalism" (p. 193). The effect of agile capitalism on the news industry, as well as other knowledge-based industries, has been "an astonishing proliferation of goods and segmentation of markets" (p. 191) characterized by rapid innovation.

Unfortunately, traditional news media have lagged behind the innovation trend. For example, the Project for Excellence in Journalism found that 62 percent of Web journalists reported newsroom cuts in 2004—a greater level of cutbacks than any other news media that year. The authors speculated that Internet outfits had faced the biggest cuts because of relatively low revenues in an industry accustomed to unusually high profit margins. Now that they can no longer take market domination for granted, newspapers and the broadcast networks risk losing the upper hand to non-journalistic companies and individuals who are more willing to experiment and invest online (Meyer, 2004b; Project for Excellence in Journalism, 2005). Although data for the 2006 update indicated an increase in online investments, the industry has a lot of catching up to do, and it is not doing it particularly well. There are so many sources of "content" now that journalists also are bending their standards to gain access to sources in what has become a "seller's market for information," according to the Project for Excellence in Journalism. The authors of the 2004 report concluded that the press is simultaneously being pulled in the directions of fragmentation and convergence as audiences disperse into niches and news outlets get swallowed up by ever-bigger conglomerates. The result: "Journalism is in the middle of an epochal transformation, as momentous probably as the invention of the telegraph or television" (p. 4).

The Ethical Costs of Commodification

Jane Jacobs (1992) talks about two survival strategies that provide the moral foundations for different occupational specialties. The commercial syndrome is the strategy of those who trade for a living and provide for a society's basic needs—in the case of the news industry, the executives and advertisers. The guardian syndrome is the strategy of those who administer, acquire or protect various kinds of territories. Its aim is to prevent corruption and fight enemies, including foes such as disease and ignorance. In the case of reporters, the aim is to guard the moral order itself, according to Ettema & Glasser (1998), who aptly describe this role as "moral custodianship" (p. 63). Other guardians include professionals and artists, who may protect learning and art by monopolizing knowledge, for example, or protecting the creative process. They perfect their talents primarily for the sake of their work's intrinsic value—not economic gain—within traditional frameworks that are themselves carefully guarded. The commercial and guardian syndromes contradict each other because they rely on different moral precepts. Therefore certain things are virtuous in one syndrome but vicious in the other. Each syndrome, taken by itself, is morally legitimate and internally consistent. However, when one syndrome arbitrarily chooses moral precepts from both spheres, it can become systematically corrupt, losing its meaning and failing to check its own worst vices. The result is degeneration into what Jacobs calls "monstrous moral hybrids" (p. 80).

Journalism is in danger of becoming such a monster. Gardner, Csikszentmihalyi & Damon (2001) in *Good Work* argue that journalism has been corrupted because editors, rather than being its guardians as before, have become "agents of the corporate hierarchy" (p. 134). Unfortunately, executives tend to see wealth as the ultimate good. Executives are not the only ones guilty of this, of course. Money is what drives not only the investment market, but medicine, law, education, and a host of other spheres in which excellence should not be defined in monetary terms (Ohmann, 2003). Governing these spheres on the basis of market principles distorts the meaning of health, justice, and learning just as surely as the meaning of an honor is lost if one could merely buy it. In a similar way, making the news nothing but a commodity to be shaped according to a market's taste leaves it with no intrinsic value.

Nevertheless, the managers' sphere and the journalists' sphere are necessarily linked by circumstance. Journalism in the United States is a private business that relies on advertising revenues and (to a lesser and lesser extent) subscribers to underwrite its good works. Journalism needs business to finance news production and distribution, and to retain its independence from the state. At the same time, business needs journalism. Evidence has accumulated in the newspaper industry, at least, to show that quality is positively associated with audience loyalty and higher household penetration in the long run.[4] When quality goes down beyond a minimal level, circulation drops too. Advertisers go where the readers are. "Aggressive dilution of the quality of their journalism can make managers look like geniuses to

---

4   However, actual causation cannot be proven in non-competitive markets, where the effects of newsroom investments are difficult to determine (Meyer, 2004b).

their investors for a while. But, in time, the inevitable price is paid" (Meyer, 2004b, p. 215). The symbiosis between business and journalism, in short, is a difficult but necessary one.

For this symbiosis to work well, trade-offs are required on both sides to preserve the integrity of each sphere. Unfortunately, the trade-offs that take place in news organizations tend to be tacit and to disproportionately favor commercial interests. MacIntyre (1979) notes that organizations tend to tie profit to other organizational goals (for example, if we increase our ad revenue, then we have more newshole). This is how news organizations can combine commercial and guardian priorities together in a way that disguises potential clashes between the two camps. Organizations also prevent open conflict with commercial goals by compartmentalizing expertise and responsibility so that the two kinds of values do not appear to contradict each other (Keough & Lake, 1993).

> Such partitioning of human experience enables people to operate with two discourses that are logically contradictory; they use each when situationally appropriate (Silverman, 1993). This is essentially a coping strategy—necessary for everyday functioning, but undesirable insofar as it obscures value tradeoffs and corrupts the integrity of each domain (Jacobs, 1992). Deep-seated contradictions between the two syndromes may emerge only when traditional roles become blurred (Keough & Lake, 1993), as when one party views as a journalism issue what another sees as a purely business matter. (Borden, 1997, p. 39)

An example would be closing a news bureau. Journalists would see the news bureau as an important way to stay abreast of developments in an important location, to cultivate sources, and so on. A manager may look at closing the bureau as simply a matter of cutting costs and using resources more efficiently (perhaps substituting wire coverage for the correspondents who used to report out of the bureau).

Loss of Public Confidence

Some observers have pointed to newsroom cuts and competitive market pressures to explain a rash of recent press scandals:

- *USA TODAY* discovers that its best foreign correspondent is guilty of repeated fabrication and plagiarism.
- Local television stations get caught airing unlabeled "video news releases" from the government as news.
- The *New York Times* investigates substandard reporting of government officials' statements leading up to the Iraq War.
- CBS News relies on unauthenticated documents to back up an explosive election-year story questioning the president's military service.
- *Newsweek* retracts an incendiary story reporting that the government had found evidence of Qu'ran desecration by US military officers at Guantanamo Bay.
- Reuters distributes doctored photographs of fighting in Lebanon from its understaffed global photo desk in Singapore.

It is little wonder that the sources for Jayson Blair's fabricated stories never reported his inaccuracies to the *New York Times*. "It may be that the expectations of the press have sunk enough that they will not sink much further. People are not dismayed by disappointments in the press. They expect them" (Project for Excellence in Journalism, 2005, Overview: public attitudes, ¶21). Lack of confidence makes it hard for journalists to serve the public well. From a business standpoint, it also affects journalism's ability to sell audiences to advertisers (Meyer, 2004b).

The American public's low opinion of both newspaper and television journalists was confirmed in Gallup Poll results released at the end of 2004 indicating that journalists ranked lower on honesty and ethical standards than bankers and auto mechanics (Mitchell, 2004). Between 1985 and 2002, in fact, the percentage of people rating news organizations as highly professional and moral fell dramatically, while the proportion who thought the news media tried to hide their foul-ups jumped from 13 to 67 percent, according to survey trends aggregated by the Project for Excellence in Journalism (2005). Cable news—with its opinionated programming airing 24 hours a day alongside more traditional journalism—ranked highest, at 38 percent, in "doing the best job of covering news lately" in a survey conducted by the Pew Research Center for the People and the Press in early 2002. For perspective, the 2004 Project for Excellence report notes that this percentage is "more than twice that of network, nearly three times that of local television and nearly four times that of newspapers" (p. 19).

These shifts in audience confidence crystallized during the 2004 US presidential election. Voters relied on the Internet for election news to an unprecedented degree. According to a survey of 1209 voters conducted after the election by Pew Research Center for the People and the Press (2004a), 21 percent used the Internet as their main source of campaign information, compared with 3 percent in 1996 and 11 percent in 2000. Although reliance on newspapers increased to 46 percent from 39 percent in 2000, it pales in comparison to the 60 percent of voters who cited newspapers as their main source in 1996. Continuing earlier trends from the 1990s and 2000, television remained the major source of campaign news for 76 percent of voters. Yet the single most dominant television source was not a traditional journalism outlet, but Fox News, with its partisan journalism format. Fox News was cited by the single largest percentage of voters (21 percent); the most cited network source was NBC News (13 percent). In a separate Internet survey of 2543 wired newspaper readers from around the country, the Associated Press Managing Editors' National Credibility Roundtables Project reported that those who considered blogs especially useful cited the new online journals' willingness to question the mainstream media as a major aspect of their appeal. Michael Hodges of Nashua, NH, said in his e-mail response to the survey: "In the aggregate, bloggers are much more balanced because they instantly call one another on bias, slant, errors in logic, and inadequate information. It's a network effect that is better than the mainstream 'networks'" (Pitts, 2004, ¶5).

The View from Journalists

Traditional journalists have become defensive in response to such attitudes. Their pessimism just seemed to be confirmed when they discovered in early 2005 that a correspondent for an online "news" service owned by a Texas GOP activist had been given daily passes to White House press briefings and news conferences for two years, despite using an alias. The correspondent, James D. Guckert, wrote for a conservative web site called Talon News under the pseudonym Jeff Gannon. Guckert first drew attention because of the perception that he asked easy, partisan questions at briefings and news conferences, in effect passing off propaganda as news with the Bush Administration's complicity (a role lampooned for several weeks by Garry Trudeau in the daily political cartoon Doonesbury). Guckert, who had no journalistic experience, later resigned from Talon News; the site itself shut down for revamping in the wake of the scandal, according to a message posted to the site (www.talonnews.com). Besides questioning the decision by the White House press secretary to give a daily press pass to someone not using his real name, veteran White House reporters questioned the scrutiny being given to the legitimacy of news organizations allowed representation in the White House briefing room. *New York Times* reporter Richard Stevenson complained in an interview with trade magazine *Editor & Publisher*: "I don't think it is good for our profession to have the briefing room hijacked" (Strupp, 2005).

Later that year, Hollywood actor Sean Penn went to Iran to report for the *San Francisco Chronicle* (Fathi, 2005) and Yahoo! News started testing a search tool that would pull up results from blogs as well as mainstream news sources (DiCarlo, 2005). In this kind of climate, it may not be surprising that a substantial majority of the nearly 550 journalists surveyed in 2004 by the Research Center for the People and the Press "believe that increased bottom line pressure is 'seriously hurting' the quality of news coverage" (Pew Research Center for the People and the Press, 2004b, ¶2). The report noted that the percentages of both national and local journalists concerned about business pressures were considerably higher than in earlier surveys conducted in 1995 and 1999. Journalists associate profit-driven news decisions with infringements on their autonomy and with potential conflicts of interest (Borden, 2000), as reflected in all the codes suggesting that "journalists—individually or in the aggregate—are, or should be, free of business-related constraints imposed by those who pay them and distribute their work" (McManus, 1997, p. 8). They also worry that bottom-line pressures lead to sloppy, simplistic, timid reporting (Pew Research Center for the People and the Press, 2004b). A former newspaper reporter, who is now a book editor, complained in a letter sent to the Romenesko blog run by the Poynter Institute:

> You still have many good newspapers and reporters out there. But you run a bank, you hire bank tellers. You run a fast-food joint, you get people flipping burgers. You run a newspaper where the priority is high profits for distant shareholders, where stories become "product," where staffers become "human resources," where frightened reporters worry themselves sick over byline counts and "getting beat" by their shallow stories in the

competition, where pre-fab, art-driven layouts take priority over story content, then you get more dullards working for a Revenue Stream. (Henry, 2005)

In its 2006 report, the Project for Excellence in Journalism minced no words about who is winning the argument at the top levels of US news organizations:

> From here on, at many companies, the fight on behalf of the public interest will come from the rank and file of the newsroom, with the news executive as mediator with the boardroom. There are some notable exceptions, and journalists who work in those situations today consider themselves lucky. Meanwhile, at many new-media companies, it is not clear if advocates for the public interest are present at all. (Project for Excellence in Journalism, 2006, Major trends, ¶4)

Journalism as Practice

When a local news broadcast in a major market hires Jerry Springer as a commentator or the White House admits a reporter from a fake news agency to its press briefings, journalists' status as communicators with special claims to legitimacy is indeed precarious. From an ethical standpoint, journalism has to have a distinct identity if journalists are to clearly understand what they are and what they are not, if they are to stand for some things and against others. Without a clear articulation of their collective purpose, no one will have any kind of yardstick by which to judge journalistic performance. Former *Minneapolis Tribune* readers' representative Richard P. Cunningham (1995), writing soon after the Associated Press Managing Editors approved new ethical guidelines, underscored the importance of this step. "As the trash piles up higher around us," he wrote, "we need to convince readers and viewers that we are different! What better way than to publish a clear set of ideal guidelines, to say publicly that we live and work by them and to invite readers and viewers to cite particular clauses in the guidelines when they think we have violated them?" (p. 12).

Unfortunately, Springer's crack about local television news not even being journalism hits close to home. The handling of former President Clinton's affair with intern Monica Lewinsky continues to be an instructive example of how blurred the boundaries between journalism and other non-fiction media have become. When the story first broke, Lewinsky led the network broadcasts—and also *Entertainment Tonight*. Some Associated Press photographers, in their zeal to get a picture, followed the car in which Lewinsky was driving so closely that they actually bumped into it—no better than the mercenary paparazzi. Meanwhile, the esteemed Washington Post was taking its cues from the notoriously unreliable Drudge Report on the Internet. In subsequent weeks, the Lewinsky story overshadowed the collapse of the Russian economy, the Serbian assault on ethnic Albanians in Kosovo, and the first US federal budget surplus in decades. When journalists act too much like entertainers, people just assume that journalists are in it for the money, for the fame, for the titillation. When journalists act too much like partisans, people assume that they are not making a serious effort to rein in their prejudices. The stakes are high. If journalists are unable to clarify journalistic goals in relation to other occupations (Winch, 1997, p.

3), they may not be able to ensure meaningful control over what is defined as news, command substantial autonomy in how they do their work, or summon enough credibility to perform their social functions.

Practice Makes Perfect

American journalists have tried to stand out by identifying themselves as the only occupation tagged for constitutional protection and by taking on the trappings and obligations of professionals. So far, these arguments have not succeeded in giving journalists a group identity that can withstand the pressures of commodification in current market conditions. I hope to show that journalism as practice has the potential to serve this function. Journalism as practice is a normative concept that entails the following characteristics: an institutional context, an overriding purpose, a viable moral community, collective organization, and internal goods that can only be realized and extended through the practice.

The outline of my argument is as follows. Chapter 2 lays out the virtue-ethics framework upon which MacIntyre (2007) relies and critically discusses the notion of a practice as it applies to journalism. Chapter 3 details journalism's tradition. A tradition, as MacIntyre describes it, is an historically situated, ongoing argument about what constitutes the good life. Journalism's tradition articulates what constitutes good journalism and being a good journalist. I will focus on ideas related to the development of reporting as an occupation and as a distinct identity. In the first of four *Practically Speaking* features that discuss relevant examples at length, a sidebar to Chapter 3 examines an important *character*, or model, of virtue in journalism: CBS reporter Edward R. Murrow.

Chapter 4 sets out the distinguishing marks of *journalism as practice*, as well as its *telos*, or ultimate purpose. A theory of journalism is proposed that relies on a communitarian account of participatory citizenship and Code's (1987) notion of epistemic responsibility. This chapter, finally, offers a preliminary account of the practice's internal goods—those that are oriented toward the realization of the *telos* and that can only be realized as a journalist.

Chapter 5 explains the intellectual and moral virtues needed to realize and extend journalism's internal goods, including intellectual honesty and moral courage. It identifies institutional goods external to the practice of journalism that have the potential to corrupt the practice, including profit. The emphasis of the discussion will be on virtues needed to sustain the practice, rather than on individual virtues needed to demonstrate good character. The *Practically Speaking* feature takes a look at how *Newsweek's* Qu'ran desecration story from 2005 failed to meet the highest standards of journalism's discipline of verification.

Chapter 6 focuses on the practice as a moral community that can support journalists who resist ethically questionable business requirements. The concepts of shame and solidarity will be analyzed to argue that an effective moral community fosters a true willingness among journalists to sanction each other and also to go to each other's aid. The chapter concludes with a discussion of individual resistance in the absence of such support, including a model for evaluating resistance options. The *Practically Speaking* feature illustrates how the practice provides an interpretive framework for collectively understanding and refining important moral concepts, using as an example journalists' evaluation of the 1981 Janet Cooke fabrication case at the *Washington Post*.

Chapter 7 critically analyzes the potential of professionalism as a form of collective organization for *journalism as practice*. Two key functions of professionalism are analyzed—ethical motivation and occupational power—in terms of both their potential usefulness and their potential problems. A range of options for the organization of journalists are presented. The *Practically Speaking* feature discusses rhetoric produced by journalists to differentiate themselves from the bloggers who discredited *60 Minutes Wednesday's* 2004 report on the National Guard service of President George W. Bush.

The final chapter discusses some promising developments, including recent efforts by non-profit organizations and media-reform groups to promote quality journalism. Attention also is given to the responsibility of news managers and news organizations for sustaining *journalism as practice*. The chapter concludes by suggesting steps that journalists and citizens must take to launch a successful social movement aimed at protecting virtuous journalism from the excesses of commodification.

Chapter 2

Journalism as Practice

Journalism seems to come into its own during natural disasters. The sheer drama of such events makes for great storytelling and provides a national showcase for the talents of local reporters. However, the extraordinary lengths to which journalists go to report the news suggest something much deeper is going on than the thrill of what-a-story or the calculations of career climbing. Whether it is Los Angeles during the 1994 earthquake or Grand Forks, ND, during the 1997 flood, journalists set aside competitive considerations to help their colleagues and endure extreme personal hardships to give communities the news they need. This was illustrated again in 2005 when the great flood caused by Hurricane Katrina overcame the historic American city of New Orleans and chased out the staff of the *Times-Picayune*.

The paper had warned its readers about the likelihood of just such a tragedy a few years earlier; *Picayune* reporters were the first to spot a levee breach after Katrina rifled through the area. The staff evacuated the newspaper building and set up shop temporarily at *The Courier* in Houma and *The Advocate* in Baton Rouge. Meanwhile, an intrepid band of eight reporters and one photographer returned to the city to report on the fate of its citizens amid the heat, the violence, and the chaos of post-Katrina New Orleans. At first, the paper was unable to put out a print edition and instead published on its affiliated Nola.com web site. HELP US, PLEASE was the headline read by millions around the country and around the world. When the *Picayune* finally was able to produce a print edition, staffers distributed it free at the Convention Center, where thousands of trapped survivors eagerly sought copies to get news of missing family members and of help on the way (Guernsey, 2005; Rosenthal, 2005).

Summing up the significance of what these journalists did, *Columbia Journalism Review* contributor Douglas McCollam (2005b) wrote, "Living mostly in borrowed houses, often separated from friends and family, wearing donated clothes, and working with hand-me-down equipment and donated office space, the paper managed to produce coverage of the disaster that serves to remind us all of just how deep is the connection between a city and its newspaper, how much they need each other" (¶4). McCollam noted that the parent company of the *Picayune* is privately owned and, therefore, "insulated from the quarterly earnings metric that drives so much newspapering today" (¶7). Whether there would be anyone to advertise in the paper or even to buy the paper was set aside, at least for the time being. This decision was made despite uncertainty about the paper's own ability to continue operating in coming months. Journalism transcended business.

The work that has been done in virtue ethics is helpful for understanding the deeper meaning of journalistic work. Klaidman & Beauchamp (1987) were the first to flesh out a virtue-ethics framework for analyzing journalistic morality.

Lambeth (1992) relied on virtue theory for deducing "habits" of good journalism (p. 25) that lead to the achievement of standards of excellence, preferably enforced through accountability mechanisms such as media criticism. More recently, Gardner, Csikszentmihalyi & Damon (2001) referenced virtue theory when they proposed that practitioners who do good work are those who perform proficiently with a sense of social responsibility and self-reflection. They recommended that good practitioners confronted with ethical dilemmas should consider their mission, the standards embodied in their profession, and their personal sense of identity—guidelines easily translated into the virtue-ethics concepts of a *telos*, the internal goods of a practice, and character.

Focus on Virtues

Virtue theory suggests that the way to understand ethics is in terms of pursuing a *telos*, that is, the good of a whole human life; the *telos* hinges partly on doing one's role-related work well. This goal-oriented, or teleological, feature of virtue ethics makes the theory especially useful when examining the ethic of a group united behind a common purpose (Oakley & Cocking, 2001; Pellegrino, 1995) or moral ideal (Davis, 1987). General agreement on such a purpose informs a mutual understanding of what it means to be good and helps those participating in such groups to recognize models of virtue. An occupation's purpose provides it with moral justification, from a virtue perspective, if it can be integrated into a broader conception of what is good for humans. This is a feature of classical virtue theory called *eudaimonia*.[1] Human flourishing is more than just human welfare, or benefit, or utility—it is human excellence, "maxing out" as a human being. For Aristotle, human flourishing was associated with reason and was exemplified in the man of practical wisdom (the role of practical wisdom and the other intellectual virtues will be discussed in Chapter 5).

To achieve the *telos*, one must practice standards of excellence that express the virtues. A virtue, or *habitus*, is a "predictable disposition to choose the good whenever confronted with a choice" (Pellegrino, 1995, p. 257). A virtuous person is said to have good character. The relevance and application of the virtues vary from context to context. However, the theory's recognition that there are objective conditions for human flourishing keeps virtue from being relativistic: "It is the *telos* of man as a species which determines what human qualities are virtues" (MacIntyre, 2007, p. 184). All of the virtues are good in themselves; they do not boil down to some ultimate good such as utility (Oakley & Cocking, 2001).[2] One advantage of virtue ethics is that it accepts the agent-relative quality of some virtues such as

---

1   Prior (2001) suggests that many modern virtue theories have gotten away from *eudaimonia* because of its association with discredited theories of human nature and provides an Aristotelian defense of the concept.

2   MacIntyre (2007) notes that the virtues in an Aristotelian ethic are a means to the end of achieving the *telos* for human beings, but only in an internal sense. In other words, "the end cannot be adequately characterized independently of a characterization of the means" (p. 184).

friendship. Thus, the theory can explain why members of some groups have rights and responsibilities that do not apply to outsiders (such as cutting someone's chest open with a surgical instrument or going into a war zone to take photographs). It also can explain why it may be morally desirable to prefer one person over another when faced with conflicting interests (the way a professional prioritizes her clients). Virtue theory's emphasis on the habitual disposition to do the right thing also takes morality out of the realm of calculations and into the realm of moral responsiveness. This ethical constancy can be an important asset. As Klaidman & Beauchamp (1987) note, "Virtuous traits of all kinds are especially significant in crises and in environments such as journalism that are often too pressured to permit prolonged and careful reflection" (p. 19).

Although principle-based theories do not outright exclude the virtues, they usually relegate them to supporting roles: Virtues predispose people to do their duty, maximize utility (MacIntyre, 2007; Pellegrino, 1995), or follow a profession's code of ethics (Davis, 1999), but are not needed to justify responsible conduct.[3] Virtue theory is less interested in the rightness or wrongness of discrete actions—the main concern of principle-based theories—because it does not consider these to be meaningful when abstracted from the context of a specific quest for excellence. Instead of focusing primarily on journalists' scope of obligation when deciding issues such as deception and privacy invasion, for example, we would ask what it means to be a good journalist in the context of journalism's mission. Indeed, virtue theory sometimes would require journalists to go above and beyond the call of duty:

> Act-based ethicists have invented the category of the supererogatory to handle acts that are better than what duty requires, but this category gets little attention, and its analysis is generally peripheral to the heart of the theory. In contrast, an act that is not only something a virtuous person might do but expresses the virtuous agent's virtue is morally praiseworthy, not simply free from blame, and is the central concept in virtue ethics. (Zagzebski, 1996, p. 233)

Moral and Intellectual Virtues

Aristotle (trans. 1984) thought there were two kinds of virtues: intellectual virtues, acquired inductively through accumulated experience with actual cases; and moral virtues, acquired through habit with the help of proper examples and guidance. The end of intellectual virtues is knowledge; the end of the moral virtues is goodness. The two kinds of virtues are intimately connected. Some virtues, including patience and perseverance, "are causally necessary for having intellectual virtues." Some

---

3   Principle-based theories include utilitarianism, which justifies particular moral judgments on the basis of whether the possible consequences maximize the welfare of as many stakeholders as possible; and deontology, which bases justification on whether the moral agent has obeyed moral laws that make some actions intrinsically right and others intrinsically wrong. Arjoon (2000) sums up the kinds of questions typically asked by principle-based theories: "What is one's moral obligation? What ought we to do? What is our duty? What is the ultimate principle of right and wrong?" (p. 160).

virtues, including honesty and modesty, "have both moral and intellectual forms" (Zagzebski, 1996, p. 159). No rules or limitations constrain the exercise of the virtues except for "those acts and dispositions that do not allow of a mean," for example, murder and spite (Pellegrino, 1995, p. 257). Virtuous dispositions are found in the mean between excess and deficiency. Code (1987) suggests this idea can even be applied to the virtue of integrity: Too little and you do not deserve to be called virtuous; too much, and you drift toward dogmatism. In any case, "Virtues, both moral and intellectual, have more to do with ways of relating to the world than with the 'content' of particular actions or knowledge claims" (pp. 52–53).

Just as there are temptations that thwart our moral efforts, there are temptations that interfere with our efforts to know well:

> Intellectually virtuous persons value knowing and understanding how things really are. They resist the temptation to live with partial explanations where fuller ones are attainable; they resist the temptation to live in fantasy or in a world of dream or illusion, considering it better to know, despite the tempting comfort and complacency a life of fantasy or illusion (or one well tinged with fantasy or illusion) can offer. (Code, 1987, p. 59)

Code (1987) identifies the nexus of ethics and epistemology as "responsibilism" (p. 50). She says moral reasoning typically proceeds "from epistemic to ethical (from what I know to what I do)"[4] and that the epistemic efforts involved in such reasoning can be criticized, *as well as* the ethical action ultimately taken on the basis of those efforts. This notion of epistemic responsibility is clearly illustrated in the "Memogate" case from 2004.[5] The *60 Minutes Wednesday* team that produced the segment on President Bush's National Guard service can be faulted *both* for the shoddy verification processes that undercut the story's reliability, *and* the decision to rush the story to air despite reasons to question the source and authenticity of key documents.

The classic Aristotelian virtue that "fuses the intellectual virtues … with the moral virtues" (Pellegrino, 1995, p. 257) is *phronesis* (referred to variously as practical wisdom, prudence, or discernment in the virtue literature). Moral virtues identify the right desires and human goods that constitute the good life. *Phronesis* is the intellectual virtue that identifies virtuous means for achieving those goods; it performs a coordination function. Zagzebski (1996) says *phronesis* also performs a coordination function when it comes to cognitive activity: *Phronesis* ultimately mediates *both* moral and intellectual justification.

Despite the importance of *phronesis*, Aristotle thought the primary intellectual virtue was what he called philosophic wisdom: a capacity for contemplation of universal truths. Code (1987), however, prefers to think of philosophic wisdom as the "ultimate, possibly unattainable, goal toward which the epistemically

---

4   Code (1987) notes, however, that sometimes "ethical considerations are permitted to create epistemic constraints" (p. 79). A journalistic example might be a reporting team that stops digging for information that would invade someone's privacy, even though truncating the investigation in this way means they will not arrive at the best possible approximation of the truth.

5   This case is discussed at length in the *Practically Speaking* feature for Chapter 7.

responsible strive" (p. 54). Code suggests epistemic responsibility should be the major intellectual virtue instead because it better conveys the "active nature of human cognitive life" (p. 54) and because knowledge is necessarily situated in experience or human narrative, in MacIntyre's (2007) sense. Intellectual virtue, then, consists fundamentally of a "kind of humility toward the experienced world that curbs any excessive desire to impose one's cognitive structurings upon it" (p. 20). This humility is similar to journalistic skepticism. Altschull (1990) notes that skepticism, as understood by journalists, is not stubborn pessimism, but a belief that "absolute knowledge is impossible" and that inquiry must, therefore, "involve continual testing" (p. 355). Journalistic skepticism also incorporates an adversarial impulse that, when used responsibly, can "keep the epistemic community on its toes, to prevent it from settling into complacency or inertia" (Code, p. 55).

Cooper (1993) underlines the relevance of epistemic responsibility to journalism:

> If the news were perceived as a type of serialized fiction or daily distraction or entertainment "bait" for the advertisers' hook, then perhaps there need be no discussion of the journalists' epistemic responsibility. However, because most consumers treat news as a direct, even if somewhat distorted, conduit of "knowledge"—about an "outside world," about life's unveiling, about a collective reality—a discussion of epistemic responsibility among journalists becomes paramount. (p. 95)

Any attempt to exercise epistemic responsibility would seem to require intellectual modesty; that is, an appropriate degree of humility about knowledge claims based on recognition of their transitory and incomplete nature. This virtue is evident in tentative statements about knowledge claims. For example, a news story should explicitly and accurately describe the basis of any factual statements (actual examination of legislative language versus quoting a legislator's interpretation of the bill in question), invoking no more and no less authority than warranted and including any appropriate disclaimers (for instance, acknowledgment that the veracity of the legislator's statement could not be determined). Intellectual modesty also would be evident in a willingness to re-visit claims in light of new evidence.

Epistemic responsibility also requires intellectual honesty and intellectual reliability. Intellectual honesty consists of making a good-faith effort to be truthful and exercising independent judgment—or failing that, to disclose any known biases or conflicts of interest that might interfere with such judgment. Intellectual reliability is a virtue achieved and demonstrated through a cooperative discipline of verification on deadline. This discipline, which will be discussed in Chapter 5, depends on the right sort of collegial relationships among journalists, as well as an adequate level of institutional support in the form of resources for gathering, constructing, and editing the news responsibly.

The Corrective Nature of Virtues

Unlike an art or a skill, a virtue is "not a mere capacity: it must actually engage the will" (Foot, 1978, p. 8). Besides being consciously exercised, virtues must be rationally exercised. Otherwise, according to Aristotle (trans. 1984), a virtue would be more like a rudimentary instinct. True virtue "involves the proper use of reason and the pursuit of the good" (p. 333). Thus, virtues provide a basis for both moral accountability and credit. Reason and habit are available to all; therefore, virtue is something for which everyone can strive (Pellegrino, 1995; Prior, 2001). However, such human temptations as fear and the desire for pleasure encourage us to act against reason, necessitating virtues such as courage and temperance. "As with courage and temperance so with many other virtues: there is, for instance, a virtue of industriousness only because idleness is a temptation; and of humility only because men tend to think too well of themselves," writes philosopher Philippa Foot (1978). However, some compensatory virtues exist because of a "deficiency of motivation" (p. 9). Hence, the need for the virtue of charity (whereas there is no need for a virtue of self-love). For Foot, this corrective dimension of the virtues is so essential that she deems actions to be morally praiseworthy if they do not conflict with any virtue and, further, if they *require* a virtue to compensate for a specific human tendency or lack of motivation. Oakley & Cocking (2001) speak of motive as being an integral part of some virtues, such as friendship, where concern for the other person is entailed by the meaning of friendship. In any case, it will be helpful to think about specific temptations lurking in journalism that may require compensatory virtues.

What About Principles?

The appeal of virtue ethics has endured "because one cannot completely separate the character of a moral agent from his or her acts, the nature of those acts, the circumstances under which they are performed, or their consequences" (Pellegrino, 1995, p. 254). Still, ethicists disagree about the place of virtue ethics in normative ethical theory compared with principle-based approaches. Virtue theorists criticize principle-based theories for focusing on procedures for making right choices without necessarily offering an account of what kinds of goals one should pursue in the first place. They also object to these theories on the grounds that they encourage an excessively rational and minimalistic approach to ethics. Principle-based theorists, for their part, are concerned that virtue theory fails to adequately safeguard the "causal autonomy" (Lucas, 1988, p. 297) of agents or provide a transcendent perspective in situations that question the culture itself. Critics also are bothered by the vagueness of its terms and its decision-making procedures, as well as its circular logic, such that "the good is that which the virtuous person does and the virtuous person is the person who does what is good for humans" (Pellegrino, p. 262).[6]

For the purposes of my argument, it is not necessary to settle whether virtues or principles constitute the foundation of morality. There are ways to think about ethics that can encompass both virtues and principles. Hursthouse (2001), for example, suggests that virtue theory can come up with rules grounded in their relationship to virtue and vice without excluding rules grounded in deontological correctness. Oakley & Cocking (2001) propose a "regulative ideal" (p. 25), or internalized

---

6   For more background on the debate between principle-based and virtue-based theorists, see Davis (1999), Donahue (1990), Gewirth (1985), Hursthouse (2001), Rosen (1990), and Oakley & Cocking (2001).

model of excellence, as a criterion of right action that may include principles. To explain the relationship between virtues and principles, they suggest the analogy of fluency. When you speak a language fluently, you do not have to consciously refer to grammatical principles when you speak. It is not that the rules are no longer relevant; they still guide your speech, but it is precisely when you do *not* have to refer to the rules any longer that you know you are finally fluent; this ability is a dimension of excellence. Oakley & Cocking conclude that a regulative ideal may consist of both standards of correctness and standards of excellence. The former govern actions along the lines of right or wrong, while the latter govern actions and motivations "beyond the merely correct or incorrect" (p. 27). Thus, the regulative ideal encompasses the relatively narrow concerns of principle-based theories, as well as the more morally ambitious scope of virtue ethics.

Oakley & Cocking's (2001) conceptualization of virtue ethics broadly agrees with that of Alasdair MacIntyre (2007), who notes that virtues promote the common good, while principles are necessary to prevent harm. Although my argument does not necessarily depend on MacIntyre's version of virtue ethics, his ideas about virtuous practices provide a useful framework for thinking about journalism as a cooperative endeavor guided by a sense of moral purpose.

A Practice as a Context for Moral Action

In *After Virtue*, MacIntyre (2007) argues that the virtues are inherently contextual. Virtue "always requires for its application the acceptance of some prior account of certain features of social and moral life in terms of which it has to be defined and explained" (p. 186). For MacIntyre, practices are the context that actually give virtues their point and function. Practices are ground zero for appreciating the virtues because they "generate new ends and new conceptions of ends" (p. 273). Although MacIntyre was not the first to suggest that certain occupations could be considered in terms of cooperative practices (see, for example, Arrow, 1963), his conceptualization of a practice has been particularly influential. He provides this definition:

> By a "practice" I am going to mean any coherent and complex form of socially established cooperative human activity through which goods internal to that form of activity are realised in the course of trying to achieve those standards of excellence which are appropriate to, and partially definitive of, that form of activity, with the result that human powers to achieve excellence, and human conceptions of the ends and good involved, are systematically extended. (p. 187)

Internal goods can only be specified in terms of the practice, and they "can only be identified and recognized by the experience of participating in the practice in question. Those who lack the relevant experience are incompetent thereby as judges of internal goods" (pp. 188–189). Besides achieving internal goods, practices involve "standards of excellence and obedience to rules" (p. 190). External goods, on the other hand, are only "contingently attached" (p. 188) to practices and can be achieved in other ways besides participation in the practice. Both external and internal goods are the result of competition—one for possession and one for excellence. However, external goods "are always some individual's property and possession" (p. 190), thus constituting a zero-sum victory for the winner, who gets more of them while others in the practice get less. Internal goods, in contrast, are a win–win benefiting everyone involved in the activity. External goods belong only to individuals; virtues might actually get in the way of achieving them. Internal goods belong to the whole community; they cannot be achieved without the virtues.

MacIntyre (2007) uses the example of chess. Making a brilliant move in chess makes sense only within the context of the game and can be mastered, appreciated, and enjoyed only within that context. To interject goods external to the practice—such as fame or money—endangers the very nature of the enterprise. Chess players, for example, might become tempted to "throw" a game for money or become more interested in becoming celebrities than perfecting their game. Winning itself is an external good because chess players can win and reap the associated rewards in other activities besides chess. All they have to do is develop the requisite skills. Thus, MacIntyre points out that a less-skilled chess player who plays just for the sake of the game may actually surpass the excellence of the master player who plays only to win.

The practice specifies the context of a self in its roles (one can belong to more than one practice). Roles make us accountable to others even when we do not choose them; they entail expectations that affect how we, and others, perceive us. When one chooses a role, one must submit to the expectations that accompany that role. To enter into a practice, you must submit to the authority of the standards and the internal goods of that practice and place yourself into a relationship with that practice's history and previous practitioners (MacIntyre, 2007). Thus, if journalism is to be understood as a practice, it will not do to say that one is a journalist simply by learning and sharing information with lots of other people who may be interested in it. If you do not accept the standards of excellence that have been established for journalism, either you are not a journalist or you are a bad one.

Another important aspect of MacIntyre's (2007) definition is the dynamic nature of a practice's goals. As Lambeth (1992) explains it:

> MacIntyre's argument is that the pursuit of standards of excellence within a practice accounts substantially for the achievement of internal goods. More important, such pursuit sets in motion a dynamic by which a practice's very capacity to achieve excellence can be systematically elevated and extended. As a result, new concepts of the goods and ends involved in a practice emerge. (pp. 73–74)

As an example of this dynamic in journalism, Lambeth (1992) discusses the pioneering of survey methodology in reporting by Philip Meyer, then with the Knight newspapers, and the subsequent expansion of computer-assisted reporting by investigative journalists in the years since, such that "a new measure of reportorial mastery" was established (p. 76). Lambeth calls such opportunities "MacIntyrean moments" (p. 78). Another example is the civic journalism movement, which began with special projects at local newspapers in the mid-1980s aimed at encouraging civic participation. These projects were subsequently expanded to include multimedia partnerships all over the country, thanks in part to funding from the Pew Charitable

Trusts. A recent study estimated that one-fifth of all US newspapers between 1995 and 2000 employed community outreach, interactivity, or some other technique characteristic of civic journalism projects (Friedland & Nichols, 2002). As a result of the movement's influence, journalists have re-considered journalism's civic aims, the means it should use to achieve those aims, and the relationship it should have with citizens.

Figure 2.1 summarizes the teleological structure of practices. At the collective level of the practice itself, virtues enable the achievement of internal goods, which, in turn, are oriented toward the realization of the practice's overriding goal. Vices are those qualities that prevent the achievement of internal goods. At the individual level of practitioners, standards of excellence and standards of correctness are integrated into a regulative ideal (Oakley & Cocking, 2001) that guides the actions and motives of a practice's members. Standards of excellence express the virtues, while standards of correctness restrain the vices. My argument, as noted earlier, will be concerned with the collective level of practices. When I deal with the individual level, it will be with an eye to socially grounded concepts, including moral identity and moral support.

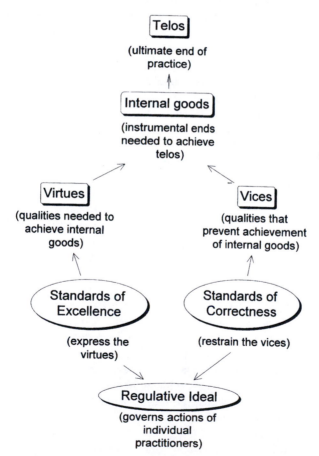

Figure 2.1 Teleological structure of practices

What is and What is Not a Practice?

Besides chess, MacIntyre (2007) offers painting and creating/sustaining family life as examples of practices. These examples have raised questions about the precise boundaries of practices and whether participation in practices is necessary for exercising the virtues. One area of disagreement involves MacIntyre's position regarding external goods. He describes these as legitimate goods, but ones that can stand in the way of achieving a practice's internal goods; they also are often hindered by possession of the virtues.

> Thus although we may hope that we can not only achieve the standards of excellence and the internal goods of certain practices by possessing the virtues *and* become rich, famous and powerful, the virtues are always a potential stumbling block to this comfortable ambition. We should therefore expect that, if in a particular society the pursuit of external goods were to become dominant, the concept of the virtues might suffer first attrition and then perhaps something near total effacement, although simulacra might abound. (p. 196)

MacIntyre (2007) says most people do not work within practices any more because modern work mostly embodies means–end relationships that are "necessarily external to the goods which those who work seek" (p. 227). The prime example would be factory work, which MacIntyre cannot see as a practice even if those who engage in such labor see its overriding goal as the "larger project of survival," as Putman (1997, p. 310) suggests. When production was still located within the household, work was understood as "part of the sustaining of the community of the household and of those wider forms of community which the household in turn sustains" (MacIntyre, p. 227). Modern wage labor, in contrast, makes work about "biological survival and the reproduction of the labor force, on the one hand, and that of institutionalized acquisitiveness, on the other. *Pleonexia*, a vice in the Aristotelian scheme, is now the driving force of modern productive work" (p. 227). To paraphrase the film *Wall Street*, greed is good. The bureaucratic manager and "their social kindred," MacIntyre says, have become today's role models.

Despite the potentially adversarial relationship between internal goods and external goods, Moore (2002) suggests that business can be a practice housed within corporations because allegiance to internal goods does not *necessarily* preclude allegiance to external goods, and vice versa. He concludes that "[A] full reading of MacIntyre potentially hints at a dynamic and creative tension rather than a static and destructive one" (p. 28). To preserve the integrity of business as practice, Moore would require corporations to limit their emphasis on external goods (although it is not clear what he considers the practice's internal goods to be). He does not acknowledge the possibility that other practices may co-exist within the same corporation alongside business (as would be the case in journalism), and that the goals of different practices may conflict in irreconcilable ways (MacIntyre, 2007).

Applbaum (1999) notes that goods that are external to one practice may be internal to another. He uses the example of medicine. If a practice becomes different enough from "doctoring" by emphasizing financial rewards over healing, maybe we could call it "schmoctoring." He does not see any moral problem as long as the new practice's goals are morally permissible and those seeking services know whether they are getting a doctor or a schmoctor. If those with medical training abandon their commitment to doctoring, "they indeed are morally free from the collective judgments of a social practice that is not their own and that does not apply to them" (p. 59). So, the winning-minded chess player might belong to the practice of "schmess playing," with internal goods oriented toward winning. Would-be journalists who endorse entertainment as their overriding goal might belong to some practice called "schmournalism" with corresponding internal goods such as humor and charisma. MacIntyre's (2007) reply, I think, would be to say that winning and entertaining can be achieved through lots of different kinds of activities and, therefore, cannot define any practice, whether it be called journalism or schmournalism.

Besides the question of external goods, MacIntyre (2007) has stirred debate regarding skills. Every practice requires skills, but a practice "is never just a set of technical skills, even when directed towards some unified purpose and even if the exercise of those skills can on occasion be valued or enjoyed for their own sake" (p. 193). Improvements in skills—such as the innovations in brick-laying techniques and materials cited by Putman (1997)—are morally neutral in themselves. Skills have moral significance only to the degree that they contribute to the excellence of a practice. Indeed, as Klaidman & Beauchamp (1987) point out, competence within a practice is partly defined by moral criteria. They use as an example the journalistic skill involved in deciding how many credible sources are enough to report something as factual. They note that there is no way to decide without "taking a view about what constitutes a responsible use of sources" (p. 25). Other skills relevant to journalism include recognizing news, using language well, and organizing stories.

Putman (1997) agrees that there is a distinction between skills and virtues, but denies that one is any better than the other. "All intentional voluntary human activities can be done more or less well. To do them requires virtue. Conversely, all such activities, simple or complex, can be done viciously" (p. 309). MacIntyre (2007) does not deny that the virtues may be exercised in other contexts besides practices. In fact, "someone who genuinely possesses a virtue can be expected to manifest it in very different types of situation, many of them situations where the practice of a virtue cannot be expected to be effective" (p. 205). It is precisely this consistency of disposition that distinguishes virtues from skills. Virtues are deployed in every facet of a virtuous person's life; skills are used only where they can work. Virtues are embedded in the very conception of a practice's ends, whereas they function more as moral side constraints for those whose activities are defined by proficiency.[7] In short, skills are about effectiveness, while virtues are about excellence.

---

7 Although the virtues aim at internal goods, they are not concerned with calculating consequences for particular situations, as Klaidman & Beauchamp (1987) suggest in their discussion of public service in journalism. The goodness of the virtues is *aretaic* (tending toward excellence), rather than *welfaristic* (tending toward benefit) (Oakley & Cocking, 2001). What this means is that you ought to habitually exercise the virtues because they tend toward the achievement of internal goods, but you do not choose to exercise a virtue based upon some calculation of whether it will actually produce those goods in any one particular situation. There may even be instances in which virtue may require sacrificing our lives (a consequential harm) in order to preserve our character (an intrinsic benefit) (Prior, 2001). It is

Requirements for *Journalism as Practice*

To sum up, an activity is considered a practice, according to MacIntyre's (2007) definition (p. 87), if it:

- is coherent and complex;
- is socially established;
- is cooperative in nature;
- possesses goods internal to that form of activity;
- realizes those internal goods as the natural outcome of trying to meet suitable standards of excellence;
- systematically extends human powers to achieve excellence as a result of realizing its internal goods (results in self-improvement);
- systematically extends human conceptions of the ends and goods involved in the practice as a result of realizing its internal goods.

The first couple of criteria set minimum qualifications that journalism meets easily. The first suggests that a practice must be intelligible as a whole and that it must require some experience and knowledge to understand. Journalism—with its web of norms, methods, and ideology—constitutes a bona fide domain of knowledge, according to Gardner, Csikszentmihalyi & Damon (2001), thus meeting this criterion. Journalism also is widely recognized as a distinct human activity (the second criterion), with a long tradition that will be examined in Chapter 3. The next few criteria are directly relevant to establishing journalism as an enterprise distinct from other activities, including other practices. For example, the requirement of cooperation is a key difference between journalism and personal publishing activities such as blogging. Journalism requires joint action by gatekeepers, reporters, artists, and technical staffers to create, present, and share the news through the mass media. One could make an argument that blogging is a cooperative activity because of its interactive character and because of its reliance on social networks. However, the act of blogging (posting to a personal web page) does not, in itself, require joint action with others. If no one posted feedback to a blog, it would still be a blog—albeit not a very lively one. Journalism also is distinguished by its internal goods and how their achievement promotes self-improvement and goal transformation. These matters will be examined in Chapter 4. The virtues required to sustain *journalism as practice* will be discussed in Chapter 5.[8]

A close reading of MacIntyre (2007) yields additional conditions for a practice that are not spelled out in his formal definition (Table 2.1 provides a summary of the requirements for practices). Besides the exercise of technical skills, other requirements are: an overriding purpose that distinguishes the practice (journalism's

---

not that the virtuous journalist should be oblivious to the harm she may cause by being honest, brave, or whatever; it is that she is honest, brave, and so on because she wants to further the practice's specific *telos* (not a general "benefit").

8   However, standards of excellence that express these virtues will not be discussed in detail, as action guides for individual practitioners are not a major focus of my argument.

Table 2.1   Requirements for a practice

It is coherent and complex.

It is socially established.

It is cooperative in nature.

It possesses goods internal to that form of activity.

It realizes those internal goods as the natural outcome of trying to meet suitable standards of excellence.

It systematically extends human powers to achieve excellence as a result of realizing its internal goods.

It systematically extends human conceptions of the ends and goods involved in the practice as a result of realizing its internal goods.

It involves the exercise of technical skills.

It has a distinctive overriding purpose.

It constitutes a moral community that can effectively maintain the kind of relationships needed to achieve the practice's internal goods.

It partly defines members' way of life.

It operates within an institutional context.

It has a formal social organization to effectively push back institutional corruption.

Note. Based on MacIntyre (2007)

purpose will be analyzed in Chapter 4), and a moral community that can effectively maintain the kind of relationships needed to achieve the practice's internal goods (to be examined in Chapter 6). Practices also must partly define one's way of life (the vocational aspect of journalism will be discussed in Chapter 7). Finally, a practice requires an institutional context. This last criterion is directly relevant to the problem of commodification in journalism and will be discussed next.

Institutional Contexts in Journalism

Lambeth (1992) identifies the following external goods in journalism: "wealth, fame, prestige, and position" (p. 73). These are precisely the kinds of rewards that tempt the Stephen Glasses and Jayson Blairs of the journalistic world to cut ethical corners. These temptations are ever-present, however, because of the intimate relationship between practices and institutions:

> Institutions are characteristically and necessarily concerned with what I have called external goods. They are involved in acquiring money and other material goods; they are structured in terms of power and status, and they distribute money, power and status as rewards. ... For no practices can survive for any length of time unsustained by institutions. (MacIntyre, 2007, p. 194)

In short, institutions are both necessary and dangerous for practices. Innovations and improvements at the institutional level can function as "levers" for good work in journalism, according to Gardner, Csikszentmihalyi & Damon (2001, p. 212). These can include creating new institutions (for example, CNN); expanding the functions of existing institutions (for example, creating ombuds positions); reconfiguring the membership of existing institutions (for example, diversifying news staffs); and reaffirming the values of existing institutions, especially benchmark ones (for example, the *New York Times*'s 2005 announcement that it would implement procedures to systematically track errors appearing in the paper). Similarly, Meyer's (2004b) influence model demonstrates that the institutions and the practice of journalism can be mutually beneficial.

However, institutions can warp the practice's sense of mission by providing alternative rewards and standards that benefit individual practitioners instead of the practice as a whole. In the worst-case scenario, external goods actually contradict the practice. For example, many critics have pointed out that the reimbursement practices of health maintenance organizations, or HMOs (prepaid insurance networks that contract with groups of health professionals for a flat rate), create incentives for physicians to refrain from recommending tests that, in their professional judgment, would help patients. Thus, medicine's very reason for being—patient health—is undermined. Similarly, journalism's mission is undermined when newspapers write off entire segments of their coverage area (the unprofitable ones) and cater news content, instead, to the tastes of a (profitable) few. The "essential function of the virtues" in a practice is to resist "the corrupting power of institutions" (MacIntyre, 2007, p. 194). However, they may not be enough. The tendency of media corporations and news organizations to warp journalism's goals suggests an additional criterion for *journalism as practice* that MacIntyre (2007) does not specify: a formal organization that can effectively push back institutional corruption. The prospects of professionalism serving this function will be critically examined in Chapter 7.

Stephanie Craft (in Adam, Craft & Cohen, 2004) wants to pin responsibility for good journalism on corporations as well as journalists. She says media corporations straddle business and public service realms "in ways that other corporations do not" (p. 263). However, media corporations and journalists disagree about what the institutional "product" is. "The lack of a shared idea about the purpose of the corporation, its product, frustrates the practice of journalism and ... the corporation's ability to sustain that practice" (p. 264). Craft, like Moore (2002) and Cohen (Adam, Craft & Cohen, 2004), say it is the practice's responsibility to bring this harm to light, a claim that will be discussed in Chapter 5. The responsibility of media corporations to sustain good journalism will be discussed at more length in Chapter 8.

Gardner, Csikszentmihalyi & Damon (2001) note the dynamic interplay between external forces and the specialized knowledge of a practice, which they call a domain. A domain is stable when it is in alignment. This is a rare sociological condition in which the values of the culture and the domain are in line; the expectations of stakeholders and practitioners match; and the domain and its practitioners are in sync. A domain becomes unstable when misaligned due to external conditions (e.g. technological change or population trends) or internal pathologies (e.g. sudden wealth or power)—this is the condition they ascribe to journalism as a domain. A domain also can be superficially aligned when there is only the appearance (or simulacrum) of alignment because of underlying corruptive forces or ongoing neglect of discrepancies (including the unrestrained pursuit of external goods).

Gardner, Csikszentmihalyi & Damon's (2001) focus on broad forces influencing journalism draws attention to the fact that its institutions do not have to be limited to news organizations or media corporations. There has been a tendency to interpret MacIntyre's (2007) notion of institutions in this narrow sense of for-profit entities, despite the fact that MacIntyre himself includes chess clubs and laboratories as examples of practice-bearing institutions. An institution is any social structure that bears a practice; it can take many forms. One of the most ancient forms is that of the state. For American journalism, the state is a key institution because of the way the practice is legally and philosophically grounded in the First Amendment guarantee of press freedom. In fact, the most common way of deducing journalism's purpose among American ethicists is to make reference to the First Amendment and its implied rights and obligations (see, e.g., Adam, Craft & Cohen, 2004; Hodges, 1986; May, 2001). Journalists themselves tend to make this move. Press observer Jay Rosen (2004a) goes so far as to characterize journalism as a First Amendment religion with the press clause as the sacred text in journalism and the public as the God term. The faith of journalism, he writes, is "that people can make a difference when they know what is happening in their world" (Seven: A breakaway church in the press, ¶8). The role of the First Amendment in journalism's tradition will be examined in Chapter 3; its effect on the professionalization efforts of journalists will be studied in Chapter 7.[9]

Other Contexts for Exercising the Virtues

MacIntyre (2007) describes two other relevant contexts for the application of the virtues: the narrative of a single human life and a moral tradition. No quality can be properly called a virtue unless it satisfies the requirements of a practice and these other contexts. A virtue must not only enable one to achieve a practice's internal goods, but it must be integrated into "an overall pattern of goals" that defines a good human life. A good human life, for its part, integrates the goods of particular practices. A tradition, finally, integrates the goods of particular lives into an overall pattern "informed by a quest for *the* good and *the* best" (p. 275).

Regarding the context of a single human life, MacIntyre (2007) says we need to look at an individual's history and the history of the settings to which that individual belongs. It is only this context that makes intentions intelligible, to the agent and to others. Knowledge of intentions is necessary to evaluate moral behavior: "An action is a moment in a possible or actual history or in a number of such histories. The notion of a history is as fundamental a notion as the notion of an action. Each requires the other" (p. 214). Personal identity, or selfhood, is then necessarily linked to the ideas of narrative, intelligibility, and accountability. It is only when we know someone's whole "story" that we can understand her actions and attribute to her a good or bad character in light of the "plot" that has played over the course of her

---

9   Adopting a professional organization would, in effect, constitute an additional institutional context for journalism. This one would be an occupational one, in addition to the state institution of the First Amendment and the economic institutions of the media industry and particular news organizations.

life. This narrative aspect of morality entails accountability to others because our individual narratives are nested within others' narratives. The virtues sustain us in our quest for the good human life. They enable us, as the protagonists of our own narratives, to "overcome the harms, dangers, temptations and distractions which we encounter" (p. 219). Chapter 5 will focus on the harms, dangers, temptations, and distractions faced by journalists and suggest virtues necessary to defeat them at the level of a practice.

Likewise, the exercise of the virtues sustains traditions; their absence corrupts traditions, "just as they do those institutions and practices which derive their life from the traditions of which they are contemporary embodiments" (MacIntyre, 2007, p. 223). A tradition, as MacIntyre describes it, is an historically situated, ongoing argument about what constitutes the good life. Bondi (1984) puts it in terms of the "normative story of a community," which is passed down in various "sites of storytelling activity" (p. 213). Using Christianity as an example, he cites scripture, preaching, sacraments, liturgy, the lives of the saints, church teaching, church history, and the lives of current Christians as storytelling sites. Journalistic counterparts might include published media criticism in trade reviews, news council proceedings, blogs, ethics codes and policies, recorded journalistic history, newsroom war stories, and the lives of former and current journalists.

Key to a moral community's stories are its *characters*, analogical to stock characters in some forms of literature and popular culture. These constitute social roles with moral constraints built into them. As "moral representatives of their culture," they "embody moral beliefs, doctrines and theories" (MacIntyre, 2007, p. 28). These *characters* do not have universal acceptance, but "provide a culture with focal points for conflict and disagreement, catalysts of moral change" (Code, 1987, p. 30). In journalism, these might include Watergate sleuths Bob Woodward and Jim Bernstein, war correspondent Ernie Pyle, broadcast pioneer Edward R. Murrow, and revolutionary pamphleteer Thomas Payne. Journalism's tradition, including its stories and *characters*, are the topic of the next chapter.

Chapter 3

The Tradition of Journalism

When 91-year-old W. Mark Felt revealed himself as the mysterious Deep Throat of Watergate legend in the summer of 2005, Bob Woodward and Carl Bernstein were the toast of their colleagues again. Journalists recalled, often in heroic terms, how these two scrappy *Washington Post* reporters helped expose a corrupt president (see, for example, Rich, 2005b; Woestendiek & West, 2005). Never mind that the pair's part in forcing Richard Nixon to resign in 1974 had become exaggerated over the years relative to the influence of the Senate hearings, the White House tapes, and the courts (Von Drehle, 2005). The book and the film *All the President's Men* had captured the imagination of a generation of journalists, contributing to an increase in J-school enrollments and providing journalism with its central narrative in modern times. Journalists enthusiastically reminded the public of the good that they can accomplish when they do their work to the highest standards. Former *CBS Evening News* anchor Dan Rather told Larry King on his CNN talk show:

> Those of us who know how difficult it is to do this kind of work and can only aspire to do the kind of work that they did. It wasn't just "Deep Throat." Mark Felt deserves all the credit in the world as far as I'm concerned. But they worked hard. They had lots of sources. They had dozens of sources. They made telephone calls, they wore out the shoe leather, they did it the old-fashioned way. (Cable News Network, 2005)

The news that the FBI's former no. 2 official had been Woodward's secret source broke at a time when journalists were becoming alarmed at the increasing willingness of prosecutors to subpoena reporters about their anonymous sources. The Deep Throat story became an occasion for American journalists to revisit and reflect on their tradition. This chapter describes and critiques selected elements from this tradition—what Moriarty (1995) might call the practice's ethos by destiny—in light of current scholarship, and circumstances facing the practice. This look at journalism's tradition sets the stage for deriving a theory of journalism in the next chapter that describes the practice's distinctive marks, its internal goods, and its *telos*.

Traditions and Practices

An activity's *telos* determines which goods its practitioners should pursue and which means they should use to achieve those goods. For example, a journalism oriented toward maximizing profits will have different implications than a journalism oriented toward creating knowledge. To understand a practice's *telos*, we must look to its tradition. "Practices always have histories and ... at any given moment what a practice is depends on a mode of understanding it which has been transmitted often through many generations" (MacIntyre, 2007, p. 221). Traditions themselves are narratives in progress. When we keep in mind the inherently transitory nature of traditions, it encourages us to be open to ongoing critical reflection about the traditions we inherit, perhaps even culminating in the realization that previous conceptions of a practice's *telos* were incomplete. In the case of American journalism, that may include reconsidering the journalist's typical interpretation of the First Amendment or her adherence to the ideal of objectivity. At the same time, MacIntyre says we have to respect traditions: "What I am, therefore, is in key part what I inherit, a specific past that is present to some degree in my present. I find myself part of a history and that is generally to say, whether I like it or not, whether I recognize it or not, one of the bearers of a tradition" (p. 221).

Appreciation for journalism's tradition has prompted some media critics and commentators to prefer the terms "journalism" (Adam, Craft & Cohen, 2004; Demers, 1989) or "press" (Miller, 1997; Rosen, 2003) to the ubiquitous "media" when writing about journalism ethics. Miller identifies the normative concepts of the "press" with print journalism, which developed a certain idealism independent of money. Entertainment, he notes, has always been the primary content of television and so television journalism has moved in that direction, despite its start as basically newspapers on television (a history preserved in such residual expressions as "a look at the headlines"). "Television confirms, anoints, and dramatizes news, and when it covers events live, it witnesses news. But it rarely finds news. That remains almost entirely the task of print" (Schudson, 1998, p. 287). Writing in the introduction to his web log *PressTHINK* (2003), New York University professor and media critic Jay Rosen noted, however, that journalism is not wedded to any specific technology:

> We need to keep the press from being absorbed into The Media. This means keeping the word press, which is antiquated. But included under its modern umbrella should be all who do the serious work in journalism, regardless of what technology they use. The people who will invent the next press in America—and who are doing it now online— continue an experiment at least 250 years old. It has a powerful social history and political legend attached. (¶1)

This powerful social history and political legend of the press is located within the larger discourse of American thought regarding the meanings of democracy, citizenship, knowledge, and freedom. This legend supplies a tradition that makes journalism intelligible as an activity and also an ideology that guides the practice's beliefs about itself and the world. As is the case with all ideologies, journalism's is the product of both power struggles and good faith (Gieryn, 1983). Altschull (1990), who analyzes the influence of major philosophical ideas in the various stages of journalism's development, includes the following major elements in journalists' ideology:

- *Optimism*: a belief in progress, opportunity, equality, and belonging based on faith in science and technology, capitalism, the common man, individualism, and local community.

- *Pragmatism*: an emphasis on the practical, on facts, observation, and common sense—ideas that contributed to the concept of the people's right to know and empiricist objectivity.
- *Criticism and self-criticism*: embodied in muckraking, investigative journalism, and media criticism by the Hutchins Commission and others.
- *Power*: a belief that the media are highly influential (for good or bad).
- *Skepticism*: "which as an ideal may in fact represent the expressed professional ideology of contemporary American journalists" (p. 185).

Altschull (1990) says journalistic ideology is broadly compatible with America's notion of the "can do" society:

> It is one into which nearly all the ideas of the American journalist can fit comfortably. It is optimistic; it believes without qualification in progress and growth under the banner of science and empirical inquiry; its social order is democratic and moral; education is the key to the future; and the people have a right to education in their schools and in their newspapers. In this system of beliefs, under this set of attributes, the press is without a doubt an instrument of vast power with an enormous potential for good. (p. 238)

For Demers (1989), professional autonomy has been a key theme as the press has evolved over the centuries. He identifies three key periods in the development of the press, marked by what he calls essential myths of journalism ethics:

- *Independence* (eighteenth century and first half of nineteenth century), wherein ethics was characterized by the no-holds-barred approach of the partisan press. The imperative was having an authentic voice and giving an honest rendition of one's views. This phase was a reaction to censorship attempts.
- *Neutrality* (second half of the nineteenth century and first half of the twentieth century), wherein ethics was characterized by following the procedures of objectivity. The imperative was to accurately describe events and to produce information that could be distinguished from opinion. This phase was a reaction to the experience of journalism becoming a commodity.
- *Public service* (starting with the release of the Hutchins Commission report in 1947), wherein ethics is characterized by safeguarding the public's right to know. "This model extends the idea of news as 'objective data' which reporters are entrusted to circulate without distortion in order to fulfill their public service function" (p. 22). This phase was in reaction to concerns about concentration of media ownership.

Demers (1989) claims that these three models, which rest on disparate premises, have become blended into one. The current model incorporates the notion of independence from the era of censorship, the notion of neutrality and individual thought from the era of objectivity, and the notion of guardianship of the public's right to know from the era of social responsibility. This new model gives journalists the right to resist all potential obstacles to serving the public, including commercialism, propaganda, and consumer desires, and to insist on publishing a wide variety of viewpoints.

Lambeth (1992) relied on interviews with editors and analysis of journalism ethics codes to come up with the following set of principles for journalism: truth telling, humaneness, justice, freedom, and stewardship of free expression. Gardner, Csikszentmihalyi, & Damon (2001) came up with a different list based on interviews with journalists: diversity of opinion, open forum for debate, dedication to craft, integrity, and objectivity. Kovach and Rosenstiel (2001) offered a "theory and culture of journalism" (p. 12) based on three years of research conducted by the Committee of Concerned Journalists in partnership with a team of academic researchers. The "elements of journalism" (p. 12) include a primary obligation to the truth, first loyalty to citizens, a discipline of verification, and independence. This study is the most ambitious effort to date to capture how journalists themselves see their mission and distinguishing characteristics.

The Essence of Journalism?

In recent debates aimed at distinguishing journalism from blogging, commentators have zeroed in on the role of reporter. For example, blogger Rebecca Blood (2005), writes, "So, when I say weblogs and journalism are fundamentally different, one thing I mean is that the vast majority of weblogs do not provide original reporting—for me, the heart of all journalism" (¶14). Another blogger agreed with this assessment, contrasting what (ideally) happens in reporting versus most blogging:

> For example, in the political realm, bloggers on the left and right opine on the policy of the day but few actually do the legwork of polling the public, reading through complete legislations, associating those parts to other existing laws, or going through the federal budget line by line … Yes, journalism can sometimes be a boring job … and that's why it's a job. (Louis, 2004, Looking back, looking forward, ¶4)

The reporter as the embodiment of "real" journalism has been referenced in popular culture as well, as exemplified in satirical references to celebrity television anchors in the television series *Murphy Brown* and the Academy Award-nominated motion picture *Broadcast News*. Altschull (1990) has suggested that the Investigative Reporter, in particular, is the quintessential *character* in contemporary journalistic ideology:

> The chief task of the skeptic is inevitably defined in terms of asking questions. Only by posing questions can one approach the truth about the facts. The image of the investigative journalist is that of the skeptical watchdog par excellence. He or she trusts no one who cannot document his case with verifiable evidence. Truth can be arrived at only by empirical—that is to say, verifiable—proof. Facts are sacred, but first they must be verified. (p. 335)

The most current data on the characteristics of American journalists bear out these intuitions. Nearly 80 percent of the 1149 journalists responding to a 2002 national survey conducted by Weaver, Bean, Brownlee, Voakes & Wilhoit (2007) said that they engaged in reporting at least occasionally. When online journalists were excluded from the analysis, the proportion of journalists who described themselves as reporters climbed to nine out of every 10. Taking into account that most high-level editors probably engaged in substantial reporting activities earlier in their careers, it is reasonable to assume that reporting is central to the experience of being a journalist in the United States.

If the reporter is indeed the defining role in American journalism, it provides a useful lens for analyzing journalism's tradition. By understanding what a reporter is and is not, what he believes and does not believe, we can distinguish journalism from other kinds of public communication and we can clarify our thinking about less clear-cut journalistic roles, such as camera operator, graphic artist, and copy-editor. What follows, therefore, is a brief "MacIntyrean history" (Lambeth, 1992, p. 79) focusing roughly on the same ideas and tensions as Demers (1989), but with an eye to the development of reporting as a distinct occupation and identity. Reporting is an American invention historically situated in the society and institutions of urban America in the nineteenth century. Since then, however, it has become "a vocation with a distinctive outlook and a distinctive meaning" (Schudson, 1988, p. 228). Schudson traces this self-consciousness from eighteenth-century printer Benjamin Franklin and nineteenth-century muckraker Lincoln Steffens to twentieth-century foreign correspondent Harrison Salisbury. "The shift from Steffens to Salisbury is a shift from an individual with a mission to an individual with a role (the detached reporter), a role within a profession that has a collective mission or, at least, a collective responsibility" (p. 243).

The Reporter's Inheritance

The main themes I will examine are: storytelling and authorship, truth and objectivity, professionalism and social responsibility, power of the press and the people's right to know, participatory citizenship and the press. These ideas—the reporter's inheritance—are embodied in key *characters* (MacIntyre, 2007*)* and events that most journalists would recognize, including the Zenger trial, the muckrakers, Edward R. Murrow's broadcast exposing Senator Joseph McCarthy, and Watergate.[1] Once the key elements of journalistic tradition have been examined, a theory of journalism can be proposed that incorporates or modifies those elements that are most definitive of the practice. The aim is to articulate a *telos* for journalism that preserves the best of the past and provides direction for the future.[2]

---

1   The legacy of Edward R. Murrow is discussed in this chapter's *Practically Speaking* feature.

2   This strategy for describing journalism's tradition, however, happens at a time when the centrality of reporting may be fading. Meyer (2004b) notes that technology is pushing the industry toward a focus on processing instead of producing information; editing is becoming more important than reporting. At the same time, many younger people from non-journalistic backgrounds are getting recruited into journalism because of the industry's need for skills related to new technologies. So whether reporting will continue to define journalism's tradition remains to be seen.

Storytelling and Authorship

Critics have noted how storytelling conventions in journalism tend to oversimplify complex issues (for example, by looking for heroes and villains instead of recognizing nuance). However, Kovach & Rosenstiel (2001) argue that "journalists must make the significant interesting and relevant" (p. 148) and that "storytelling and information are not contradictory" (p. 149). While noting that newsroom cutbacks make it more difficult for reporters to make stories compelling, they recommend a number of storytelling techniques such as use of insightful detail. Besides the functional aspect of good writing, reporters value excellence in storytelling because they have pride of authorship: They sweat over their ledes. They delight in the clever phrase. They celebrate the insightful metaphor. They try to put just the right quote in just the right spot. They do not gather facts just to serve democracy. They also want to order and interpret those facts with literary flair and distinctive style. They are storytellers, writers. In fact, writing is what draws most journalists into the practice (Weaver, Bean, Brownlee, Voakes & Wilhoit (2007). This element of journalistic tradition explains the allure of the so-called New Journalism in the 1960s and 1970s. Although many journalists viewed this as a dangerous phenomenon because of the genre's use of fiction writing techniques, many also admired the literary style of such reporters as Gay Talese, Norman Mailer, and Hunter S. Thompson. In a tribute to Thompson after his death in 2005, *New York Times* writer David Carr noted the influence of the hard-living pioneer: "For all of the pharmacological foundations of his stories, Mr. Thompson was a reporter, taking to the task of finding out what other people knew with an avidity that earned the respect of even those who found his personal hobbies reprehensible. Hunter S. Thompson knew stuff and wrote about it in a way that could leave his colleagues breathless and vowing to do better" (¶9).

The New Journalist is one of journalism's most interesting *characters*— illustrating at once the practice's irreverent, passionate quest for truth through the artistic use of language, as well as the enticement of placing a higher value on style than on truth. "New Journalism turned epistemic authority upside down by changing the emphasis of reporting from fact to scene, moving from official sources to 'saturation reporting,' and utilizing literary techniques that made the writer, not the fact, the primary source of authority" (Jackson, 1988, p. 23). Indeed, taken to an extreme, the desire for the "perfect" story can come at the expense of truthfulness: This seems to be the case with some of the practice's best-known representatives of another *character* in journalism, the Hoaxer or Fabricator. These include Janet Cooke, who won a Pulitzer at the *Washington Post* for a compelling story she wrote about an 8-year-old heroin addict who never existed, and Stephen Glass, who made up people and anecdotes in a number of stories he wrote for the *New Republic* in the late 1990s. In this age, when commercial pressures are so salient in newsrooms, it is easier and easier to succumb to the temptation to juice up a story to get the attention of higher-ups. Many critics thought this motivation was at work when *Dateline NBC* decided in 1992 to outfit a couple of GM trucks with incendiary devices to dramatize claims the trucks were prone to catching fire in side collisions. These incidents are a reminder that authorship implies an audience. Ideally, journalists write for citizens, but sometimes they write for their editors or prize juries, who can reward them with awards, job opportunities, and the prestige of being on the cover or on Page One. Sometimes journalists write just for each other, as when the Washington press corps focuses excessively on the strategic aspects of political campaigns.

Authorship also is an ethical role in itself, as Adam points out (in Adam, Craft & Cohen, 2004). Understood as a "literary and moral craft" (p. 248), journalism's mission is to "write well and truly" by mastering "technical proficiency, liveliness, originality, precision, and eloquence" (p. 253). This perspective fits into the larger tradition of literature viewed as an art form and a vehicle for social criticism— the idea that the pen is mightier than the sword. Unlike other kinds of writing, however, American journalism is distinguished by its commitment to factuality and its democratic functions. "Facts are sacred in journalism and democracies because experience, and its factual rendering, matters. From a writer's view, the language in which such facts are presented also matters in a moral sense" (p. 253). Adam sees writing as intimately connected with the other role dimensions of journalism:

> The reporter in the journalist investigates and uncovers facts and prepares the way for the creation of texts; the writer in the same journalist writes faithful documents and stories based on these facts; the critic in the journalist provides the meaning of the facts of the stories, judges their significance, and explains why and how things happen. (p. 254)

McDevitt (2003) sheds light on how a journalist can fuse these aspects together through "covert writing techniques" (p. 163), including what he calls "disdained news" (p. 159). This is a writing style that conveys the reporter's disgust with the competitive need to report stories that are tainted because of their origins in the tabloids or some other dubious reason. McDevitt sees such strategies as individual expressions of journalistic autonomy, an important aspect of the literary element of journalism's tradition. As an author, a reporter wishes to have an authentic voice—a difficult proposition given the way the role has developed.

The role of reporter initially was contrasted with the role of correspondent, which had been around since the earliest colonial newspapers.[3] Correspondents were paid letter writers from far-away places who "could opine and should comment; they should also have a literary voice" (Nerone & Barnhurst, 2003, p. 439). Reporters, on the other hand, joined newspapers beginning around 1830 as "pieceworkers, voiceless writers assigned to record proceedings at public events, speeches in the legislature, facts from police courts and hospitals, and other matters that could be more or less automatically compiled" (p. 439). The reporting role we now take as the standard did not develop until newspapers reorganized as professional organizations in response to public concerns about newspaper monopolies in the early twentieth century. The modern, professional reporter combined the previous two roles by faithfully recording facts and arranging them intelligibly, displaying an impartial expertise, much like the scientist's. However, reporters' voices continued to be

---

3   The correspondent may be the closest historical antecedent to the blogger. Lacking formal affiliation, the blogger (and those who post feedback on blogs) send in their comments from "afar." Their authority, if any, resides in their expertise *outside* media institutions and in the authenticity of their voice.

effaced: "As experts, they deserved a byline, not to lay claim to authorship, but to reassure the public that their authorship didn't matter" (p. 439).

Truth and Objectivity

The place of truth looms so large that Meyer (2004b) boils down journalism's tradition to "Get the truth and print it" (p. 228). Tradition often points to the 1735 trial of political party paper owner John Peter Zenger as a turning point in America's history of free expression. Zenger's lawyer, paid by a group of fellow printers, convinced a jury for the first time in the American colonies that truth should be a legal defense in libel cases. British common law held just the opposite: that the libel was worse if it were true. The actual legal and political significance of the Zenger case is questionable, but it certainly became an early symbol of an emerging "belief that people should have the right to speak the truth" (Nord, 2001, p. 67). Later, this belief became part of liberal democratic philosophy, linked to ideas about individualism, government accountability, and the power of the truth to win out in what Supreme Court Justice Oliver Wendell Holmes would later call the marketplace of ideas.

Yet what is truth? Bok (1989a) argues in *Lying* that perfect Truth is unattainable and that we should settle for the more reasonable standard of truthfulness. Borden & Pritchard (2001) endorse this view for journalists:

> Seeking the truth and making a sincere effort to report the truth insofar as one has been able to ascertain it can be expected. That is what truthfulness requires. Furthermore, although "the whole truth and nothing but the truth" may not be attainable, departures from truth are often readily determinable; and deliberately reporting what one knows to be false is not acceptable. (p. 77)

Journalists, however, often fail to meet even this threshold. In fact, hoaxes were common (and accepted) features of American journalism in the early penny press (Tucher, 1994). The best-known fraud is the moon hoax of 1835, in which the *New York Sun* ran a series reporting that a non-existent astronomer had published findings of bat-men and other life on the moon in a defunct scientific journal (Thornton, 2000). Against the backdrop of showman P.T. Barnum's antics at the time, such hoaxes were understood as harmless humbugs—little deceptions in which the deceived willingly participated to have a little fun.

Since the days of the humbug, however, journalism has come to rest its authority and legitimacy in large part on its commitment to ferreting out the truth and reporting it in accurate detail without prejudice or hidden motives. In time, journalists developed routines for accomplishing objective reporting, or the "disinterested reporting of verified facts" (Borden, 2002, p. 158). These routines include using quotation marks to mark verbatim statements, and balancing he said–she said statements (Tuchman, 1972). Schudson (2001) describes objectivity as an occupational norm that "is at once a moral ideal, a set of reporting and editing practices, and an observable pattern of news writing" (p. 149). It has some strategic functions as well: increasing efficiency for the businesses that employ journalists, deflecting criticism, and standardizing journalistic judgment (Soloski, 1989; Tuchman, 1972).

Objectivity also has a tendency to reproduce hegemonic relationships in society (Fishman, 1980). The best-known example in journalistic tradition is the rise of Senator Joseph R. McCarthy, whose Communist witch-hunt ruined many careers and lives at the height of the Cold War. He was aided by the conventions of objectivity, which forced journalists to report McCarthy's charges (accurately, of course) even though they knew that these were based on deception. The same dynamic was at work in press coverage of the Swift Boat Veterans for Truth political ad during the 2004 presidential election. Journalists dutifully reported the ad's attacks against the Vietnam service record of Democratic candidate John Kerry, even after they had established that the charges were unsubstantiated.

Despite objectivity's conservative tendencies, Schudson (1988) observes its inherent potential for subversion. Recalling Salisbury's trip to Hanoi during the Vietnam War, Schudson says, "It was the sort of nonpartisanship that makes journalistic objectivity inevitably an impertinence and a challenge to authority. He showed forcefully the unending capacity of the objective stance to be seditious" (p. 242). It was the same when CNN war correspondent Peter Arnett stayed behind in 1991 as the only American journalist behind enemy lines during the Gulf War. Reporting live (and admittedly censored) from Baghdad, Arnett was branded a traitor by several members of Congress and the White House because of his reports of civilian casualties and an interview with Saddam Hussein. The same fate met those journalists who objected—on the grounds of objectivity—to wearing flag lapels and other patriotic symbols in the days following the September 11, 2001, terrorist attacks on Washington and New York City (Borden, 2005).

Objectivity, in short, is at once expected and suspected these days. Journalists get criticized for showing bias at the same time that they are impugned for following the conventions of objectivity. *National Journal* writer William Powers (2005b) commented in a column:

> Referring to oneself in the third person is a noble journalistic tradition, a symbol of reporterly distance and modesty. I've been reading the self-abnegating adventures of 'a reporter' my entire adult life. When I was a newspaper reporter, I was often that faceless wraith myself, and I appreciate what traditional media outlets are implicitly saying when they use this device: *The story isn't about us, folks—we're just taking notes and writing it up for you.* (¶4)

The problem is that this artifice may actually be hurting journalists' credibility because they seem less authentic and honest than other voices in the media marketplace. In fact, audiences and media watchers enthusiastically embraced television anchors and reporters who showed their emotions during coverage of Hurricane Katrina in 2005.

The implications of the shift in audience expectations became obvious during the 2004 presidential campaign. There appeared to be a blue reality and a red reality, proffered in increasingly opinionated news formats on cable and the Internet. *Time* magazine wondered on its September 27, 2004, cover: "Who owns the truth?" Meanwhile, the looser broadcast ownership rules that allowed the amassment of capital also allowed folks like the owners of Sinclair Broadcasting to form media fiefdoms with expressly political agendas. Sinclair had planned to force all of its affiliates to air an anti-Kerry program the week before the election until advertisers and stockholders cried foul. Frank Rich, writing in the *New York Times*, bemoaned the trend in a November 2004 column: "The facts of current events can become as ideologically fungible as the scientific evidence supporting evolution. Whatever comforting version of events supports your politics is the 'news'" (¶8).

Rosen (2004d) wrote in his weblog *PRESSthink* after the election that traditional media may be better off turning partisan than remaining un-aligned: "As we know from politics, if you don't watch out you can be defined by your opponents. Opponents want to define the national press as the liberal media, and they are well along in their cultural project, which does not require the participation—or consent—of journalists" (¶6). AP television writer David Bauder (2004), on the other hand, suggested there might be a backlash in store against "opinionated news, most personified by those cable segments that set people up to argue political points, or outshout each other" (¶1). Nerone and Barnhurst (2003) worry, more basically, about losing the notion of news as truth:

> Although scholars have for decades anatomized and critiqued the ideal of objectivity, still, shouldn't everyone panic if Rupert Murdoch takes the critique seriously? No one believes Fox News is fair and balanced—who could?—but that doesn't make it undesirable to live up to their motto. (p. 449)

Professionalism and Social Responsibility

The ideal of objectivity has been at the center of journalism's professional ethos from the start. It disciplined reporters (making professionalization palatable to owners) and mitigated partisanship in the news (making professionalization appealing to the public). With the institutionalization of the wall between the editorial and business sides in the early twentieth century, it seemed as if the modern newspaper had organized news work in a way that was both "rational and inevitable" (Nerone & Barnhurst, 2003, p. 447).

University training in the new professional model gradually supplanted the apprenticeship system that had trained journalists since the days of the colonial printer. It helped standardize reporters' performance even further and also instilled another idea crucial to the professional project: "The notion of public service was now part of a newspaper reporter's individualism—a spirit and outlook now fostered as part of a reporter's professional training in the classroom" (Salcetti, 1995, pp. 63–64). Public service was hardly an alien concept to journalists, steeped in the lore of a free press. Horace Greeley, who founded the crusading *New York Tribune* in 1841, recoiled at the sensationalistic excesses of the penny press because of his belief that newspapers should be a source of moral education (Altschull, 1990). Populist editors in the late nineteenth century defended equal opportunity against the robber barons, and muckrakers in the early twentieth century went after corporate abuse and political corruption. Early media critics, including Will Irwin and George Seldes, had long sounded the call for public service. However, clearly, the *character* of The Professional has had a distinct impact on how reporters view their role. Compared with The Muckraker before him, The Professional is more devoted to fact and detachment (being an observer rather than a participant), more cooperative (working jointly with others in a community of journalists), and more likely to see reporting as a defining identity in which the reporter's "aim is defined within reporting itself" (Schudson, 1988, p. 237), rather than in some external political cause.[4]

Professionalism gave journalists some authority to insist on high standards and resist "commercial tricks like sensationalism and infotainment" (Rosenstiel, 2003, ¶88). However, concerns with press performance continued, reaching such a level after World War II that a special commission was appointed to look into them. The commission, chaired by Robert M. Hutchins, introduced a new term that has dominated the language of journalism ethics ever since: social responsibility, later labeled as a theory of the press by Siebert, Peterson & Schramm (1956). The Hutchins Commission's 1947 report concluded that the press is obligated to serve a number of social functions and implied that, if it did not, government regulation may be in order. At a more basic level, the doctrine linked freedom and responsibility together as necessary partners, rather than inherent adversaries. This was a departure from the libertarian outlook of most journalists at the time (and many today), who tended to view any call for responsibility as an undue limitation on their rights and professionalism as a step toward licensing. The report also institutionalized the idea of the public's right to know—not just the facts, but the truth behind the facts (Altschull, 1990; Demers, 1989). The most lasting effect of the social responsibility doctrine within the journalistic tradition has been to legitimize accountability. However, American journalistic tradition continues to rely largely on libertarian assumptions concerning the power of the press, the common man, the nature of citizenship, and self-government.

Power of the Press and the Common Man

Rosen (2004a) and Watson (2005) characterize the press clause of the First Amendment as the sacred text in journalism's religion. The faith of journalism, Rosen writes, is "that people can make a difference when they know what is happening in their world" (Seven: A breakaway church in the press, ¶8). Altschull (1990) notes the influence of revolutionary journalist/pamphleteer Thomas Paine, whose "passionate adoration of free expression" (p. 131) has had an enduring influence on journalism's tradition. In *Common Sense, The Rights of Man* and other late eighteenth-century writings, he defended "democracy, representative democracy, and the power of a free press" (p. 127), making him the "patron saint of the activist journalist, of the fearless seeker after truth in the public print" (p. 129). This element of journalistic tradition—the belief that the press has the power to make democracy work and that the press represents the people against the tyranny of the powerful—can be seen at work throughout the history of the American press. The idea of the press as the champion of the people can be seen in Greeley's crusades, in the muckraking

---

4   The way in which the two key functions of professionalism—ethical motivation and occupational power—affect journalism's integrity as a practice will be explored further in Chapter 7.

campaigns of magazine reporters Steffens, Sinclair Lewis and Ida Tarbell later in the same century, in Ernie Pyle's World War II dispatches chronicling the hell of war from the GI's point of view, and in Woodward and Bernstein's Watergate investigation in the early 1970s. Inspired by democratic ideals and by the desire to make a difference, this watchdog aspect of the reporter's heritage is also the most romantic. Like all good romantics, Altschull says, journalists believe their practice should be irreverent, unpredictable, and "just a little bit disreputable" (p. 22).

This strain in journalism's tradition includes a legal saga (Rosen, 2004a). In addition to Watergate, other milestones include the 1964 *Times v. Sullivan* libel opinion that made it harder for public figures to win defamation lawsuits and the 1971 *Pentagon Papers* case, in which the Supreme Court made it clear that the government had to meet a very high threshold to justify prior restraint in the name of national security. Not coincidentally, these legal skirmishes often happened in the context of war and other national conflicts, testing the limits of the press's independence and the press's own understanding of patriotism. Rosen (2004a) notes, however, that journalism's tradition does not address the public's First Amendment claims to media access and participation. Firmly entrenched in the tradition, as well, is the notion of press freedom as belonging primarily to the owners of the press and (indirectly) to the members of the press—a notion being challenged with increasing effectiveness by bloggers and others engaged in so-called citizen or participatory journalism.

Participatory Citizenship and the Press

Political scientist Doris Graber (2003) observes that the traditional First Amendment argument for a free press is premised on the ideal of a participatory democracy, "where politically well-informed citizens play an active role in government" (p. 143). It is this belief that inspires writers such as Adam (Adam, Craft & Cohen, 2004) and others to talk about journalism as a "democratic art" (p. 249). However, even if participatory democracy *were* the ideal (and she is not sure it is), Graber argues that it is unrealistic in current American society. Further, she says, the media typically do not perform the constitutional functions attributed to them. Rather than be critical of the media's performance, however, Graber says the media are doing rather well, considering that they are structured primarily around the profit motive and that most people do not dutifully attend to the news. The media look even better if one does not judge them based on the needs of an idealized citizen who does not exist and probably never will. Graber relies on Schudson's (1998) analysis of American citizenship to reach her conclusions. Schudson argued that the original model of American citizenship was the deferential citizen of the colonial period, still evident in the Founding Fathers' decision to make the Electoral College decisive in presidential elections. The informed citizen presupposed by the press did not arise until the Progressive era at the end of the nineteenth century. This notion of citizenship reflected the Progressive movement's faith in knowledge, democracy, and the common man (Altschull, 1990). Although this period has had an enduring influence on journalistic values (Gans, 1980), the rest of the country has moved on. Since the 1950s, according to Schudson, American citizenship has been characterized by the more passive monitorial citizen, who looks up occasionally from her private affairs to keep tabs on threats to her well-being, often construed in terms of individual rights. This kind of citizen needs "knowledge that is essential to performing ordinary civic tasks, such as voting and political discussions" (Graber, 2003, p. 151). Graber says current media coverage meets this requirement, especially when you consider everything on offer in the marketplace. Graber suggests that even hegemonic coverage is functional because it offers monitorial citizens a practical way to deal with the prevailing power structure.

Kovach & Rosenstiel's (2001) theory of the interlocking public suggests that there are different levels of monitoring, depending on the issue. The same person may resemble the ideal informed citizen when it comes to monitoring news about clean water legislation but pay no attention whatsoever to news about teen pregnancy rates. Indeed, it may be better this way, so that the most involved citizens do not hijack public policy to narrowly reflect their own interests and the uninvolved do not prevent the resolution of issues that affect everyone. Kovach & Rosenstiel's analysis implies that there are at least two potential publics for every news story: one expecting in-depth, knowledgeable coverage; the other, a kind of index to the basics. Even the uninvolved public can be persuaded to join in the conversation if the topic becomes a prominent enough agenda item. The authors conclude, "[T]his more pluralistic vision of the Interlocking Public suggests that the requirements of the old press, of serving the interests of the widest community possible, remain as strong as ever" (p. 29). On the other hand, proponents of niche journalism could just as easily argue that it makes more sense to serve each public separately or, better yet, allow each citizen to tailor the news to her own needs and interests. What is to preserve community bonds in this vision?

Philosopher William May (2001) suggests such bonds require a return to the idea of public virtue. Like MacIntyre (2007), May adopts a communitarian view of democracy grounded in virtue theory's claim that human flourishing depends on participation in a community constituted by a shared conception of the common good. He notes that "communitarianism is a native, not a foreign, tongue" (p. 168). For example, the Founding Fathers emphasized public virtue in their rhetoric, second only to liberty. However, May says the idea of public virtue has been all but lost to four procedural mechanisms that enable US democracy to operate without asking its citizens to sacrifice their private interests:

- *The Constitution*, which provides an arena for the pursuit of happiness conceived as an individual property.
- *The marketplace*, which encourages self-interest in this pursuit, justified by the belief that doing so contributes indirectly to everyone's well-being.
- *The large-scale organization*, which "mobilizes purely technical skills and provides economies of scale" (p. 251).
- *The university*, which gives people salable skills to succeed in this environment.

The monitorial citizen has successfully expanded individual rights and established a healthy "institutionalized distrust" (p. 301) necessary to avoid state domination; the notion of a "monitorial obligation" (p. 310) is one that should be retained (Schudson, 1998). However, in key respects, the monitorial citizen is a poor shadow of the citizen seeking public happiness envisioned by the leaders of the American Revolution.

Collectivism has been unacceptable both to American and journalistic ideology (Altschull, 1990). However, those who position communitarianism as the opposite of individualism are missing the point. Communitarianism does not prioritize the collective over the individual; rather, it claims that individuals cannot be fully realized except as members of communities. Put another way, social obligation is not a matter of me versus community, but two different "aspects of our own nature: our self-interest as individuals and our self-interest as members of a community" (Prior, 2001, p. 331).

The modern conception of incommensurable individual goods makes it impossible to determine what the common good consists of because there is no shared conception of what is good for the community, "as specified by the good for man" (MacIntyre, 2007, p. 215). Rather, the emphasis is on atomistic individuals that naturally "seek to satisfy their own desires" (p. 213). Taken to the extreme, this tendency manifests itself as egoism, which leads some people to exclude themselves from community and thus unwittingly deprive themselves of what actually is good. MacIntyre explains, "There is no way of my pursuing my good which is necessarily antagonistic to your pursuing yours because *the* good is neither mine peculiarly nor yours peculiarly—goods are not private property" (p. 213).[5] A more helpful view is to think of community as a "social web of relationships," in which competing conceptions of the good can co-exist, suggests philosopher Larry May (1996):

> The challenge of living among diversity is to construe morality in such a way that it is flexible enough to accommodate very diverse circumstances and life-styles, but not yet to give up on a vision of a shared conception of the good life. (p. 104)

Viewed within a communitarian framework, the ideal of a participatory democracy is no longer an irrelevant anachronism from the nineteenth century, but part of a coherent philosophy that incorporates the best of journalism's tradition and that gives purpose to *journalism as practice*. An informed citizenry becomes part of the larger project of human flourishing, which is "deeply dependent upon knowing well," according to Lorraine Code (1987, p. 9), who also writes in the Aristotelian tradition. This is especially true in an information society. Bovens (2002) describes this as a society in which geographical boundaries are becoming less relevant, new technologies are developing at an unpredictable pace, corporations and governments are being overshadowed by markets and networks, and data processing is becoming the primary mode of production. These conditions, Bovens says, have the potential to bring "the classic republican ideal of politics as a debate between well-informed citizens into the realm of reality" (p. 325).

---

5   MacIntyre (2007) takes pains in the prologue to the third edition of *After Virtue* to renounce the communitarian label. Nevertheless, his views about the common good and the role of communities in helping people lead the best lives they can are broadly compatible with my argument.

After analyzing the autobiographies of Steffens and Salisbury, Schudson (1988) comes up with a definition of reporting that is not very flattering. Noting the influence of organizational constraints, personal beliefs, and peers on news selection, he offers: "a reporter is someone faithful to sources, attuned to the conventional wisdom, serving the political culture of media institutions, and committed to a narrow range of public, literary expression" (p. 239). Yet a look at journalism's tradition, mixed bag that it is, suggests that the enduring ideas that have informed reporting can serve as the basis for a theory of journalism with a suitable *telos*. Chapter 4 takes up this theory, proposing five distinctive marks of *journalism as practice*, the creation of "news" as the practice's immediate goal, and a tentative list of internal goods.

The Legacy of a Key Character in Journalism

If ever there was a paradigm of virtue for journalists, it was Edward R. Murrow. His influence continues to be felt, especially among television journalists, decades after his death from lung cancer in 1965. The ultimate compliment in broadcast journalism is to be compared with him, as could be seen in the numerous tributes to ABC News anchor Peter Jennings upon his death in 2005 (see, for example, Simpson, 2005). Murrow's name graces at least two journalism excellence awards and the school of communication at his alma mater, Washington State University. A plaque at CBS headquarters holds him up as the best—still.

> It was not his specific attitude on any question that gave him his authority and credit. He often tended to take a conservative view. But his general attitude of open-mindedness, which is the core of liberalism, influenced the people who worked with him and the CBS way of handling the news, raising the level of reporting and heightening the climate of inquiry. The "Murrow style" became, and to some degree still remains, the CBS style. (Kendrick, 1969, p. 26)

In short, Murrow is a powerful *character* in journalism because he embodied the best of journalism's tradition. As such, he continues to provide a standard by which to judge journalistic quality and dedication. He often is credited with perseverance in search of the truth. The truth he spoke was not just about others, but about his own in broadcast news: He was one of the first to openly criticize the increasing emphasis on profits in television news in a controversial 1958 speech to the Radio Television News Directors Association (RTNDA), dramatized in the 2005 film about Murrow, *Good Night and Good Luck*. He recognized the unique challenges faced by journalism when it tries to meet its public service responsibilities while housed within the institution of the television industry:

> One of the basic troubles with radio and television news is that both instruments have grown up as an incompatible combination of show business, advertising and news. Each of the three is a rather bizarre and demanding profession. And when you get all three under one roof, the dust never settles. (Murrow, 2004, p. 20)

Although he was not snobbish about television's potential for entertainment—he was one of the first broadcasters to do prime-time interviews with celebrities—he was dismayed at the medium's emphasis on entertainment over education. "This instrument can teach, it can illuminate; yes, and it can even inspire," he noted in the most-quoted excerpt from his speech. "But it can do so only to the extent that humans are determined to use it to those ends. Otherwise it is merely wires and lights in a box" (p. 22).

Murrow first became a star with his rooftop reporting of the Nazi bombings of London during World War II. With his team of CBS war correspondents, known as "Murrow's Boys," he played a pivotal role in the development of radio news and, later, television news and TV documentaries. He received five individual Emmy awards during his career, as well as four for his seminal documentary series on CBS, *See It Now*, which aired in prime time from 1952 to 1958. His legacy touches on each of the main elements of the reporter's inheritance.

Murrow was a master storyteller. Recalls Joseph Wershba (n.d.), a former *60 Minutes* producer who worked with Murrow as a reporter at CBS News: "His writing was simple, direct. He used strong, active verbs. On paper, it looked plain. The voice made the words catch fire. He regarded the news as a sacred trust. Accuracy was everything. And, always, fairness" (¶4). Murrow's skillful use of language is evident in his 1945 report from the Buchenwald Nazi death camp shortly after it was liberated by Allied troops. He was one of the first two reporters there to convey the awful truth of the Holocaust. In his first-person account, he told radio listeners that the daily ration for prisoners was some stew and "one piece of brown bread about as thick as your thumb, on top of it a piece of margarine as big as three sticks of chewing gum" (Murrow, 2005, ¶7). He described walking into a warehouse where he saw "two rows of bodies stacked up like cordwood" (¶8). It appeared, he said, that the dead men and boys had starved. "But the manner of death seemed unimportant. Murder had been done at Buchenwald" (¶9).

As these examples demonstrate, Murrow prized accuracy and observation— standards that are at home in an objective framework. At the same time, his broadcasts had a definite point of view:

> He acknowledged himself to be part of the honorable tradition of muckraking, but the muckrakers were not ideologues. Lincoln Steffens, who was one of them, described them as more interested in exposure than in analysis. They dealt not so much in objective or subjective as in what might be called corrective journalism. Murrow always regarded himself as a reporter rather than an analyst, but was more. He was a disturber of the peace and a collector of injustices. Radio and television are by their very nature ephemeral. He endowed them with a sense of permanent substance by giving them a purpose. (Kendrick, 1969, p. 4)

Nevertheless, it took quite a while for Murrow to transcend objectivity's conventions when Sen. Joseph McCarthy started running amok during the Cold War. When he did, in a 1954 episode of his series *See It Now*, he was widely credited for hastening McCarthy's demise and transforming the role of television news while providing his own career with its defining moment (Thornton, 2002). He and his associate, Fred Friendly, accomplished this largely by using McCarthy's words against him. An admiring Wershba (n.d.), declared: "On the night of the broadcast, March 9, 1954, the night the spear was hurled against the terror that held America in thrall, Edward R. Murrow spoke words that should be handed down as legacy to every generation of Americans:

We will not walk in fear, one of another. We will not be driven by fear into an age of unreason if we dig deep in our history and doctrine and remember that we are not descended from fearful men, not from men who feared to write, to speak, to associate and to defend causes which were for the moment unpopular. We can deny our heritage and our history, but we cannot escape responsibility for the result. There is no way for a citizen of the Republic to abdicate his responsibility" (Final section, ¶2–3)

Former CBS news anchor Walter Cronkite, himself an icon in journalism, reflected on the McCarthy program in an essay on National Public Radio commemorating the famous broadcast. Describing Murrow's report, Cronkite (2004) said, "Ed's summation was a model of editorial rectitude, and one I tried very much to live up to 14 years later when the Vietnam War would be the issue" (¶9).

Another important Murrow contribution was his last *See It Now* program, called "Harvest of Shame," which aired in 1960. This documentary portrayed the dismal conditions of migrant work on Floridian farms and included two passionate speeches by Murrow at the beginning and at the end. Although "Harvest of Shame" was perhaps the most dramatic of Murrow's investigations, it was not unusual for him to focus on common folk. Although CBS got thousands of sympathetic responses, powerful critics included CBS's own network chief, William S. Paley. The "Shame" documentary, along with the McCarthy program and the RTNDA speech, caused CBS to gradually distance itself from the legendary Murrow. Eventually, he accepted a position as head of the US Information Agency, where he worked until 1964. Gary Edgerton (n.d.), writing for the web site of the Museum of Broadcast Communications (www.museum.tv/), notes: "The apparent irony between Edward R. Murrow's life and the way that he is subsequently remembered today is that the industry that finally had no place for him, now holds Murrow up as their model citizen—the 'patron saint of American broadcasting'" (¶1).

Chapter 4

A Theory of Journalism[1]

Coming up with a definition of journalism is notoriously hard. Blogger Rebecca Blood (2004) writes, "Journalism is like pornography. The specific definition varies from person to person, but in general, you know it when you see it" (¶2). Some who have taken a stab at it emphasize journalism's role in preserving a record of events: "Journal" was the original term for what came to be known as newspapers (Schudson, 1988), a word that itself is derived from the French word "jour," or day. "It is our day book, our collective diary, which records our common life. That which goes unrecorded goes unpreserved except in the vanishing moment of our individual lives" (Carey, 1995, ¶5). However, journalism is not the only practice that provides such a record. The Congress and the courts keep their own records (the use of "reporter" in journalism is derived from the courts), and so do many organizations and individuals on the Web. Nor is journalism defined by medium or organization. "Journalism can be practiced virtually anywhere and under almost any circumstances" (Carey, 1995, ¶7).

Rosen (2004c) says that journalism's "strengths are in reporting, verification and access—as in getting your calls returned" (¶16). Blood (2005) agrees:

> Research alone does not qualify an activity as journalism. Bloggers may point to reader comments as sources of information about the items they post, but these are equivalent to letters to the editor, not reporting. ... Credible journalists make a point of speaking directly to witnesses and experts, an activity so rare among bloggers as to be, for all practical purposes, non-existent. (¶12)

For Blood (2004), verifying facts is a central part of any definition of journalism:

> When a blogger interviews an author about their new book, that is journalism. When an opinion columnist manipulates facts in order to create a false impression, that is not. When a blogger searches the existing record of fact and discovers that a public figure's claim is untrue, that is journalism. When a reporter repeats a politician's assertions without verifying whether they are true, that is not. (¶7)

A virtue framework directs us toward a teleological definition grounded in a theory of journalism that provides a morally substantive link between the practice's product and purpose. Such a theory should include at least five elements: a link to human flourishing, commitment to the common good, reporting as the defining activity of journalism, a desire to make a difference, and a way to make a living. These

---

1   A revised version of this chapter was presented in August 2006 to the Association for Education in Journalism and Mass Communication in San Francisco.

constitute the marks that distinguish *journalism as practice* as a normative activity
and clarify its relationships to the "public." These marks are represented in Figure 4.1
as concentric circles, with the most important mark located in the innermost circle.
Like all practices, journalism also relies for excellence on a set of skills, a vocational
aspect, and certain institutional resources. Relying on a communitarian account
of participatory citizenship and Code's (1987) notion of epistemic responsibility,
this theory proposes that journalism's immediate goal is to create a special type of
knowledge necessary for community members to flourish; journalists produce and
disseminate this knowledge in the form of "news." The ultimate goal, or *telos*, is to
help citizens know well in the public sphere. The chapter concludes with a tentative
list of the practice's internal goods—those that promote the *telos* and can only be
realized as a journalist.

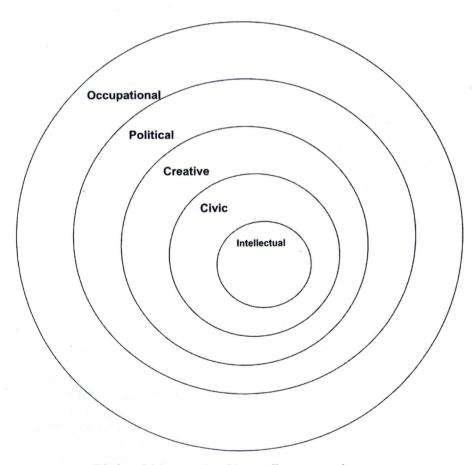

Figure 4.1   Distinguishing marks of *journalism as practice*

The Distinguishing Marks of *Journalism as Practice*

A Link to Human Flourishing

Americans live in a complex society increasingly defined by the power and abundance of information. This makes people dependent on the media to orient themselves to their communities. In response to this vulnerability, journalism is responsible for meeting the surveillance requirements of monitorial citizens.[2] However, to be a *virtuous* practice, journalism must go beyond the minimum required by moral obligation. Instead, it must embrace the more morally ambitious goal of helping people flourish as human beings. To flourish, people need to know *well* so that they can actually participate in (not just casually monitor) civic life. Epistemic responsibility binds journalists and citizens together by highlighting the moral significance of the investigative processes *both* use to make sense of the world. Code (1987) suggests that we are all responsible for using a good-enough process of investigation when we want to know something. Within the constraints of the "nature of the world and of human cognitive capacity," there is much freedom but also a limit to "what kinds of sense can *responsibly* be made of the world" (p. 9). This element of the theory recognizes journalism's commitment to truth and the evolution of reporting from a mechanical job (connected to the printer's trade) to an *intellectual* practice with an important role to play in an information society. Cooper (1993), who first suggested applying Code's theory to journalism, referred to this dimension of the practice when he suggested that journalism is a site for both "moral and collective knowing" (p. 87).[3] This element highlights journalism's *servant* role in its relationship with the public, which is the *beneficiary* of the practice's efforts.

Commitment to the Common Good

American journalists have committed themselves to helping citizens in explicit promises they have made over the centuries in ethics codes, policies, pamphlets, and other kinds of professional and political discourse. Such promises also are implicit in journalists' acceptance of First Amendment protections predicated on beliefs about the press's democratic functions. Through these promises, journalists have created legitimate expectations of altruistic motivations and trustworthy performance

---

2   So far, what I have said is true even of journalism carried out in non-democratic societies. People everywhere have what Kovach & Rosenstiel (2001) call the "Awareness Instinct" (p. 10), which is a need to know what is going on beyond their direct experience so they can feel safe, secure, and in control. Of course, other kinds of public communication can serve this function as well—National Weather Service warnings and web sites alerting people to out-of-state job opportunities are examples. However, if we allow that communities characterized by democratic values are those where human flourishing is most likely to occur, then *journalism as practice* inherently presumes, if not a democratic context *per se*, at least "the aspiration for … institutions of democratic life," in the words of James W. Carey (1995, ¶6).

3   The role of the intellectual virtues in journalism will be discussed in the next chapter.

directed toward the common good. This element of the theory defines journalism as a *civic* practice, which directs its activities outward to the community, rather than inward toward its practitioners (as in the case of MacIntyre's, 2007, chess example). It also highlights journalism's role as a *partner* with the public in promoting the common good.

Reporting as Defining Activity and News as Immediate Goal

Original reporting is at the core of journalism's tradition in the United States, distinguishing it from other practices embedded within media institutions. The centrality of reporting to journalism's identity is illustrated by recent announcements to hire salaried reporters at weblogs with journalistic aspirations, including the liberal *TalkingPointsMemo.com* and Arianna Huffington's *The Huffington Post*. Reporting consists of gathering evidence for the purpose of creating timely, practical civic knowledge called "news." The basic unit of news is the news story, an established literary genre that enjoys privileged status in American culture (McNair, 1998). Although reporting can be separated from writing, these processes are intertwined in news creation. Typically, the journalist who gathers evidence also writes the story based on that evidence.

An excellent news story results from proficiency in storytelling and a cooperative "discipline of verification" (Kovach & Rosenstiel, 2001, p. 71) on deadline. Although the latter implies a high degree of news processing, it is not accurate to conclude, as Meyer (2004b) does, that "[e]diting should be gaining importance relative to reporting" (¶10). Numerous non-journalists aggregate and organize information for easy retrieval. The *sina qua non* of journalism is reporting. The seven Ds of good reporting are:

- *Dig*—investigate, research, interview, witness.
- *Document*—write down or tape statements and data, duplicate documents, produce a record.
- *Debunk*—check veracity of statements, validity of data.
- *Digest*—interpret meaning, put into perspective, relate to the common good.
- *Describe*—narrate sequence of events, relate quotes and interpretations.
- *Demystify*—translate technical terms, relate to possible collective action.
- *Divulge*—expose, reveal, bring out into the open what was hidden or unknown.

Journalism derives its cultural authority from excellent reporting, which backs up the practice's claim to produce truthful, non-fictional accounts of "some *hitherto unknown* (new) feature of the *actual, social* world" (McNair, 1998, p. 4). However, journalists do not just passively transmit observations of empirical phenomena. Reporters actively construct news by giving narrative form to their sense making. "[N]o reporter just 'gets the facts.' Reporters make stories. Making is not faking, not lying, but neither is it a passive mechanical recording. It cannot be done without play and imagination" (Schudson, 1988, p. 230). In other words, journalism is not stenography, or merely passing on knowledge possessed and produced by others, as

May (2001) suggests. It is authorship. This element of the theory makes journalism a *creative* practice that puts journalists in an *performative* relationship to the public as *audience*.

An Instrument of Reform

Modern journalists eschew politics. Objectivity's first goal was to remove journalism from the fray of partisan politics and establish it as an independent activity. However, the crusading strain in the practice's tradition puts the practice squarely on the side of reform in the sense of righting wrongs and promoting positive change (Gans, 1980). Journalists hope to make a difference, not by being affiliated with partisan causes, but by shedding light on corruption and injustice (which also helps explain journalism's emphasis on the negative). A number of common newspaper names testify to the reformist impulses of the press, suggesting the roles of champion, revealer, instrument of progress: the *Advance*, the *Advocate*, the *Guardian*, the *Voice*, the *Beacon*, the *Herald*, the *Sun*. The act of investigative reporting, in particular, is thus a persuasive activity that selects "breaches in the moral order for public attention" with the goal of provoking public outrage against abuse of power by government and other influential institutions (Glasser & Ettema, 1991, p. 219). This element of the theory makes journalism a *political* practice that acts as the public's *guardian* in the public sphere.

Way to Make a Living

Journalists are not amateur communicators or occasional volunteers for a cause. Journalists gain competence through degree programs and/or through formative experiences working with veteran journalists so that they can be qualified for a career. Journalists aspire to jobs with news organizations that have established themselves as prestigious bearers of journalism's tradition, either as salaried employees or freelancers. The journalistic community consists of people who have decided to make a living doing journalism. This element of the theory makes journalism an *occupational* practice—a prerequisite for consideration as a profession, which will be taken up in Chapter 7. As an occupation, journalism functions within the marketplace as a *provider* of goods for the public as its *patron*.

The *Telos* of Journalism

Many scholars and journalists have made statements about the purpose of journalism within an American democratic context. These statements usually are based on an interpretation of the First Amendment that gives the press a mandate to make democracy work. Kovach & Rosenstiel (2001), for example, suggest that journalism's purpose is "to provide citizens with the information they need to be free and self-governing" (p. 17). Gardner, Csikszentmihalyi & Damon (2001) say that their interviewees articulated the primary mission of journalism as informing the public about important events, empowering the powerless, supporting democracy, and promoting social change. Cohen (in Adam, Craft & Cohen, 2004) writes that a central purpose of journalism is to "provide an independent source of information by which the governed can exert autonomous control over their own lives" (p. 268). These definitions rely on an Enlightenment conception of the self finding happiness in the possession of private goods, free from others' interference. Virtue approaches have been rightly criticized for glossing over protection of individual human rights. These are, after all, necessary for the "equal possession of the necessary conditions" for purposive action (Gewirth, 1985, p. 761). However, the common good cannot be reduced to the protection of individual rights either. Journalism's guardian dimension provides only a partial rationale for *journalism as practice*.

A growing trend is to stress a deliberative function for the press. Barger & Barney (2004) say journalism's essential purpose is production of what might be called shared democratic knowledge, which requires pluralistic forums for debate. May (2001) likewise offers enhancing democratic deliberation to "create the possibility of vigorous public life in a republic" (p. 199). Demers (1989) says "the major task of journalists is to disseminate the kind of information that illuminates collective choices" (p. 26).[4] Definitions focused on deliberation more closely resemble MacIntyre's (2007) framework, which relies on the Aristotelean notion of a self whose happiness depends on community membership and joint action with others. In fact, MacIntyre suggests that citizenship itself is a practice. This notion is echoed, as well, by Carey (1995), who argues that journalism's reason for being is the "development and enhancement of public life, a common life which we can all share as citizens" (¶8). Croteau & Hoynes (2001), laying out a public sphere model of the media (versus a market model), say "the principal way that mass media can contribute to democratic processes is by helping to cultivate social spaces for public dialogue" (p. 20). Kovach & Rosenstiel (2001), when they extend their thinking beyond what is suggested by the First Amendment, suggest that the purpose of journalism flows from the function of news and that journalism has been intrinsically bound up with forming community. May (2001) likewise concludes that, at a deeper level, the role of the press is "to give citizens a sense of belonging. To belong, people need to feel clued in. They want to know what's up, what's new" (p. 204). May traces this mission to the yellow journalism of the nineteenth century, when scrappy dailies looked beyond the elite audiences of earlier newspapers and swung their appeal to the masses of immigrants who were pouring into America's emerging urban centers:

> At a still deeper level, the media—emphasizing as they do, what's new, what wasn't there yesterday—continue to make immigrants of us all. They redefine us daily as the newly arrived, those who need constant reorientation. When we have been too busy and distracted for a few days to read the newspaper or watch TV, we talk about catching up on the news, as though we have lagged in a caravan that moved off ahead of us into unfamiliar terrain. Or, more accurately, as though the landscape itself has changed while we slept. (p. 205)

---

4   Although journalism does not have to be limited to this content, Demers' requirement illuminates a key difference in function between journalism and consumer-oriented media content.

It is because human flourishing is conditional on community membership that May (2001) argues for membership, or belonging, as "first in social goods not only because it supplies the member with a claim on other goods but because it is a good in itself" (p. 252). If so, journalism may be among the most important practices of all. However, is fostering community membership an expansive enough goal to provide the *telos* for *journalism as practice*? Belonging is necessary for human flourishing, but not sufficient. Flourishing requires participation in the quest for the common good, and that requires knowing well. A theory of news that helps citizens know well is discussed next.

What Kind of News Does the Telos *of Journalism Require?*

The fact of a complex—some would say hostile—public sphere is the single most relevant context for news (Rosen, 2004b), more so than any specific political or economic system. It is this fact that makes knowing well so challenging. At the most basic level of human need, we need to "understand the emerging environment" (Barger & Barney, 2004, p. 201) so that we can look out for our safety and general well-being. As individual moral agents, we need to understand our world so that we can exercise autonomous choice. As social beings, we need information about others for "creating community, making human connections" (Kovach & Rosenstiel, 2001, p. 21)—a need so intense that news binds people together even in tyrannical societies.

However, as citizens, we also need to feel oriented to the public sphere to enjoy true membership and meaningful participation in civic life—and thus to engage in a viable quest for the good life as humans. The public sphere is that "space" outside of government and Big Business where private individuals come together through various civic institutions to constitute a "public" that can effectively assert the interests of the community (Habermas, 1989). Excellent news oriented toward a *telos* of civic participation is not, then, just *any* kind of information. If I need to find out something that affects only me, I can go find it. I can do a Google search, make a phone call, look through a catalog. "News," on the other hand, is never just about one person. Even human interest stories are properly called "news" only if they shed light on some broader social phenomenon illustrated by an individual case, just as all true art provides insight about the human condition. "News," then is *inherently communal* in nature. Rosen (2004b) notes:

> Philosophers disagree on whether a tree falling in the forest makes a sound, if no one hears it. But it is certain that the tree does not make news. Until it hits a house, and civilization gets involved. Then a public interest is at stake. Now there can be news. (Journalism is done for a public, ¶3)

Journalism's tradition has emphasized localism, or geographically bound communities (Altschull, 1990), but news also can be about an ideological community, a community of shared interests, a community of shared beliefs, and so on. What specifically counts as news for each of these communities will depend on what determines membership and which values they share. In other words, relevance of content varies by community, much as virtues do. This is the realm of niche journalism, which is valuable to the *telos* of civic participation if it enhances intra-group deliberation.[5] The purpose is for communities to properly examine their separate interests, in addition to interests they may have in common with others in the larger public sphere. This is especially relevant to subordinate communities, which might not have a chance to engage in such deliberation otherwise (Haas and Steiner, 2001).

Journalists are not the only ones who help fellow citizens in this regard— religious denominations and political parties come to mind. Yet, unlike most other groups, journalists are called by their practice's *telos* to consistently address all the overlapping communities of the public sphere with the common good for all in mind. Christians, Ferre & Fackler (1993) note that the common good in this sense does not refer to majority opinion or some false consensus, but rather a commitment to transnational human norms that foster good communities, such as truthfulness, justice, and empowerment. News directed at a general audience (the traditional emphasis of American journalism) attempts to go beyond the particularities of specific communities and generate the possibility for constructive collective action in the public sphere. General news should strive to promote significant overlap in the knowledge possessed by different communities. The goal is not to gloss over differences, but to surface and accommodate differences (Anderson, Dardenne & Killenberg, 1997; Haas & Steiner, 2001), so that it is possible for all citizens to participate meaningfully in the public sphere and to take concerted action on behalf of public concerns. Excellent news is common knowledge that is inclusive and empowering, rather than coercive and subordinating—a "normative pluralism," in the words of Christians, Ferre & Fackler (1993, p. 194). No citizen left behind. Such interaction with fellow citizens must be frequent and timely to keep them in the loop. When news meets the practice's standards of excellence, it empowers citizens to perform the following civic functions necessary for full participation in community life (these are summarized in Table 4.1). Non-journalists possessing certain skills and resources also may help citizens perform these functions. However, journalism has the rare ability to promote these functions in ways that are timely (unlike most scholarship), independent (unlike political parties or special-interest groups), and contemporaneously available to most segments of society (unlike classroom discussions or weblogs). From most to least basic, these functions are:

- *Surveillance.* This function consists of monitoring people, events, and things that affect citizens as individuals and community members. To perform this minimal function, journalists require training and experience with investigation and access to centers of power. This kind of news is what Hendry (2004) calls "common sense knowledge" (p. 117). As Graber (2003) suggests, journalists have had the best track record with this particular civic function.
- *Interpretation.* This function consists of assessing the relative importance and relevance of specific civic knowledge to the common good. To help citizens

---

5   Hendry (2004) points out that identifying strictly with others who are similar (e.g. those who share the same "lifestyle") unduly narrows the moral focus of individuals, compared with the moral demands of "traditional communities of diversity" (p. 170).

Table 4.1   Civic functions promoted by excellent news

Function	Purpose	Journalistic Requirements
Surveillance	Monitoring people, events and things that affect citizens as individuals and community members	Training and experience with investigation and access to centers of power
Interpretation	Assessing the relative importance and relevance of specific civic knowledge to the common good	High standards of reliability and demonstrable independence
Reckoning	Evaluating the realistic possibility of influencing specific public issues through collective action	Knowing the system and its players, judging extent of public concern, assessing risks and benefits, analyzing possible solutions on their merits

perform this function, excellent news meets high standards of reliability and demonstrates independence. In these regards, traditional journalistic practices of gatekeeping remain relevant. Excellent performance of this function also entails a commitment to community service backed up by transparency, self-reflection, self-criticism, and other disciplines rendering journalists accountable for their performance. As far as these standards are concerned, journalism should be more open about how it creates news, providing access to raw interviews, documents, and other sources, and explaining the process of verification. Journalists also need to provide citizens with a wide diversity of viewpoints, opportunities to try out ideas, and help in assessing presuppositions. To achieve these goals, news stories might fruitfully incorporate an interactive component (Matheson, 2004).

* *Reckoning.* This function consists of evaluating the *actionability* of specific issues arising in the public sphere; that is, the realistic possibility of influencing them through collective action. This requires knowing: the system and its players; grassroots movements; whether there are enough people concerned about the problem to have an influence on policy; a reliable assessment of risks and benefits; and views on a range of possible approaches and their costs, effectiveness, and durability. Depending on the problem, collective action may consist of "voluntary community intervention" or lobbying of "relevant political actors and institutions" (Haas & Steiner, 2001, p. 137). Practitioners engaged in civic journalism projects have been interested in correcting for journalism's traditional lack of attention to the reckoning

function by broadening the range of sources they interview, focusing as much on solutions as they do on problems, conducting public surveys, and other strategies.

Press coverage of Hurricane Katrina in 2005 illustrates the need for journalists to carry out these civic functions when they create news. Initial reporting of Hurricane Katrina neglected issues of race and class and failed to question the government's response. However, as the scope and causes of the human misery became clearer, the press eventually began asking the right questions. News organizations ranging from the flooded-out local newspaper, the *Times-Picayune*, to national powerhouses like the television networks helped citizens monitor the situation through traditional reporting and also through innovative approaches, such as online tools to help victims locate missing relatives. Reporters were guilty of spreading misinformation about rapes and other crimes at the Convention Center and elsewhere in the city, partly because of logistical problems that made getting accurate accounts difficult and partly because of failure to verify rumors. This, coupled with lack of local perspective about the dynamics of race in New Orleans, resulted in negative stereotypes about poor black people (O'Keefe, 2005). On the other hand, the eyewitness accounts of reporters on the scene successfully conveyed the dire need of those trapped by the floodwaters. "[C]ameras captured the immediate reality of what was happening at the New Orleans Convention Center, making a mockery of the stalling and excuses being put forward by those in power" (Wells, 2005, ¶3).

There were numerous stories as part of continuing coverage of Katrina that offered perspective on hurricane planning in the Gulf region and on public policy affecting minorities and the poor in the South and elsewhere (Alterman, 2005b). By spelling out the implications of the failure to plan properly for the evacuation and rescue of the city's poorest residents, journalists highlighted important questions about the terms of the social compact in the United States. "What's more American: The public good? Or individual profit? Frankness? Or posturing? A safety net? Or tax cuts? The bloated corpses floating in the toxic New Orleans waters seem to demand an answer" (Gurnett, 2005, ¶2).

Reporters and anchors demonstrated more independence than usual, prompting *NBC Nightly News* anchor Brian Williams to hope that "this is the story that brings a healthy amount of cynicism back to a news media known for it" (Bauder, 2005, p. D5). Journalists shouted at cops, lectured politicians, and blocked artful dodges they normally would have let slide. In effect, they personally lobbied those who had the means to do something about the desperate conditions caused by Katrina and, at least by example, encouraged readers and viewers to do so as well. The tone was so uncharacteristically aggressive that the *Salon* magazine web site talked of "Reporters Gone Wild" (Bauder, 2005).

This kind of activist stance, which would have drawn flak had it come from American reporters in Iraq, seemed utterly appropriate when applied to the yawning gap between mounting casualties and reassuring rhetoric. For once, reporters were acting like concerned citizens, not passive observers. (Kurtz, 2005, ¶8)

However, journalists may have allowed their emotions and physical isolation to interfere with the skepticism and larger perspective that characterizes good reporting (O'Keefe, 2005). This illustrates the need for a cooperative verification process that can mitigate the cognitive limitations of individual journalists and correct for institutional pressure to be first with the story.

Right after the hurricane, journalists did a remarkable job of helping citizens take action—whether it be accessing assistance, finding out about volunteering opportunities, or making monetary donations to the American Red Cross and other aid organizations. Three months after the disaster, major news organizations were still reporting on the recovery of towns affected by the hurricane and scrutinizing federal contracts awarded for rebuilding efforts. However, excellent news demands more, as Brent Cunningham (2005) noted in the *Columbia Journalism Review*:

> Extensive coverage of the rebuilding of New Orleans is certainly something readers and viewers deserve, but they also deserve a form of journalism that has always been difficult for the press in the United States to produce: stories grounded in solid reporting about what is possible, rather than simply what is probable; stories that shatter the official zeitgeist; stories that help set the agenda. (¶3)

Re-casting their democratic role in terms of public virtue would mean journalists would strive to promote as much civic participation as possible. It also would mean defining and covering news in ways that reflect the kind of knowledge citizens need to jointly discover to achieve the common good. This would mean no more framing issues in the black-and-white rhetoric of warring interest group leaders, no more reducing public opinion to the aggregation of fleeting individual preferences (May, 2001; Schudson, 1998). This would mean more analysis of the values at stake in public policy, and more coverage of opportunities and strategies for joint action. It also would mean a greater focus—borrowing from bloggers—on helping citizens choose materials and access multiple perspectives, rather than offering a singular synthesis of the day's news (Matheson, 2004). In the process of meeting such performance standards, journalists would also realize the internal goods that uniquely define their practice.

The Internal Goods of *Journalism as Practice*

According to MacIntyre (2007), the distinguishing features of internal goods are:

- They cannot be realized outside of "some particular kind of practice" (p. 188).
- They can be evaluated only by "the experience of participating in the practice in question" (p. 189).
- They are realized as the natural outcome of achieving standards of excellence that partially define that kind of practice.

In his chess example, MacIntyre (2007) talks about the game's internal goods as consisting of the "achievement of a certain kind of highly particular kind of analytical skill, strategic imagination and competitive intensity" that offer reasons for "trying to excel in whatever way the game of chess demands" (p. 188). These goods are internal to chess because "we can only specify them in terms of chess or some other game of that specific kind and by means of examples from such games" (p. 188). In another example, portrait painting, MacIntyre distinguishes between two types of excellence internal to practices: the "excellence of the products" themselves (p. 189)—evident in the end results and the performances that went into generating them—and "the good of a certain kind of life" found in the self-conscious pursuit of achieving that excellence (p. 190). In other words, the dimensions that are key to distinguishing among different kinds of activities are product and purpose.

Internal goods are the reasons why practitioners participate in a particular kind of practice; if a good can be achieved or gotten in some other way, it is not internal to the practice. Lambeth (1992) has proposed "telling the whole story" (p. 74); "choosing clear, vivid, and precise prose" (p. 73); and "keeping the reader squarely in mind" (p. 73) as goods internal to journalism. However, telling the whole story is a goal of documentary filmmaking as well as journalism. Writing clear and precise prose with your reader in mind is the objective of any writer, not just a journalist. Further, Lambeth's ideas take the form of action guides, or standards of excellence, rather than goods to be achieved within the practice. Later, Lambeth equates internal goods with "professional values of in-depth truth-telling, humaneness, and fairness" (p. 85). However, qualities such as fairness, honesty, and loyalty are best characterized as virtues because they are habitual dispositions applicable to a whole human life (in fact, Klaidman & Beauchamp, 1987, include these among the virtues required to be a good journalist).

What counts as a good that can only be achieved by practicing journalism or something like it? To answer this question, it might be helpful to think through an exemplary journalistic achievement. The quintessential achievement in journalistic tradition is the expose that brings to light wrong-doing by government officials through the compelling presentation of carefully verified original evidence. Even better is when such news directly prompts government and/or citizen action to rectify or prevent the problem journalists have identified. This achievement is especially gratifying when the story or series has been the result of intense effort—in the form of "good old fashioned shoe leather reporting," sophisticated data analysis, repeated Freedom of Information Act requests, persistence despite intense pressure—and when the news is disseminated widely to a mass audience in a publication or program of recognized quality. If the story is an exclusive and comes at a crucial time, even better. Because it resembles this scenario so closely, the Watergate investigation has become paradigmatic of excellence in journalism's tradition, as noted in Chapter 3. However, is not the exemplary story of scientific excellence quite similar? A team of scientists conducts a meticulously designed scientific study that, at long last, determines the cause of an environmental calamity. The findings are judged groundbreaking by the scientific community. Better yet, the study inspires further research that can ultimately form the basis of sound environmental policy. The achievement is especially gratifying if the breakthrough has come after many years of failed experiments and fund-raising obstacles. Prouder yet will be the scientists be if their work is published first in a distinguished peer-reviewed journal of wide circulation at a pivotal time for research in their field.

Science as an Exemplary Intellectual Practice

Excellence in journalism and science are similar because they are both a "particular kind of practice" (MacIntyre, 2007, p. 188), namely, intellectual practices. Ward (2005) recognizes this aspect of *journalism as practice* when he describes journalism as a "practical, truth-directed form of inquiry" (p. 314). Kovach & Rosenstiel (2001) likewise identify verification as the essence of journalism and suggest that it is a discipline characterized by five "intellectual principles of a science of reporting" (p. 78). Intellectual practices—such as science, journalism and teaching—cooperatively determine what counts as a particular kind of knowledge, what is worthy of investigation, what is worthy of dissemination, and in what form. Each, in its own sphere, is engaged in seeking and sharing an authoritative account of the "truth."[6] It is this knowledge quest, how it is conducted and how it is internally and externally validated that constitute the essence of science, on the one hand, and journalism, on the other. To be a scientist is to know the world in a certain way. The same is true for a journalist. Both practices require acceptance of a specific way of knowing, or epistemology; certain methodological procedures, and writing conventions that enact that epistemology; gatekeeping procedures that enforce that epistemology; and conditions for accepting the authority of that epistemology. Indeed, when we think of the worst cases of journalistic misconduct, they come down to grievous violations of this code: fabrication, plagiarism, lack of corroboration, gross bias. This is not to imply that other kinds of activities do not also need intellectual virtues to flourish. This seems to be the case with some arts, crafts, and games, for instance. However, as Zagzebski (1996) points out, the object of such activities "is more a matter of knowing-how rather than knowing-that" (p. 179).

Code (1987) suggests that science can serve as a model for all intellectual practices. She says "what happens in a scientific community can profitably be taken as an example of the importance of an interdependent, responsible approach in intellectual activity as such" (p. 229). Scientists produce shared knowledge within a "complex network of interdependence" (p. 230) resting on a "tacit basis of trust and trustworthiness" (p. 230). Similarly, reporters and editors must trust each other to evaluate news on the basis of rules and standards passed down by the forebears of journalistic tradition and not to commit wanton violations of these rules and standards, such as fabricating events or plagiarizing someone else's copy. The necessity of mutual collegial trust makes these practices extremely vulnerable to practitioners with no regard for traditional rules and standards, as illustrated by the

---

6   Zagzebski (1996) says that truth is only one component of knowledge and that truth-conducive processes, such as journalism's discipline of verification, function to promote reliable success in justifying true beliefs. These processes may not be useful, however, for promoting other epistemic goals, such as understanding or creativity. These goals may require different kinds of epistemic processes—perhaps in different kinds of practices (such as philosophy or painting) or in different divisions of epistemic labor within the same practice.

gross cases of misconduct that occasionally surprise and shame both scientists and journalists.

Collegiality exerts itself among scientists in a mixture of accountability, criticism, and esteem. Peer review (analogous to the layers of editing in journalism) lets only the most plausible findings see the light of day. Although Code (1987) acknowledges the potential tyranny of such a system, she notes that, "[w]ith such mutual control, epistemic authority is established and dogmatic or fantastical excesses are checked" (p. 231). This system recognizes that knowledge is essentially "commonable," (p. 167) or interdependent, and that, therefore, there are limits on individual cognitive autonomy. Hence, the need for a system of checks and balances. Like journalism, science "welds tradition and freedom together in pursuit of the truth" (p. 236), creating "constant tension between independent thought and institutionalized expertise" (p. 233). In science, this tension is manifest in the process of paradigm-driven research described by science sociologist Thomas Kuhn (1970). In journalism, it has been surfacing recently in skirmishes between those who argue for the superiority of the stand-alone Internet journalist freed from newsroom hoops and those who think there is a need for the traditional gatekeeping functions of editors and fact checkers.

Science's system is well-developed and rigorous, whereas journalism's techniques and conventions fall short of being an actual "*system* for testing the reliability of journalistic interpretation" (Kovach & Rosenstiel, 2001, p. 75). Rather, it uses a relatively loose "discipline of verification" (p. 71). Meyer (2004b) is among those who believe that, if anything, journalism should try to resemble science more closely by adopting such scientific techniques as replication so others can "get the same answer" (¶14) and playing "devil's advocate with your data" (¶16).[7] Code (1987) points out that science (and, by implication, other intellectual practices) need standards of verification, yes, but also recognition of knowledge's limitations. Knowledge is an interim product subject to revision. It also is a constructed product necessarily situated in a particular context. For example, journalistic epistemology is largely structured by the presentational, scheduling, and audience demands of each particular medium and news genre (Ekström, 2002).

Code's (1987) observation pinpoints another tension being experienced within all intellectual practices resting on modernist assumptions. Jackson (1998) describes this as a struggle between epistemic authority—reflected in the use of datelines, quotations, and other journalistic conventions vouching for the objectivity of news stories—and interpretive authority—reflected in the rejection of objectivity among those involved in new media formats on cable and the Internet. Kovach & Rosenstiel (2001) frame the tension as a contest between the journalism of verification and the journalism of assertion. In this regard, the outpouring of journalistic nostalgia about Watergate in 2005 can be seen as the mourning of what Hallin (1992) has called the "high modernism" (p. 16) of American journalism during the early 1970s. Now, many agree with McNair (1998) that there is "no universal, *objective* journalism … only journal*isms*, with different styles and hierarchies of news values, shaped

---

7   Code (1987) specifies, however, that science is paradigmatic in terms of "the nature and extent of human cognitive interdependence" (p. 230), not in its methodology *per se*.

by and specific to particular societies at particular times" (p. 12). Modern science, likewise, has been challenged by postmodernism and other interpretive research paradigms, which now co-exist with the positivist model in an uneasy dialogue. Yet, perhaps because science's epistemological framework was much more developed than journalism's, its authority has not eroded to the same degree. Chapter 5 will examine the virtues most appropriate for sustaining journalism's traditional strengths as an intellectual practice while also accounting for new insights into the nature of knowledge.

The Unique Configuration of Journalism

So what goods can be achieved or gotten in intellectual practices that cannot be achieved or gotten any other way? Those would be the goods internal to this "particular kind of practice" (MacIntyre, 2007, p. 188). They include *knowledge* and *inquiry* as goods in themselves (not as mere means to other ends such as career advancement), *discovery* (in the senses of both finding out and making known), *originality* (in the sense of doing your own investigation and thinking), and *newness* (in the sense of being the first to find out, think, or experience something). The achievement of these goods requires a certain "analytical skill, strategic imagination and competitive intensity" (MacIntyre, 2007, p. 188) particularly suited to the rational pursuit of knowledge, using cooperative standards of investigation and interpretation that allow practitioners to vouch authoritatively for their products.

All intellectual practices have similar internal goods, although their emphasis may differ depending on each practice's particular tradition, *telos*, and product. These differences raise questions when people go back and forth between different intellectual practices. Science produces knowledge that is more specialized and authoritative than journalism. Therefore, the conventions and procedures it has developed to achieve its internal goods are more rigorous and difficult to master; they result in products that are inaccessible to all but a small audience versed in the jargon and techniques of scientific inquiry. Advancement of specialized knowledge in this highly particular way is the *telos* of science. News, on the other hand, is practical common knowledge typically aimed at a general audience for the purpose of helping citizens know well in the public sphere. Normatively, news is not knowledge created for its own sake, but to provide the opportunity for civic participation—and, thus, human flourishing—in a complex society. In this respect, journalism resembles the intellectual practice of teaching, which also has a civic dimension in its goal of cultivating citizenship in the young.

On the other hand, journalism emphasizes newness as a good more than other intellectual practices. In fact, time itself—particularly the present—seems to be a good in journalism. Journalists value the present in the sense of being present—wanting to be a witness, to be in the know—and in the sense of the current times—wanting to record what is happening now, to get the word out now, to make sure that today is not forgotten. If historians hope to recapture the past for present times, journalists hope to capture the present so that it may one day become a record of the past; it is in this sense that journalists write the first draft of history. Indeed, history as an intellectual practice resembles journalism in several ways: It is a relatively open discipline (meaning it does not have a monopoly on historical knowledge); it is practiced in a range of venues (including universities, but also museums and other places); it has an interest in affecting the present through its knowledge products; it privileges a narrative form of presentation; and its knowledge claims are open to multiple interpretations (see the American Historical Association's Statement on Standards of Professional Conduct, adopted in 2005, for more background on the goals and values of professional historians).

Science is an occupational practice like journalism, but it does not as clearly possess the civic, political, and creative marks of *journalism as practice* (although arguments have been made for each). In these respects, journalism more closely resembles politics and literature. It is the specific configuration of a practice—its intersection with different traditions informing different kinds of practices—that provide it with a unique combination of internal goods. These determine what will be required for the excellence of its products, but also what counts as living an excellent life as a journalist, rather than a scientist, teacher, novelist, or public official. The thrill of a scoop, the pleasure of a well-written lede, the satisfaction of pinning down a pattern of wrong-doing, the honor of witnessing history. For a journalist, it does not get any better—as only a journalist can truly understand.

Chapter 5

Practice-Sustaining Virtues[1]

The late *Los Angeles Times* media critic David Shaw (2005b) attributed the growing "list of media miscreants" (¶1) to the transformation of journalism from a fairly modest occupation into a high-paying profession for elite practitioners who can parlay their success "into even more lucrative careers writing books and going on the lecture circuit" (¶9). As an example of how this state of affairs can impinge on good journalistic performance, Shaw cited the case of best-selling author Mitch Albom. Albom pre-wrote a Sunday column for the Detroit *Free Press*, in the past tense, about the attendance of two basketball players at a Saturday game. The players ended up not showing up to cheer their alma mater, so the column (which was printed in advance) was flat-out wrong on that point. In this case, wrote Shaw, the problem probably had to do with a surplus of fame and fortune. "Maybe he was just careless, too busy with his book writing, radio hosting, ESPN appearances and the other demands of celebrity to pay attention to the fundamental rules of journalism. Maybe journalism, and adherence to its rules, is no longer the first priority for journalists who become multimedia celebrities" (¶15).

This chapter explores five functions of virtues in sustaining *journalism as practice* at a time when commercial news organizations have increased the availability and appeal of power, status, money, and other material goods. This approach is a departure from other virtue treatments that underscore the virtues required of *individuals* or that focus on practices as the context for the *individual* exercise of the virtues. Oakley & Cocking (2001), for example, define professional virtues as those dispositions that help individual practitioners meet the profession's overriding goal with regard for relevant moral side constraints. Pellegrino (1995), writing in the context of medical ethics, suggests that professional virtues are "those dispositions that impart the capacity to [perform one's role] well" (p. 268). In the journalistic context, Lambeth (1992) identified truth, justice, freedom, humaneness, and individual responsibility as moral virtues in journalism (which he contrasted with non-moral values). Klaidman & Beauchamp (1987) covered the essential "traits of virtuous journalists" (p. 19), including reaching for truth, avoiding bias and harm, serving the public, and maintaining trust. Cohen (in Adam, Craft & Cohen, 2004) likewise focused on defining the virtues of individual journalists in relation to the "stated end of journalistic practice" (p. 268); these constitute competence in journalism. Adam, in the same article, conceptualized journalism as consisting essentially of authorship, so he specified virtues associated with writing. In my own

---

1   A slightly different version of this chapter was presented in March 2006 at the 15th annual meeting of the Association for Practical and Professional Ethics held in Jacksonville, FL.

work, I have written about individual virtues journalists should possess to overcome potential problems with case-based reasoning (Borden, 1999).

The purpose of this chapter is to seriously consider the significance of virtues at the level of the practice itself. The following practice-sustaining functions of virtues are discussed: (1) protecting the practice from the corruptive influence of external goods; (2) keeping the institutions that house the practice healthy, including the First Amendment and the news organizations that employ most journalists; (3) maintaining the kind of relationships that are necessary for achieving the practice's internal goods, especially collegial ties that support the practice's discipline of verification before news is disseminated; (4) preserving continuity with the practice's tradition; and (5) supporting the practice's regenerative capacities by making possible a cooperative discipline of confirmation after news is disseminated.

Protecting the Practice from Corruption by External Goods

MacIntyre (2007) says practices require cooperation, recognition of authority and achievement, respect for standards, and risk-taking. Business imperatives often threaten these basic requirements. The cooperation vital to good practice is distorted by the intense competitiveness of the market. Organizational reward systems do not necessarily honor journalistic achievement (as opposed to business goals) and often undermine journalistic authority by blurring the practice's boundaries. Likewise, managerial objectives often go directly against journalistic standards, for example, by insisting on efficiency over completeness. Finally, businesses are reluctant to tamper with money-making formulas, upset political allies, or otherwise rock the boat. In fact, Thompson (1967) suggested that reducing uncertainty is a fundamental organizational principle.

Organizational efforts to reduce uncertainty hinge on the efficient use of resources and on control. Being efficient in news organizations means getting and disseminating as much news as possible as quickly as possible (Nord, 1985). To that end, news organizations try to routinize news. Deadlines and news bureaus determine when and where something has to happen to make headlines. "Beats" limit the domain of potential news to predictable areas such as city government and police (Tuchman, 1977). Efficiency has even come to be viewed as a professional value in journalism: Failure to get news implies incompetence (Breed, 1955; Shoemaker & Reese, 1991). Formulas that routinize news are thus not only efficient, but also control workers by standardizing their behavior, just like supervision, performance evaluations, and other traditional management strategies. Formulas also maximize market share because they are widely accepted, albeit not necessarily desired (Ettema, Whitney & Wackman, 1987). Growth motivates commercial news organizations to adopt standards of excellence pertaining to productivity (usually measured in output of news stories or some other relevant unit), innovation (usually based on marketing research suggesting which kinds of novelty will appeal to the demographics most desired by advertisers), and quality (in customer service, marketing and other growth-oriented organizational functions, as well as in the product itself). The most ambitious form of control goes beyond internal adaptations to actually trying to control the market environment by merging with other companies in the information sector to accomplish vertical integration and/or neutralize a competitive threat (for example, Disney buying the ABC television network to ensure promotion and distribution for its various entertainment products).

The organizational imperative to reduce uncertainty comes into direct conflict with the internal good of reform. Far from rewarding journalism's impulse to bring attention to social injustice and official wrong-doing, news organizations put pressure on journalists to play it safe so they will not alienate advertisers, political allies, and audiences. In response, journalists need to be even bolder, to insist even more on the righting of wrongs, and to try even harder to contribute to the common good. This will be the pattern for all the virtues threatened by organizational priorities. Compensating for such pressures also requires, at times, the exercise of additional virtues that can help journalists to overcome specific threats to good practice and to restrain specific vices.

News organizations may be willing to loosen formulas if this is perceived as a useful strategy to attract new audiences. On the surface, then, it might appear that the institution supports the journalistic good of newness under certain circumstances. However, the institution's version of newness is often quite shallow. Efficiency considerations, such as closing bureaus or limiting travel, often prevent the practice from having the kind of access it needs to keep abreast of significant events as they happen. Rather than genuinely seeking to break ground, newness as an institutional priority often degenerates into mere novelty aimed at turning people's heads. Newness as gimmick is evident in organizational policies that require reporters to constantly update stories even when they cannot confirm developments or when it forces them to rush printing, airing, or posting "new" information just to beat the competition. With the capacity for real-time reporting provided by 24-hour cable news stations and the Internet, it would be a deficiency to stick with old production cycles that offered news updates just once or twice a day. Striking the appropriate mean requires the virtues of initiative and curiosity that characterize any good intellectual endeavor, but with an appreciation of what constitutes true knowledge as opposed to mere trivia or gossip.

Cost-cutting measures—such as closing bureaus, limiting travel, and reducing staff levels—also pose threats to the internal goods of originality (doing your own work, coming up with your own ideas) and discovery (learning about the world through observation and other evidence). For example, using the wire, other news publications, or press releases as sources of news stories prevents reporters from finding out information independently. In its 2005 report on American journalism, the Project for Excellence in Journalism noted, "Much of the investment and effort is in repackaging and presenting information, not in gathering it. For all that the number of outlets has grown, the number of people engaged in collecting original information has not. Americans are frankly more likely to see the same pictures across multiple TV channels or read the same wire story in different venues than they were a generation ago" (Project for Excellence in Journalism, 2005, Overview: news investment, ¶8).

Limiting access to news sources and events can preclude finding out about entire topics (even entire continents) altogether, thwarting the good of discovery. To compensate, journalists need to cultivate ingenuity or cleverness to overcome the resource constraints so commonly imposed by the institution. For example, they may be able to convince superiors of the necessity of on-the-scene reporting by appealing to values supported by both the practice and the institution. Failing that, journalists can come up with dependable substitutes for finding out and corroborating evidence, such as working with a trusted stringer.[2]

The good of inquiry, or the process of "substantiating beliefs and knowledge claims" (Code, 1987, p. 53), is constantly challenged by time constraints imposed by the institution for efficiency purposes. Inquiry is also harmed by not having enough qualified colleagues; that is, practitioners who consciously self-identify as journalists and who are bound to recognize the authority and standards of the practice. This has become a factor because of staff cuts and demoralized journalists leaving the practice. Without an appropriate moral community, journalists cannot implement proper standards for ensuring intellectual reliability because these rely on a cooperative system of verification. Rutten (2006) suggested, for example, that Reuters ended up circulating a doctored photo of fighting in Lebanon around the world in 2006 because it dismantled three photo desks staffed by veterans in Washington, London, and Hong Kong in favor of one consolidated global desk manned by less experienced journalists in Singapore. There simply were not enough journalists who had achieved the practice's standards of excellence to exercise high standards of verification when freelance photographer Adnan Hajj e-mailed the image to Reuters from his laptop. Even when there are enough practitioners to vouch for the reliability of news, organizational incentives that accent external rewards dampen the motivation to act out of the virtues of curiosity, love of learning, open-mindedness, and self-reflection, while competitiveness strains collegial trust and cooperation.

The good of knowledge itself—the clear perception and presentation of truth as practitioners can best determine it—is threatened by inadequately small news holes that prevent complete presentation of news and other institutional obstacles. The desire for material rewards, meanwhile, interferes with the exercise of intellectual modesty and intellectual honesty. A case in point is the conservative cable commentator who got $240,000 from the US Department of Education in 2004 to talk up the Bush Administration's controversial No Child Left Behind education law (Toppo, 2005). Even though Armstrong Williams was not, strictly speaking, a journalist, the journalistic community reacted with palpable dismay that someone purporting to offer independent commentary would compromise his credibility, if not his actual judgment, by accepting a fee to disseminate propaganda (see, for example, Rich, 2005a).

The Williams incident showed that even non-objective commentators in the media implicitly vouch for certain standards of knowing and, of course, independence. Although it is an extreme case, it illustrates the need for journalists to compensate for such temptations. Through the exercise of prudence, for example, journalists can limit the situations that pose conflicts of interest or tempt them to overstate the evidence. Justice can help them make sure that incentives for spicing up stories do

---

2   These and other strategies are discussed in Chapter 6.

not tempt them to treat sources and subjects unfairly. Other compensating virtues will be called for depending on the specific situation. Whenever the institutional context endangers the practice's internal goods, journalists need to cultivate and exercise the virtue of courage to defend the practice's integrity. Nevertheless, the degree to which we can legitimately expect individual practitioners to be courageous depends on the level of moral support they can count on at the collective level of the practice (May, 1996). There will be more on this in Chapter 6.

In an environment in which the pursuit of external goods becomes dominant, MacIntyre (2007) warns that the virtues can be replaced by "semblance and simulacra" (p. 183): counterfeits of the real thing. This is a real concern in journalism because of the strong influence of the organizational setting and the way in which managers blur the journalism and business spheres in newsroom policies and news formulas. The practice's passion for good writing gets warped into a commercial strategy for attracting audiences; topics that are considered too "boring" are covered by wire services—or are ignored altogether—regardless of their importance. Objectivity, journalism's effort to develop a procedure for producing reliable knowledge, becomes an efficient way to produce news and to avoid offending advertisers and audiences—real insight, even truth, be damned. The practice's interest in discovering new knowledge gets turned into a market imperative to beat the competition, even if this means chasing after celebrity trivia and cutting intellectual and moral corners to be first.

Competition, in fact, has become such a powerful counterfeit virtue that it even pits colleagues of the same organization against each other. William May (2001) notes that competitive relationships among members of a practice hurt their "capacity for mutual nurture and renewal," while "service to the common good yields to the necessities of survival" (p. 11). Thus, the Janet Cookes and Jayson Blairs of the world feel that the only way they can make it at places like the *Washington Post* and the *New York Times* is to wow their editors by producing one fabulist story after another. Indeed, such episodes illustrate the vulnerability of journalists to vice, even those journalists with the potential for excellence. As MacIntyre (2007) points out:

> It is no part of my thesis that great violinists cannot be vicious or that great chess-players cannot be mean-spirited. Where the virtues are required, the vices also may flourish. It is just that the vicious and mean-spirited necessarily rely on the virtues of others for the practices in which they engage to flourish and also deny themselves the experience of achieving those internal goods which may reward even not very good chess-players and violinists. (p. 193)

However much can be explained by the competitive pressures of their respective newsrooms, it is clear that Cooke and Blair also allowed themselves to be driven by greed, dishonesty, and other vices. They took advantage of their fellow practitioners and, in the end, proved themselves to be ignorant of true excellence in journalism.

Sustaining the Institutional Bearers of the Practice

Despite the potential of institutions for corrupting practices, it is one of the jobs of virtue to help them flourish. "The ability of a practice to retain its integrity will depend on the way in which the virtues can be and are exercised in sustaining the institutional forms which are the social bearers of the practice" (MacIntyre, 2007, p. 195). This role of the virtues can be seen most clearly in the acceptance by most journalists of a responsibility for protecting the First Amendment, the institutional context that journalists love to love. This constitutional clause has been widely interpreted as a foundational document for the practice of journalism in the United States. Lambeth (1992) proposes that stewardship of free expression is a principle in journalism. He explains, "Although citizenship in a constitutional democracy makes each citizen a steward, the journalists' occupation gives them unique resources for this role. They manage their resources of communication with due regard for the rights of others, the rights of the public, and the moral health of their own occupation" (p. 32).

Lambeth (1992) says stewardship includes taking First Amendment cases to court, as long as these are not likely to result in an unfavorable ruling that ultimately constricts expression. Stewardship also involves insisting on the openness of government documents and meetings. Lambeth's analysis suggests that journalists should oppose recent efforts to increase government secrecy, including such initiatives as extending federal agencies' power to classify information, restricting access to unclassified information in libraries and other public sites, discouraging disclosure of information under the Freedom of Information Act, and making access to top officials contingent on anonymous attribution. At the time of this writing, there has been no effective resistance to these practices by the Washington press, which is reluctant to blow what little access it has left. The result has been a dramatic reduction in government accountability and journalistic effectiveness (Alterman, 2005a). On the other hand, some commentators have wondered whether the *New York Times* might have set back the legal recognition of journalists' right to protect confidential sources in the Valerie Plame case. This legally problematic case pitted *Times* reporter Judith Miller against the federal prosecutor investigating the leak of Plame's identity as a CIA operative to reporters (McCollam, 2005a).

The aim of stewardship should not be just to advance a particular news story, but to preserve and strengthen free expression as a fundamental context for the practice of journalism and the exercise of citizenship in the United States. "By such stewardship, [journalists] contribute not only to the health of journalism but to a civic culture dependent on both freedom and community" (Lambeth, 1992, p. 204). Lambeth notes, however, that stewardship also implies acting responsibly *as* journalists to avoid eroding support for the First Amendment among citizens fed up with media excess.

Just as the First Amendment needs the practice's stewardship, so do the other institutions that sustain journalism, including commercial news organizations. Meyer (2004a) has put forward the most compelling case yet for linking the health of news organizations to the integrity of the practice. He goes so far as to advise, "Those who would preserve the best of journalism's traditions should start with the premise that it is a business" (p. 205). He does not mean by this that *journalism as practice* is a business *per se* but, rather, that the practice's long-term health is inevitably intertwined with the commercial vitality of news organizations (he focuses particularly on newspapers). His research shows that good journalism can help newspapers succeed economically in competitive markets. When they invest in quality, newspapers inspire credibility and improve their sales. Although there is a point at which additional investments no longer outweigh the additional costs associated with improved quality, people start looking elsewhere for news if quality declines beyond a minimal level. The key, therefore, is to hit the optimal level at which newspapers recoup or exceed the investments they put into quality. Meyer calls this the influence model. The basic idea is that social influence (which is not for sale) increases commercial influence (which newspapers sell to advertisers) by fostering audience trust (which is valuable to advertisers). The evidence for this model is unclear in monopoly situations. However, Meyer's work so far suggests that the practice can help itself by shoring up the commercial organizations that employ most working journalists.

Next, I will discuss virtues that pertain to the practice as a context for performing certain social roles. MacIntyre says this aspect of participating in a practice requires virtues to perform two other practice-sustaining functions: maintaining the kind of relationships that are necessary for achieving the practice's internal goods, and preserving continuity with the practice's tradition.

Maintaining Relationships Essential to the Practice's Goals

To achieve its internal goods, *journalism as practice* requires collegial relationships that are "trust-based, covenantal ones," rather than "autonomy-based, contractual relationships" (Pellegrino, 1995, p. 264). To have such relationships, MacIntyre (2007) says that all practices require the virtues of justice, courage, and honesty. "For not to accept these ... so far bars us from achieving the standards of excellence or the goods internal to the practice that it renders the practice pointless except as a device for achieving external goods" (p. 191).

Honesty, justice, and courage are virtues that should characterize the relationship between journalists and their sources and between journalists and the public too (Klaidman & Beauchamp, 1987). However, MacIntyre's (2007) discussion of these virtues as necessary for excellence in any practice pertains specifically to the relationship of practitioners to each other. The goods of a practice can only be achieved by subordinating ourselves to "our relationship to other practitioners. We have to learn to recognize what is due to whom [justice]; we have to be prepared to take whatever self-endangering risks are demanded along the way [courage]; and we have to listen carefully to what we are told about our own inadequacies and to reply with the same carefulness for the facts [honesty]" (p. 191).

Among the goods that practitioners must distribute fairly among themselves are the authority and recognition that are due those who achieve excellence as journalists. "To depart from the standards of justice in some particular instance defines our relationship with the relevant person as in some way special or distinctive" (MacIntyre, 2007, p. 192), interfering with the trust needed for colleagues to depend on each other. As for courage, it is necessary to demonstrate the genuineness of our "care and concern for individuals, communities and causes which is so crucial to so much in practices" (p. 192). This requires a willingness to risk harm for their sakes. For example, the journalistic community should stand with individual practitioners who put their jobs on the line for the sake of the practice's goals. This is a concrete demonstration of solidarity (Borden, 2000). Such courage is also demonstrated by those practitioners who risk going to jail to protect the principle of source confidentiality—a risk that has become more common as the federal government resorts to prosecuting journalists as a way to find and punish leakers (McCollam, 2005a).

In addition to its role in constructive criticism, honesty also affects our perception of colleagues' "allegiance to each other in the pursuit of common goods" because "we define our relationship to each other, whether we acknowledge it or not, by reference to standards of truthfulness and trust" (MacIntyre, 2007, p. 192). Trust binds members of epistemic communities and makes them mutually vulnerable. In an intellectual practice, honesty is also fundamental to the epistemic contract that binds colleagues:

> *Characters* admirable as exemplars, either of moral or of intellectual virtue, do more than perform the bare minimum required by the (unwritten) letter of the contract. They would not, for example, disclose only the barest facts when asked if they know about something (the epistemic analogue of working to rule); rather, they would take cognitive interdependence to be a *value* worth some effort to sustain. (p. 179)

In the journalistic context, this implies that practitioners should openly share with each other documents, sources, observations, and other evidence to ensure that the practice *as such* can responsibly vouch for the knowledge that gets legitimized as "news"—in other words, to achieve and demonstrate intellectual reliability. To do any less is to endanger the practice's system of gatekeeping, which consists of a "discipline of verification" (Kovach & Rosenstiel, 2001, p. 71) or what Gardner, Csikszentmihalyi & Damon (2001) call journalism's "second-nature practices" (p. 185). As press critic and blogger Jay Rosen (2005b) noted, the scandal over a 2005 *Newsweek* brief would have never happened had the news magazine not created a place for speculative, gossipy news items it felt free to publish without adhering to its usual standards of verification.[3]

To produce authoritative knowledge, journalists ideally check details for accuracy, corroborate information as a way to determine its veracity, establish meaningful context to make the news intelligible and relevant to civic life, subject copy to moral scrutiny to ensure that it is not causing unjustified harm,

---

3   For more on the *Newsweek* case, see the *Practically Speaking* feature in this chapter.

and exercise transparency about the reliability of their motives, sources, and methods. All this is done on deadline. Part of what it means to be epistemically responsible in journalism, however, is knowing when to hold a story rather than to go with something that does not meet the practice's standards of excellence— a constant temptation posed by the speed of today's media technologies. The practice's verification process, in short, is characterized by intersubjectivity (which acknowledges the constructed nature of knowledge and the limits of individual cognition), redundancy (which functions as a check on individual and collective error), and skepticism (which helps to disrupt premature judgments based on unquestioned "common sense" and to surface potentially unwarranted assumptions encoded in the news).

Lambeth (1992) offers the concept of *authentic interpretation* to describe the basic process of verification I am recommending. This notion "retains the fidelity to fact central to the 'old objectivity' while furnishing perspective and fullness of meaning" that can overcome the pitfalls of he said–she said stories (p. 66). Authentic interpretation is "scientific in spirit, and the truth it portrays is subject to addition and revision" (p. 66). Likewise, Ward's (2005) *pragmatic objectivity* retains traditional objectivity's emphasis on providing good grounds for knowledge claims while, at the same time, acknowledging the role of interpretation and values in inquiry.[4] Epistemic responsibility in journalism, in other words, does not require us to give up on all factuality, but neither does it require us to buy into traditional objectivity's notion of detachment. Detachment can be a virtue in certain professional practices. However, its relevance depends on each practice's overriding goals (May, 2001). Journalists need to determine whether detachment actually furthers the practice's *telos* of helping citizens know well so that they can participate in the public sphere. Given the postmodern sensibility that characterizes the new media, the answer to that may be, "Not any more." The old markers of detachment in news stories—use of the third person, abstinence from offering one's own assessments, and so forth—may actually be lowering journalism's credibility and, therefore, its effectiveness as an authoritative intellectual practice with civic aims. Indeed, Potter (2002) implies that strict impartiality discourages trust and trustworthiness because it denies difference and suggests that practitioners are not acting out of good will. Next, I turn to the role of trustworthiness as a virtue characterizing the relationship between journalists and citizens.

The Place of Trustworthiness in Journalism

Although it is the basis on which one is fully admitted into any social group, Brien (1998) notes that trustworthiness also serves several external functions for professionals: It fulfills an implicit promise made upon entering the field, it upholds colleagues' reputations, and it promotes cooperation from clients so that they can benefit from needed professional services. Likewise, journalists recognize the connection between the level of trust they command and their credibility as sources

---

4   Ward goes so far as to suggest that an objective stance is constitutive of virtuous intellectual inquiry.

of information, ideas, and debate. Practitioners are constantly working to establish both their cognitive legitimacy—that is, trying to prove that the news they create is generally accurate and dependable—and their moral legitimacy—trying to prove that their judgments are oriented toward public service, rather than self-interest (Winch, 1997). However, the primacy of trustworthiness in professional ethics rests on several conditions that do not apply in a straightforward way to journalism. The conditions of trustworthiness discussed in the professional ethics literature include: a pronounced power asymmetry between the trusted and the truster; a significant personal investment by the truster in the decision to trust; an attribution of good will; and a proximate relationship between the two parties. The expectation of trustworthiness functions as an indirect control mechanism for the professions: If professionals want to sustain trust (and autonomy), they must act ethically (Brien, 1998). Trustworthiness is also an expression of virtuous character. "Questions of trustworthiness do not reduce to questions of justification for what one has done" (Potter, 2002, p. 50). For example, a lie might be justified, but this does not necessarily mean the client would ever trust you again. Trustworthiness can be exercised fully only within the context of a trustworthy character. Some dispositions required for being "fully trustworthy" include: giving signs and assurances of trustworthiness; taking epistemic responsibility seriously; developing sensitivity to the perspective of the trusting; responding properly to broken trust; and having additional other-regarding virtues, including compassion, justice, beneficence, and thoughtfulness (pp. 26–32).

Trustworthiness, strictly defined, is different from confidence or reliance. Confidence obtains when the truster has identifiable reasons to expect something, for example, a doctor's credentials give patients confidence that he is competent to treat them. Reliance consists of depending on another to successfully act in a certain way, for example, the way we rely on the train to be on time (Brien, 1998). Trusting someone with respect to a particular good, on the other hand, means giving someone the opportunity to take care of something you value, according to Potter (2002). Trusting makes us vulnerable with respect to the valued thing; in other words, we stand to lose it. "Trust is what people in positions of vulnerability must do in order to participate in and benefit from a relationship that contains an asymmetry of power, but which promises desirable results that are obtainable in no other way" (Newton, Hodges & Keith, 2004, p. 399). Although non-journalistic sources of social knowledge do not necessarily inspire confidence or deliver reliability, it is not clear—given the sheer number of information sources these days—that citizens are as vulnerable to journalism as trustworthiness technically requires. If we take the vulnerability requirement as far as Brien does, moreover, trustworthiness requires the truster to remain vulnerable in the trusting relationship; in other words, she is to make no back-up plans in case of betrayal. Viewed in this light, the ascendancy of blogs and other new media are a mark of *dis*trust in traditional journalism. However, it does not seem desirable to somehow make citizens *more* vulnerable to journalism. Journalism's tradition, rather, is committed to a vibrant public sphere characterized by open expression of ideas from a wide variety of sources.

The second condition for trustworthiness is a significant personal investment in the decision to trust. Brien (1998) defines trust as having certain expectations that someone "will behave in a desired way that promotes, or at least does not diminish, the putative trustee's well-being or that of something in which she has an important investment" (p. 398). Given the small percentage of American adults who attend to mainstream news, it is not clear that they value news as much as this definition of trust implies. Trustworthiness also involves an attribution of good will. "When we trust, we hold certain expectations of another. To expect is to look forward to something without anticipating disappointment" (Potter, 2002, p. 4). Trusting involves a belief in the other's good will (Brien talks about the motivation of non-maleficence), as well as good intentions and the ability to follow through. Again, given the low credibility ratings of journalists in public surveys, it is far from given that citizens would attribute good will to journalists.

Finally, Brien (1998) suggests that these conditions of trustworthiness presuppose a "proximate relationship" (p. 399). This condition is easily met in relationships among practitioners, who are participants in a community of shared goods and who work cooperatively to achieve the goals of a practice. It may even obtain in the relationship between journalists and their sources. Yet it clearly does not characterize the relationship between journalists and citizens. Citizens do not solicit journalists' services directly; they go through journalists' employing organizations (Newton, Hodges & Keith, 2004). This puts distance between them and journalists, a distance exacerbated by the sheer size of news audiences. Except for the occasional reader, viewer, or listener who calls to comment about a news story or writes a letter to the editor, journalists experience citizens as constructs, rather than as individuals with specific needs.

A good record of journalistic performance can be expected to give citizens reason to expect good performance again in the future. However, it may not be reasonable to require trustworthiness of journalists in the strict sense. Although citizens clearly are dependent on journalism for news, and are at a disadvantage in their level of knowledge compared with journalists, they are not as vulnerable or as invested as trustworthiness implies.[5] Nor can news as a mass communication genre be characterized by a proximate relationship between journalists and citizens (although interactive alternatives on the Internet can certainly help reduce the distance between them). Rather than rest the claim of trustworthiness on the fact of utter vulnerability and heavy personal investment, it may be more realistic—and more ethical—to reduce the vulnerability and investment of the trusters by producing evidence of good will (that is, being accountable) and by providing tools for assessing journalistic performance (that is, being transparent). "In effect, the era of trust-me journalism has passed, and the era of show-me journalism has begun" (Project for Excellence in Journalism, 2005, Overview: five major trends, ¶4).

---

5   And if they were, there would be further problems. As Larry May (1996) argues, absolute trustworthiness is, in fact, impossible. If that is what a practitioner conveys, she is responsible for any resulting decline in vigilance on the part of the trusted and, therefore, for any harms that result. It is more honest for a practitioner to claim that she will make a serious attempt to serve the public interest and that she will guarantee that this interest is "at least on a par with ... strongly held personal interests" (p. 136).

Preserving the Practice's Link to Tradition

By creating and sustaining the roles and relationships that define practices and institutions, traditions over time come to function as sources of moral authority for members of those groups. Traditions accomplish this by providing a common basis for the motivations and beliefs of their adherents that accounts for the strength of socialization within practices (May, 1996); journalists' identity *as* journalists is partly derived from the practice's tradition. "[I]nsofar as the virtues sustain the relationships required for practices, they have to sustain relationships to the past—and to the future—as well as in the present" (MacIntyre, 2007, p. 221). To cut oneself off from the past is to distort one's current relationships and to thwart future ones. "Traditions … provide both practices and individual lives with their necessary historical context" (p. 223).

Virtues relevant to sustaining and strengthening traditions include honesty, courage, justice, and the relevant intellectual virtues (MacIntyre, 2007). However, traditions also require a specific virtue for their flourishing: "the virtue of having an adequate sense of the traditions to which one belongs or which confront one" (p. 223). For *journalism as practice*, this means appreciating journalism's tradition, but also other traditions that intersect with journalism's, such as the traditions of American democracy and American capitalism. For example, an appreciation of the communitarian strain within the American democratic tradition can help journalists embrace a more ambitious mission than just helping monitorial citizens keep tabs on powerful institutions (May, 2001). An appreciation of capitalism's logic, meanwhile, can help journalists strengthen their employing organizations while at the same time being on guard against unwise blurring of the journalistic and business spheres (Meyer, 2004a).

This virtue of appreciating one's legacy also involves understanding the dynamic aspects of a tradition. "The adequate sense of tradition manifests itself in a grasp of those future possibilities which the past has made available to the present" (MacIntyre, 2007, p. 223). In other words, the practice's history lays the foundation for its future; it can be a resource for invention, not just continuity. For example, *journalism as practice* might look to the authorship strain in its tradition to help practitioners find an authentic voice at a time when the objective third person has lost credibility. Journalists may be able to reform objectivity along the lines suggested by Lambeth (1992) and Ward (2005) to retain the norm's emphases on independence and reliability while increasing transparency and encouraging responsible interpretation. A renewed sense of professionalism, meanwhile, could increase journalistic authority to resist commercial constraints while promoting accountability to citizens.

Just because a tradition is a source of moral authority, however, does not mean that one has to accept its moral limitations. MacIntyre (2007) notes that one way to express one's identity within a tradition is to rebel against it. Or, in the case of Ken Woodley, editor of the *Farmville (Va.) Herald*, to make amends for it. Woodley came up with the idea for a scholarship program to help people who were directly affected by school closings after the Supreme Court's 1954 *Brown v. Board of Education* decision. Some schools in Virginia, as well as other states, shut down to protest mandated school integration. The newspaper was very vocal about its support for what was known nationally as Massive Resistance. The scholarships, funded by the state legislature, will pay tuition for qualified citizens of any race who lost educational opportunities during this five-year period to finish high school or go to college. Woodley told National Public Radio that the paper, still owned by the same family that owned it during Massive Resistance, was trying to redeem itself (Williams, 2005).

Donahue (1990) has suggested a framework for decision-making that incorporates what he calls "formal processive norms" (p. 235) from virtue theory. These norms include appreciation of traditions as a context for exercising the virtues and can be easily translated to use by practices. The norms are:

- *Consistency*—habitually acting in accord with the virtues that help the practice achieve its internal goods. (Is this consistent with how the practice is known to act?)
- *Coherence*—consideration for the unity of a tradition, including how events connect over time and how different parts of a whole connect to each other. (How does this fit into the narrative of my practice and its tradition?)
- *Continuity*—validation of choices by some element of the tradition. (How does this continue my tradition? Which strain in my tradition legitimizes this choice?)
- *Communication and conversation*—comprehensive, truthful, inclusive discussion about moral choices. (Are all relevant aspects being considered? Are all relevant actors involved in the conversation? Are there adequate structures in place to enable "authentic" moral conversation?) (p. 240)
- *Conviction*—support of the practice's core beliefs. (How does this relate to my practice's internal goods and standards of excellence?)
- *Creativity*—being "open to possibilities of transformation and conversion" (Does my decision take enough stock of new insights and ideas that "challenge our traditional ways of acting and thinking?") (p. 236).

Possessors of the virtue of understanding one's traditions are able to "pursue both their own good and the good of the tradition of which they are the bearers even in situations defined by the necessity of tragic, dilemmatic choice" (p. 223). This can be true of some cases in which a journalist must choose whether to go along with a profit-oriented goal that violates the practice's standards. If the harms involved are serious enough, and the practitioner is coerced by the threat of retaliation or job loss, the stakes can be quite high, for the practitioner if no one else. For this reason, Larry May (1996) links individual integrity with group solidarity, a point that will be taken up in Chapter 6.

Integrity refers partly to coherence, or unity, among the various aspects of the self or of a practice.[6] Integrity for the individual journalist does not consist simply of being true to oneself or even to the standards of *journalism as practice*. Integrity also involves being true—at the same time—to other important principles and life plans in one's life. "All of this requires, sometimes, a difficult balancing act, rather

---

6   The other aspects of a communitarian account of moral integrity, according to Larry May (1996), are "mature development of a critical point of view, and disposition to act in a principled way" (p. 11).

than slavish conformity to one principle or to a narrow set of principles. The chief reason for this is that professional life is a part of larger personal and societal life, not a realm in which an individual is alone with his or her conscience" (May, 1996, p. 122).

This is what MacIntyre (2007) means when he says that the virtue of integrity, or constancy, is unintelligible without reference to a framework that transcends the limited and partial account of the virtues provided by practices. The good of a whole human life and, beyond that, of a tradition are needed to provide an overall pattern that can order and prioritize the "multiplicity of goods which inform practices" (p. 202). To sustain the integrity of the practice, practitioners need to consider how their own choices and how key events in the life of the practice fit into the larger narrative of the practice's tradition. This is an interpretive process carried out, not only by individuals, but collectively by journalists talking to each other as members of an interpretive community. This kind of evaluative discourse allows journalists to work out together an authoritative evaluation of events that establishes their meaning for the practice, including implications for the practice's standards (Zelizer, 1993). Such ongoing evaluation partly explains the dynamic nature of a practice's goals. This dynamic aspect of practices requires virtues to perform at least one more practice-sustaining function: supporting the practice's regenerative capacities.

Supporting the Practice's Regenerative Capacities

Just as journalism's cooperative "discipline of verification" (Kovach & Rosenstiel, 2001, p. 71) strives to achieve and demonstrate intellectual reliability *before* news is disseminated, a cooperative discipline of confirmation *afterward* could help journalists achieve and demonstrate intellectual accountability; that is, a willingness to subject one's knowledge claims to the scrutiny of others. By habitually engaging in a discipline of confirmation, journalists would be compelled to continually reflect upon the claims of their tradition, on the nature of knowledge, and on the requirements of moral and epistemic responsibility. In other words, this discipline would ensure that the practice had the capacity for systematic self-improvement and a definite procedure for pondering (and perhaps changing) its conception of good journalism.

Verification is achieved through an internal system based on collegial authority and control: Even if journalists start widely adopting innovations such as open sourcing and accuracy checks, internal gatekeepers will still be the ultimate arbiters of what gets disseminated as news. What I have in mind for a discipline of confirmation, however, is an external, iterative process by which journalists cooperate with non-journalists to confirm the reliability of the news—or to modify their knowledge claims if warranted.[7] This process would consist of interactive feedback processes characterized by accessibility, transparency, and tentativeness in the spirit of shared inquiry. Accessibility as part of a discipline of confirmation would involve letting non-journalists interact with journalists on their turf; that is, in newspapers, on news sites,

---

7   Journalists would not be excused from verifying claims during this process, however. Not all claims are created equal from the standpoint of epistemic reliability, as the well-publicized vulnerabilities of the online encyclopedia Wikipedia made clear (Seelye, 2005d).

and on news programs. Its function would be to demonstrate openness to criticism, correction, and comment—and to give such feedback a wide hearing. Many news institutions already make some provisions for such access by setting aside space for corrections and for letters and op-ed pieces from citizens. However, the Internet makes more of this kind of space available (since web space, unlike news hole or air time, is unlimited) and may increase participation and learning through interactive feedback.

Transparency, or clearly explaining one's choices so that they are readily understood, has special relevance at a time when many people are suspicious of journalistic authority and reliability. Many critics have urged journalists to be more forthcoming about how they operate, and why and how they make decisions. Klaidman & Beauchamp (1987) characterize these explanations as moral accounts when they provide justifying reasons for the action being explained. They are obligatory when journalists are, or reasonably could be, accused of wrong-doing. This has long been a function of ombuds columns, for example. However, critics are urging journalists to make such transparency a routine part of how they function, rather than reserving such accounts for times when they face criticism.[8] This could be accomplished in regular (rather than occasional) columns, as suggested by a committee looking at ways to increase reader confidence at the *New York Times*, or by posting raw source materials online for public examination, as Rosen (2005a) has suggested. Some newsrooms have gone so far as to let readers attend news meetings and editorial board meetings. The Spokane (WA) *Spokesman Review* invites readers to watch live webcasts of its 10 a.m. and 4:30 p.m. news meetings on its website at www.spokesmanreview.com. Used routinely, transparency can function to strengthen journalists' relationships with citizens by reducing citizens' vulnerability and demonstrating journalists' good will. Such transparency, as discussed earlier, is also a feature of any good intellectual practice that recognizes the necessity and value of cognitive interdependence. Although fellow practitioners have special claims to authority based on their adherence to the practice's tradition and standards, news as common civic knowledge is meant to be shared and discussed in the public sphere. Its purpose is to help citizens know well about everything of significance to the common good—including the methods, motives, and sources behind the news.

The characteristic of tentativeness, similarly, simply acknowledges the interim nature of knowledge. This is not to advocate an utterly relativistic posture toward the truth, unmoored from the wisdom of traditions and indiscriminate about the reliability of different sorts of claims. Rather, it acknowledges the epistemic limitations of even the most systematic forms of inquiry and respects human beings as makers of meaning. That is to say, tentativeness recognizes the necessity of sense making to test our interpretations and discover our values and priorities—as individuals and as community members. It functions to encourage cooperative inquiry, to push toward a fuller understanding, to promote civil discourse, to foster mutual learning.

---

8   Bovens (2002) notes that none of society's traditional institutions can assume its authority is a given in today's information society, which is starting to demand regular access to the raw materials of policies, budgets, and so forth. This movement is similar to the counter-culture of the 1960s and 1970s in its distrust of power, authority, and received wisdom (May, 2001).

Table 5.1   Practice-sustaining virtues in journalism

Virtues required	Function for practice
Courage, ingenuity	Defending against corruption by external goods
Stewardship	Sustaining institutional bearers of the practice
Justice, courage, honesty	Maintaining relationships needed to achieve practice's goals through a discipline of verification
Integrity, sense of legacy	Preserving practice's link to tradition
Accountability, modesty	Supporting practice's regenerative capabilities through a discipline of confirmation

Accomplished with intellectual modesty, tentativeness also mitigates inequality and promotes a feeling of belonging in the public sphere, rather than of merely being tolerated. These goals go far beyond the postmodernist's rebellious impulse to tear down walls; they seek stronger, shared foundations for civic knowledge.

Table 5.1 summarizes the virtues required to sustain *journalism as practice*. There may be other practice-sustaining functions performed by virtues in journalism. These should be explored in future research. This chapter's purpose was to consider seriously the importance of virtues at the level of the practice itself. As Code (1987) notes, "Practices can be created and preserved only by their practitioners; they are neither self-generating nor self-sustaining." Each practitioner should, therefore, "contribute to the creation and preservation of the best possible standards appropriate to the practices within which one lives" (p. 193). For this, practitioners need to cultivate and exercise the virtues "essential to achieving the ends of [the practice] optimally and without which those ends would be frustrated or attained in less than optimal fashion" (Pellegrino, 1995, p. 268). However, it is not just that individual virtues are necessary to achieve the practice's internal goods; they also make possible the conditions that enable practices themselves to flourish. Focusing on virtues at the individual level without also considering how they work at the *practice* level creates the false impression that good journalism is solely a function of individual character. Given the kinds of constraints and lack of moral support experienced by journalists, this is not a reasonable position to take, nor one that is likely to actually succeed in protecting journalism's mission. These issues will be discussed in Chapter 6.

Practically Speaking

Newsweek and the Breakdown of Intellectual Reliability

The furor started with one sentence in a brief article about prisoner abuse at the US detention center in Guantanamo Bay: "Among the previously unreported cases, sources tell NEWSWEEK: interrogators, in an attempt to rattle suspects, placed Qur'ans on toilets and, in at least one case, flushed a holy book down the toilet" (Isikoff & Barry, 2005).

Even before its official publication date of May 9, 2005, the *Newsweek* article was being denounced by a prominent opponent to Pakistan President Pervez Musharraf. Soon the Qur'an accusation was being repeated and condemned by clerics, government officials, and local media in Pakistan and bordering Afghanistan. Riots broke out in both countries, causing 15 deaths in Afghanistan (Thomas, 2005). The Pentagon, which had not disputed *Newsweek*'s account up to this point, set about investigating the charge. Eleven days after publication, the agency informed *Newsweek* that the internal military report referenced by the magazine did not look into accusations of desecrating the Qur'an and that similar charges had proved unfounded in the past. With criticism piling up, the magazine checked its reporting and found that the original source for the incendiary anecdote could no longer vouch for it. Bryan Whitman, speaking for the Pentagon, said: "*Newsweek* hid behind anonymous sources, which by their own admission do not withstand scrutiny. Unfortunately, they cannot retract the damage they have done to this nation or those that were viciously attacked by those false allegations" (Seelye, 2005b, ¶7).

The Qu'ran desecration story illustrates the centrality of journalism's discipline of verification to the integrity of the practice. It is the strength of this cooperative system that gives journalism its authority as a source of knowledge and, therefore, its usefulness as a catalyst for civic participation. Whenever this system's standards of excellence are grossly violated or ignored, it is the work of the entire practice that suffers. That being said, the *Newsweek* incident highlights the inherent complexities involved in knowing well as a journalist, as well as potential difficulties with exercising intellectual accountability in an adversarial news environment.

Newsweek's controversial Qu'ran brief shared page 4 with items about Iraq's new government, a promising breast cancer treatment, and a hot new rock band— all part of the mix in the magazine's flip Periscope section. As for the story itself, respected investigative reporter Michael Isikoff and national security correspondent John Barry essentially were passing along a suggestive tidbit from an anonymous source in anticipation of a probe not yet finalized. The significance of reporting the accusation was that it was coming from a US official; previous reports had come from former detainees at Guantanamo. Nevertheless, considering the seriousness of the charge, was it enough to signal the claim's provisional status through wording, attribution, and placement? Or should *Newsweek* never have vouched for it at all? Did *Newsweek*, in short, do enough to determine the item's accuracy and truthfulness? Was it sufficiently sensitive to the effects of publishing the Qu'ran accusation? Did it give readers enough information about the sources and verification methods used to determine the level of confidence they should have in the magazine's reporting? Was enough context provided to make the claim intelligible? Were Isikoff and Barry skeptical enough to question any prior assumptions about military behavior in Cuba?

Editor Mark Whitaker (2005) defended the magazine's reporting in the May 23 issue. A separate follow-up story in the same edition reconstructed the story's reporting and fallout (Thomas, 2005). "Their information came from a knowledgeable U.S. government source, and before deciding whether to publish it we approached two separate Defense Department officials for comment," Whitaker wrote (¶2). In other words, despite the phrase "sources said," the Qu'ran charge was based on a single source. However, *Newsweek* did attempt to corroborate the accusation. A Southern Command spokesman declined to comment because the military investigation in question was still in progress. A "senior Defense official" Barry consulted to check the story's accuracy disputed another part of the story "but he was silent about the rest of the item. The official had not meant to mislead, but lacked detailed knowledge of the SouthCom report" (Thomas, 2005, ¶5).

Isikoff went back to his original source after the Pentagon disputed the Qur'an accusation. The source said "he clearly recalled reading investigative reports about mishandling the Qur'an, including a toilet incident" (Thomas, 2005, ¶10). Whitaker (2005) wrote:

> Our original source later said he couldn't be certain about reading of the alleged Qur'an incident in the report we cited, and said it might have been in other investigative documents or drafts. Top administration officials have promised to continue looking into the charges, and so will we. But we regret that we got any part of our story wrong, and extend our sympathies to victims of the violence and to the U.S. soldiers caught in its midst. (¶4)

Spokesmen for the president and the Pentagon called *Newsweek*'s reporting irresponsible and pushed the magazine to retract the story, not merely apologize for any errors. The next day, the magazine issued a one-sentence press release (later appended online to the original Periscope story and follow-up reports): "Based on what we know now, we are retracting our original story that an internal military investigation had uncovered Qur'an abuse at Guantanamo Bay." Although the statement did not include an explanation for the extra step, Whitaker later said, "In order for people to understand we had made an error, we had to say 'retraction' because that's the word they were looking for" (Seelye & Lewis, 2005, ¶10). Presidential spokesman Scott McClellan said the retraction was a "good first step" (Nichols, 2005, ¶7).

Two questions of fact remain unresolved and partly explain the different reactions to *Newsweek*'s initial apology. The first is whether the Qu'ran story actually caused the protests in Pakistan and Afghanistan. The second is whether the Qu'ran toilet incident ever actually happened. McClellan repeatedly blamed the story for the deaths in Afghanistan. Many media reports repeated the charge even after reports that Army Lt Gen. Karl Eikenberry, the US Commander in Afghanistan, had determined there was no direct link between *Newsweek*'s story and the violence. The doggedness of the criticism from the White House led to a rare confrontation on May 17 between McClellan and reporters during a routine briefing (Press briefing by Scott McClellan, 2005). Questioning implied that McClellan was being disingenuous to blame *Newsweek* for the violence and that he was trying to pressure the magazine into writing a story praising the US military.

Brian Montopoli (2005), writing for *CJR Daily*, declared media coverage of the incident "more disheartening than the original sin" (¶1) because it repeated the Administration's contention that the story directly caused the violence in Afghanistan. Montopoli correctly noted that the heart of the story—whether the Qu'ran had been flushed down the toilet as an interrogation technique at Guantanamo—was still in dispute and that *Newsweek* had only disavowed its statement that it would be confirmed in a US military report. To critics on the right, *Newsweek*'s failure to rule out Qu'ran desecration by the military was splitting hairs. Critics on the left emphasized that similar stories had been told by former detainees in lawsuits and previous press reports and accused the Bush Administration of hypocrisy (the letters *Newsweek* published on the controversy are illustrative; see "Mail call: Furor and fallout," 2005).

Did the toilet incident ever happen? In the same issue as Whitaker's apology, the magazine reported on two new claims of Qur'ans in toilets made by former detainees at Guantanamo. In a subsequent issue, it also reported on confidential reports by the International Committee of the Red Cross accusing the military of Qu'ran desecration at Guantanamo, although there was no confirmed incident of flushing one of the holy books down the toilet. However, a former warden at the detention center said an inmate dropped his holy book near his toilet in 2002. This caused unrest among other inmates, who apparently believed one of the guards had deliberately thrown it there. Guards took the inmate to every cell to explain his actions and calm down the others. *Newsweek* noted that "the incident could partly account for the multiple allegations among detainees, including one by a released British detainee in a lawsuit that claims that guards flushed Qur'ans down toilets" (Thomas & Isikoff, 2005, ¶5). Indeed, this information casts quite a different light on the Qu'ran accusation and presumably would have led Isikoff and Barry to write a different kind of story altogether.

Regardless of whether this particular incident occurred, other instances of prisoner maltreatment in 2002 and 2003 are well-documented at the Abu Ghraib prison in Iraq and the Bagram Collection Point in Afghanistan (see Golden, 2005). Some critics pointed out that *Newsweek*'s sloppiness had distracted the American public from this larger pattern. Marvin Kalb of the Shorenstein Center on Press, Politics and Public Policy at Harvard University told the *New York Times*:

> This is hardly the first time that the administration has sought to portray the American media as inadequately patriotic. They are addressing the mistake, and not the essence of

the story. The essence of the story is that the United States has been rather indelicate, to put it mildly, in the way that they have treated prisoners of war. (Bumiller, 2005, ¶21)

In fact, rigorous verification defines good journalism to such a degree that failure to meet this standard often overshadows what Kalb calls the "essence of the story." This has happened time and again—with *60 Minutes Wednesday*'s 2004 story about President Bush's Texas National Guard service, with *Dateline NBC*'s 1992 report about the dangers of sidesaddle gas tanks on GM trucks, and with *PrimeTime Live*'s 1992 investigation into the Food Lion supermarket chain's packaging and labeling practices. In each of these cases, the essential claims made by journalists were either not in dispute or backed up by a preponderance of evidence. However, the journalists doomed whatever impact their stories might have had by failing to be scrupulous in the process of documenting or sourcing these claims.

A key temptation in all such cases is lack of access to "official" information that would easily and definitively confirm controversial details. Another, in the *Newsweek* and CBS cases at least, seems to have been the temptation to defer to "star" reporters. In the Memogate incident, Dan Rather and CBS editors gave the benefit of the doubt to powerhouse producer Mary Mapes, who vouched for the source of documents related to Bush's military service; it turned out the source was questionable and that the documents were not properly authenticated (Associated Press, 2005a). In the *Newsweek* case, the magazine decided to go with a story based on one unnamed source, trusting Isikoff's sourcing. Although respect for the authority of master practitioners is necessary for practices to flourish, these examples illustrate the need for journalists to preserve procedures for optimizing intellectual reliability, even when it is one of their best whose name is on the byline or listed in the credits. These procedures recognize that any one individual is extremely limited in his or her capacity to vouch for knowledge claims. For one thing, individuals bring to reporting some working assumptions about any given topic. As Thomas (2005) noted, previous allegations of prisoner abuse at US detention camps made the Qu'ran anecdote believable. Isikoff and Barry may not have been skeptical enough to overcome any assumptions they might have had about the story given this background; a more rigorous verification process with more oversight from colleagues could have helped overcome this problem. A final challenge was the temptation to be hip. As media critic Jay Rosen (2005b) pointed out, the first question to ask about this case may be why *Newsweek* has a speculative, gossipy section like Periscope in the first place.

Given *Newsweek*'s failure to find actual corroboration for the Qu'ran charge, University of Maryland Professor Chris Hanson (2005) suggested the magazine should have held the story for verification. "This was a far cry from the laborious checking and multi-source requirements that had delayed *Newsweek*'s Lewinsky story in 1998" (¶10). In fact, Hanson traces journalism's willingness to disseminate inadequately vetted information to *Newsweek*'s Lewinsky decision. The magazine's care with Isikoff's story about President Clinton's affair earned high journalistic marks, but resulted in the magazine's getting scooped by online gossip Matt Drudge. Since then, newspapers and magazines have been posting exclusives in their online editions, sometimes ahead of their print editions. Tom Rosenstiel, director of the Project for Excellence in Journalism, likewise suggested that *Newsweek* had acted prematurely. "The news organization has to be skeptical of the information it receives, verify it independently, then run it by the subjects of the story for comment," he said (Johnson, 2005, ¶10).

Hanson's (2005) observations highlight the implications of such carelessness for citizens' ability to know well:

> Too often these days, reporters and editors seem unable or unwilling to perform a basic duty—sifting rumor from fact, salesmanship from independent analysis—and instead become conduits for falsehoods, half-truths and propaganda. Whether they know it or not, news media are helping to create a world in which we often *don't* know what we know, and don't know what we don't know, and are thus easy marks for manipulation by anyone from politicians to ideologues to self-help gurus. (¶5)

As for whether *Newsweek* reporters and editors were sufficiently sensitive to the possible consequences of running the Qu'ran story, Thomas (2005) later noted that the brief:

> arrived at a particularly delicate moment in Afghan politics. Opponents of the Karzai government, including remnants of the deposed Taliban regime, have been looking for ways to exploit public discontent. ... With Karzai scheduled to come to Washington next week, this is a good time for his enemies to make trouble. (¶7)

Further, the magazine had run a cover story in February 2002 about the Qu'ran and the Bible that made clear that flushing a Qu'ran to a Muslim would be roughly equivalent to flushing a consecrated Communion host to a Catholic. "In gospel terminology, the Qu'ran corresponds to Christ himself, as the logos, or eternal word of the Father. In short, if Christ is the word made flesh, the Qur'an is the word made book" (Woodward, 2002, Divine authority, ¶3). Still, the magazine acknowledged that the reaction to the Periscope item "came as something of a surprise" (Thomas, 2005, ¶8). Given the high stakes, *Newsweek* should have taken extra care with the Qu'ran story, not less. There was no particular reason—other than to get a scoop— for the story to be rushed into print. If Isikoff and Barry had taken their time to get it right, they also may have been in a better position to ascertain the story's potential for causing offense or even violence.

Although the discipline of verification was not conducted to the highest standards in this case, *Newsweek*'s actions immediately after the Pentagon disputed its story illustrate some key features of the discipline of confirmation proposed in Chapter 5. The magazine scrutinized its reporting, shared the findings with readers, acknowledged the tentativeness of the original brief's claims, pledged to continue the process of inquiry, and expressed regret for poor procedures and judgment. However, the process of confirmation could have begun upon publication with more information about how Isikoff and Barry had verified the charge and more opportunity for non-journalists to weigh in on the charge's authenticity, rather than awaiting a challenge from the Pentagon.[1] Unfortunately, *Newsweek* was hampered by its own entrenched habits and attitudes, as well as an adversarial environment.

A couple of weeks after publishing the Qu'ran desecration story, *Newsweek* did adopt new guidelines for the use of anonymous sources. Although the guidelines do not rule out the use of uncorroborated anonymous sources, they tighten up the magazine's standards for attribution and for getting approval to use confidential sources (Associated Press, 2005c). The magazine joined the *New York Times*, *USA TODAY*, CBS News and other news organizations that have restricted the use of unnamed sources in recent years due to a series of scandals ranging from outright fabrication to potentially bogus documents (Smolkin, 2005). This history of scandal was an important context for *Newsweek*'s story. Although the majority of Americans support the right of journalists to keep sources confidential, the abuse of this practice rightly raises their suspicions. Several surveys, including one conducted by the University of Connecticut in the spring of 2005, show that the vast majority of the public suspects the accuracy of news stories based on anonymous sources (Smolkin, 2005). *Newsweek* contributed to this problem, thus failing to exercise proper stewardship of the First Amendment as an institution that sustains *journalism as practice*.

Whether lax verification occurs because of complacency, competition, or attempts to mimic the postmodern sensibility of new media, it reflects on the entire practice. This is especially perilous at a time when journalism, if anything, requires higher standards of intellectual reliability to shore up its credibility and to compensate for organizational pressures to dilute its standards.

---

1 Proponents of open sourcing might suggest that *Newsweek* should have given readers, "citizen journalists," and bloggers a heads-up online, inviting them to check out or confirm the Qu'ran tip while Isikoff and Barry were still reporting the story. However, this is a good example of why traditional journalistic gatekeeping is still desirable, at least for certain stories. Certainly the Qu'ran abuse accusation would have caused offense if it had circulated openly at an earlier stage of *Newsweek*'s reporting—even if it did not ultimately get published in the magazine's online and print editions. In other words, the possible harms that can be caused by unfounded rumors can best be prevented in journalism by meeting the highest standards of the practice's discipline of verification.

Chapter 6

The Practice's Role as a Moral Community

As a community of intellectual workers who cooperatively create and share "news" according to shared notions of good journalism, *journalism as practice* functions as a moral community that partly constitutes the moral identity of its members. One way in which the practice makes itself felt as a moral community is through discourse that sustains, repairs, and extends standards of excellent journalism. Individual journalists enact these standards in their actions and in their discourse, establishing appropriate moral identities that can affect their acceptance by their peers (Borden, 2003). The practice, for its part, will exert more moral authority if it allows members to coordinate its goals with the goals that they have as family members, neighbors, citizens, and so forth. This coherence, or unity, among the various aspects of the self is an essential aspect of moral integrity (May, 1996). The practice also exerts influence on individuals indirectly through the moral authority that it is granted by non-members, including corporate officers and fellow citizens (what Gardner, Csikszentmihalyi & Damon, 2001, call the *field*).

This chapter focuses on the practice's function as a source of moral identity for journalists. I will give special attention to the role played by peer discourse in shaping shared understandings of excellent journalism and to the practice's potential for successfully supporting individual members who resist ethically questionable business requirements. I will rely on communitarian philosopher Larry May's analysis of the concepts of shame and solidarity to argue that an effective moral community fosters a true willingness among journalists to sanction each other and also to go to each other's aid. The chapter concludes with a discussion of individual resistance in the absence of such moral support, including an ethical model for evaluating individual resistance approaches. The types of resistance identified vary along the ethical dimensions of (a) consideration of both the organization's goals and the practice's goals and (b) openness with regard to journalists' preference for the practice's goals.[1]

---

1   This resistance model was first published in Borden (2000) A model for evaluating journalist resistance to business constraints. *Journal of Mass Media Ethics*, 15(3), 149–166. That article and accompanying table are reprinted here, slightly revised, with permission from Lawrence Erlbaum Associates.

Moral Identity and Sense Making

MacIntyre's (2007) emphasis on the narrative quality of moral agency suggests that identity is best understood discursively, as do more recent social constructionist approaches.[2] "Our social identities are not static or structurally determined, but contextually situated and interactionally emergent" (Matoesian, 1999, p. 494). Rather than a static category defined by traits such as membership in a professional organization, identity in these perspectives is a social category that "can be strategically enacted, constructed, and maintained in discourse" (Borden, 2003, p. 233). In ethical discourse, this can include managing others' assessment of our conduct and character. Notes Rymes (1995): "Through talk, people are not creating a merely random identity; rather they are actively narrating themselves relative to a moral ideal of what it is to be a good person" (p. 498). That is, they are making sense of their moral commitments and actions in light of a community's role models or, in Oakley & Cocking's (2001) terms, a regulative ideal. Weick (1995) and other constructionist scholars suggest that such identity enactment is essential to sense making. Zelizer (1993) has shown how this process can take place at the collective level of group identity. When journalists talk about journalism, she argues, they function as an interpretive community that is able to contextualize current problems within the larger tradition handed down by previous generations of journalists. Increasing concern about the influence of business constraints on good journalism, in fact, has prompted journalists to produce a large volume of discourse regarding their place in society. Peer discourse about journalism ethics can happen during newsroom discussions (Borden, 2003), in columns and news commentaries (e.g. Eason, 1988; Winch, 1997), in television commentaries, and in discussion lists on the Internet (Borden, 2002). Blogs are increasingly important carriers of such discourse. Of special note is the Romenesko blog, published daily on the Poynter Institute's web site (www.poynter.org). The blog, named after the former police reporter who started it, features items about all things journalism and is so influential among reporters and editors that it has been called the "sex-offender registry of journalism" (Buttry, 2006, ¶30) and has been credited with a "Romenesko effect" (Jurkowitz, 2005, ¶2):

> In the old days, media controversies might merit mention in places like Newsweek or the Columbia Journalism Review and would stay entombed inside the journalism world. Now, they instantly erupt into national scandals that bounce around the media echo chamber and often penetrate the broader public consciousness. Sometimes, they even end up on the pages of the media outlets where the problem originated. (¶3)

---

2   MacIntyre (2007) dismisses the social constructionist view of identity as a misguided attempt to separate the self from its social roles. In other words, social constructionism (and, by extension, related sociological approaches) appears to describe a self that can invent itself out of whole cloth, unencumbered by any social starting point. However, this reading overstates the agency of social actors. Although identity enactment is a dynamic process in which people enjoy some latitude, their available options are socially given. In other words, Goffman and other sociologists recognize that individual identity is, at least in this sense, a social category.

Sense making about moral identity is analogous to MacIntrye's (2007) argument about the narrative context of moral actions. Moral intentions—and hence the actions they motivate—are intelligible only in the context of an individual's history, and the history of her settings and roles (including practices). However, each individual is the protagonist of her own narrative, and thus must be guided by self-knowledge and knowledge of the good in making choices that can influence the plot of her own life and the lives of those with intersecting narratives. Both Weick, from a sociological perspective, and MacIntyre, from an ethical one, attribute an element of creativity to the process of identity formation. Sociologically speaking, we make sense of what happens to us through the filter of our identities, and we revise or reconfirm our identities in light of our experiences. Morally speaking, the virtuous agent learns gradually from experience and self-reflection what it is that the good life actually consists of and, therefore, what kind of character is required for human flourishing.

Because our individual narratives are nested within others' narratives, however, we can claim to be only co-authors of our life stories. This feature of moral life is what makes us accountable to others, according to MacIntyre (2007). However, it also has implications for the notions of moral identity and moral integrity. Notes Larry May (1996): "Integrity is not a withdrawal from the influences of the world into one's own core self. Understanding integrity necessarily involves understanding how groups influence the formation of even the most 'essential' aspects of the self" (p. 11).[3] For example, my (2003) study of deviance mitigation in the peer discourse of journalists at a small Midwestern daily suggested that collegial legitimacy—or acceptance by one's peers—may hinge substantially on moral legitimacy. Their interaction included a built-in incentive for shaping moral identity according to the shared values of journalism as a particular moral community. The threat of losing collegial acceptance may function to restrain vice in the same way that collegial support functions as a motivation for virtuous action.

Shame, Solidarity and Moral Support

Journalism as practice functions as an important context for sense making about good journalism in part because it makes some forms of moral identity intelligible as cause for shame. According to Larry May (1996), "Shame is best understood as the response that people feel when they believe that others (an anticipated audience) would judge them to have a particular failing or character defect" (p. 81). Socialization on the job can block feelings of shame toward certain actions by rewarding or redefining those actions. For example, a business reporter who is routinely asked to come up with complimentary stories about local advertisers may

---

3   Identity, according to Larry May (1996), is not best conceptualized as a core, but "as a web knit from the various identifications and commitments that one makes with various social groups" (p. 13), including practices. In other words, it is a "process rather than essence" (p. 16), a commitment to self-growth, rather than adherence to any specific set of beliefs. May's view does not entail uncritical absorption or accommodation to social influences, but it does suggest that moral identity is a dynamic concept along the lines suggested by social constructionists.

come to see these stories only in terms of customer service, rather than also being a potential threat to his editorial independence. *Journalism as practice* can help safeguard the integrity of journalists by providing them with an appropriate frame of reference for feeling shame within news organizations.

Shame can be experienced in a collective sense too. A group member can legitimately feel shame for "harms perpetrated by or within communities" (May, 1996, p. 93); in other words, for failures to respond well to the practice's shared responsibilities. Shame can be felt toward another's failure in this regard, as well as toward one's own failures:

> One may feel ashamed that one did not do anything to stop the harm from occurring; or one may feel shame merely for being a group member, since one's group memberships form who one is. And in many cases something like a group failure or defect is the source of the feelings of shame. (p. 93)

It is not merely a sense of duty to collective standards or pressure to conform to group norms that is at work when members of a practice feel shame in this way. Such strong feelings of association are based in a sense of solidarity.[4] According to Larry May (1996), "What binds people together as far as solidarity is concerned is their felt bond with one another and their readiness to act collectively in one another's behalf, that is, their adherence to one another rather than to a set of rules" (p. 30). These bonds are deeper than the "esprit de corps that permeates most effective newsrooms" (Lambeth, 1992, p. 52) and more stable than transitory self-interests. In other words, May is not talking here of individuals who merely like each other or who stay together for the limited purpose of securing their mutual benefit. Neither can solidarity simply be equated with other-regarding virtues such as compassion. Virtues are "rarely able to build a sense of community from which one can draw moral support and find motivation to pursue the common good" (p. 45). For May, true solidarity provides group members with the motivation to act in behalf of the shared values that constitute the common good:

> It is not enough that a person identify himself or herself with a particular group, or even that he or she have bonds of sentiment with that group and its members. For it may be that the person will still not feel motivated to go to the aid of a fellow member. The person may even form intentions to go to the aid of fellow members but never act on those intentions. What is essential … is that one have the disposition to act on such intentions. (p. 44)

Moral support has two aspects: Solidarity makes group members want to help colleagues who are in need, and it helps individuals overcome self-interest when required for the common good, as when a journalist stands up for the practice's standards at the risk of retaliation or other grave personal harms. In other words, practitioners do not have to face alone their fear or the harmful consequences of acting courageously (Miller, 2005). In addition to their own individual characters, practitioners can draw on the moral support of the practice to deal with the moral struggle necessarily entailed by the exercise of moral courage. Moral support can

---

4   However, neither vicarious pride nor vicarious shame is *necessary* for solidarity.

include actions ranging from retaliating and boycotting to sanctioning and signing petitions. It is especially relevant to journalists, who may have to pursue the practice's goals in defiance of their employing organizations. News organizations rely on journalists' individualistic streak and competitiveness to pressure them to go against what they think is right. If the practice stood ready to go to journalists' aid, however, ethical conflicts between the goals of the practice and the goals of the organization would be solved in favor of supporting the practice's goals. Potter (2002) acknowledges the role of moral support when he suggests that attending to relations of trust requires "preparing for acts of resistance" (p. 86) and forming alliances with like-minded peers to ensure back-up when needed.

If moral support is the positive expression of solidarity as a source of motivation to follow community norms, moral condemnation is the negative expression of that function. In the case of moral condemnation, solidarity helps community members to act in behalf of the common good even when this requires some damage to particular relationships. In other words, solidarity in a moral community consists both of a willingness to go to each other's aid and a willingness to sanction those who grievously violate the community's shared standards. Although ritually excluding wrongdoers from the practice is one option (see, e.g., Blanks Hindman, 2003; Borden, 2002; Winch, 1997), sanctions can take a range of forms, including public criticism. Together, moral support and moral condemnation help to implement and demonstrate the practice's accountability. On the one hand, the practice stands ready to affirm its mission, even under serious pressure; on the other, it condemns and tries to repair serious failures to meet its shared responsibilities.

Klaidman & Beauchamp (1987) stress that virtue ethics cannot *require* heroism. Nevertheless, the theory's emphasis on going beyond the demands of obligation implies that moral responsibility may exact great personal sacrifice. The exercise of moral courage, in fact, is traditionally thought to imply heroism in this sense (Miller, 2005). In the context of resisting unethical business demands, perhaps a practitioner's character or the tradition of her practice is at stake, in which case sacrificing her job or career may be for her own good. Indeed, philosopher Elliot Cohen (Adam, Craft & Cohen, 2004) puts the onus on journalists to "remain steadfast" and to call business and government on their efforts "to undermine the public trust" (p. 270). He suggests that journalists who acquiesce are just as guilty of vice as their news organizations because they choose to work there. Lambeth (1992), likewise, dismisses what he considers to be overly deterministic assessments of journalistic discretion: "The point, in fact, is that journalists, as a group, have enough professional competence and enough moral freedom to fully face and accept the responsibilities implied by the constitutional protection granted them" (pp. 70–71). He cites as examples reporters refusing to write stories and negotiating conditions for writing stories; engaging in enterprise reporting that thwarts the timidity of news organizations; quitting; "newsroom traditions against advertiser interference with the news product" (p. 70); and media criticism written by working journalists.

Both Cohen (Adam, Craft & Cohen, 2004) and Lambeth (1992) seem to underestimate the degree to which the threat of retaliation coerces journalists' options (May, 1996). Firing and other kinds of retaliation for defying organizational orders are a very real danger in today's competitive media market, as seen in the

Sinclair Broadcast Group's termination of political reporter Jon Leiberman over the anti-Kerry documentary controversy in 2004. Although Lambeth's list of options reflects appreciation of resistance strategies that fall short of heroic self-sacrifice, the examples he offers presume rather ideal circumstances; namely, practitioners who have enough clout and job security to openly contest superiors and pursue whatever stories they want, the ability to land on their feet should they resign, and newsrooms where the wall between business and editorial still exists in its traditional form.

Larry May (1996) suggests that two conditions must be met for heroism to be expected in behalf of a community's shared values: "either the good to be achieved by the principled conduct is very great indeed, or the person who is expected to sacrifice is given significant moral support from his or her community" (p. 27). Otherwise, heroic actions may be unwarranted. That being said, solidarity does not substitute for individual conscience. Indeed, there is always a danger that solidarity will degenerate into the kind of mindless followership that characterizes the groupthink phenomenon in cohesive groups (Janis & Mann, 1977). Individuals need to engage in self-reflection about group beliefs, as well as institutional practices, so they can "settle ambivalences with as much moral agency as possible" (Potter, 2002, p. 87). *Both* solidarity and individual conscience are "undeniably significant sources of morality" (May, 1996, p. 45). Moore (2002) notes that a practice is primarily responsible for keeping the institution focused on the practice. "So within those who engage directly in the practice there needs to be the commitment to exercise the virtues not only in pursuit of the internal goods of the practice that benefits them as individuals directly, but also against the corporation when it becomes, as it inevitably will at various times, too focused on external goods" (p. 29).

Resisting Business Demands

All the major codes of ethics in journalism suggest that "journalists—individually or in the aggregate—are, or should be, free of business-related constraints imposed by those who pay them and distribute their work" (McManus, 1997, p. 8). This implies an inadequate moral standard, given the constraints on journalists' autonomy and the lack of moral support that individual journalists can count on when they decide to resist unethical business demands. Meanwhile, the management perspective reflected in the organizational studies literature suggests that passively accepting unsatisfactory work conditions should be viewed as *constructive* behavior. This also falls short as a moral guide because of the importance of protecting journalism's integrity and of respecting individual conscience. This section develops a model of resistance strategies to illustrate the range of options available for resisting business constraints within a news organization. The types of strategies identified vary along the ethical dimensions of (a) consideration of both the organization's goals and the practice's goals and (b) openness with regard to journalists' preference for the practice's goals. Using these criteria, some resistance strategies can be considered more virtuous than others. What is being proposed, to be clear, is not an exhaustive primer of resistance strategies, but rather a sampler of realistic options that have ethical advantages and liabilities that may not be obvious if one looks only to professional ethics codes, on the one hand, or to the organizational studies literature, on the other.

The model assumes that journalists have broad discretion in dealing with the prevention of particular harms that may result from going along with business directives that undercut the practice's integrity—or from resisting them. It also assumes that the practitioner role will be preferred to that of employee whenever the two roles are incompatible at a basic level (such that the practice's goals are outright precluded by organizational ones). This is because the employee role concerns primarily the achievement of external goods contingently attached to *journalism as practice.* Although there are relational aspects to the typical employment relationship, this relationship has always consisted, at its most basic level, of an economic bargain based on the contribution of effort in exchange for (mostly) monetary rewards (Maguire, 2002). This transactional aspect of the employment relationship has become even more dominant with the workplace changes brought on by the new global economy. Whereas many journalists in the past might have been able to count on a relationship with their newspaper or TV station based on shared journalistic values, the best most journalists can hope for these days are employment situations that provide some relational support to compensate for the loss of job security and prestige that has accompanied the restructuring of the media industry.

Resistance from the Organizational Perspective

An influential model in the organizational literature for conceptualizing the range of options that employees may choose from when dissenting is the exit–voice–loyalty–neglect model laid out by Farrell (1983, as cited in Kassing, 1997). Which option an employee chooses depends on how she thinks her action will be received—both in terms of whether it will be effective and whether it will be punished (Kassing, 1997). It also depends on the degree of the employee's psychological investment in the organization (Withey & Cooper, 1989). Exit from the organization—including quitting and laying the groundwork for leaving your job—is perceived as an active/ destructive option for people who are not very attached to their places of work and fear the costs of expressing their concerns openly. Thus, Carol Marin's resignation from the Chicago TV station that hired Jerry Springer is a copout in this framework. Another copout is neglect. Neglect is chosen by those who stay behind in part because they perceive their choices as limited. They express their dissatisfaction passively and destructively from the organization's standpoint; examples are absenteeism and putting in less effort at work (Withey & Cooper, 1989). The two constructive responses, according to the model, are loyalty and voice. Employees who choose the loyalty option stay put and patiently support and cooperate with the organization despite their dissatisfaction. That this is construed as constructive seems to reflect the managerial bias in the organizational literature, with its focus on productivity and managerial control. From this perspective, Marin would have been admired for staying at her station and making the best of it when Springer joined the rotation of commentators. However, loyalty seems no better than "entrapment" on this account (Withey & Cooper, 1989, p. 536)—it is no accident that this option tends to be pursued by employees who perceive themselves as bound to their organizations with little chance of improving things. Kelley (1992) notes that employees have good reasons for not following orders blindly, even if there is a presumption in favor of obeying a boss's orders. Kelley suggests that the exemplary follower may be required to disobey orders when these orders: (a) are issued illegitimately due to lack of hierarchical authority, expertise, or abuse of power; or (b) threaten to hurt the best interests of the organization itself. Unlike the EVLN model, Kelley's perspective does not assume that employees ultimately must defer to the organization in order to be "constructive."

Voice, finally, refers to open attempts to improve bad conditions by talking to supervisors and others within the organization about problems. Voice traditionally has been portrayed as the best response to employee dissatisfaction because of its association with organizational commitment and its emphasis on promoting positive change within the organization. Notice, however, that voice is considered constructive in part because objections are kept in-house. Indeed, Kassing (1997), who relied partly on the EVLN model to classify forms of expressing dissent, characterizes externally oriented resistance (such as whistle blowing) as a combination of the destructive strategies of neglect and exit. He puts this option into a category he calls *displaced* dissent—a label that suggests dysfunction. Kassing says, in fact, that this form of dissent is chosen under circumstances in which retaliation is expected. This brings up a practical reality: Many workplaces discourage voice (Seeger, 1997). Further, the model's preference for voice presumes an equality between superior and subordinate that does not exist (Robison, 1991). In short, although the EVLN model rightly points out that one should prefer openness and that resistance can be undertaken in a non-adversarial manner, it also falls short as a guide for individual journalists who need advice on resisting business constraints.

Reasons for Resisting Business Constraints

Although I have argued that heroic self-sacrifice should not be expected from individual journalists without adequate moral support from the community of journalists, it does not follow that individual practitioners are never morally responsible for resisting corruptive business directives. Practitioners do, in fact, subordinate themselves to the demands of the practice, voluntarily risking self-harm when needed for the sake of excellence (MacIntyre, 2007). And there are acts of resistance that do not involve exposure to serious harm. What must be established at this point is whether there are any particular circumstances in which virtuous journalists *would* resist business constraints. At least four come to mind: when resisting is necessary to prevent the misuse of journalists' skills; to defend the practice's internal goods; to provide moral support for colleagues; or to preserve individual moral integrity.

Serving the practice's *telos* sometimes requires that practitioners withdraw their skills if the organization that employs them plans to use these skills unethically. Quite simply, these skills would cease to be instruments for achieving the practice's purpose and might even become systematically distorted if regularly misused over time. On these grounds, journalists may be responsible for resisting organizational directives in circumstances that threaten to excessively erode the performance of the practice's functions. Part of the challenge of recognizing this kind of situation, however, is that the corrosive effects of particular organizational policies or formulas may not show themselves for some time. Think of the gradual impact of newspaper design formulas that make page layouts hinge on artsy photographs rather than on the important news of the day, or of network policies that encourage news anchors to go back and forth between reporting the news and hosting reality shows.

Individual journalists also may be responsible for engaging in acts of business resistance when important internal goods are at stake—even if it is not their own journalistic skills that are being misused. This would appear to be the rationale for Marin's decision to quit in protest over Jerry Springer. Solidarity requires, further, that practitioners stick their necks out to support their colleagues in such circumstances. This kind of support might have made a difference in 2005, when *Time* magazine reporter Matthew Cooper refused to testify about an anonymous source in the Valerie Plame CIA leak case. Despite Cooper's objections, Time Inc.—part of a giant media entertainment empire with Turner Broadcasting and America Online—complied with a court order to turn over his notes (technically company property). *Time*'s editor-in-chief, Norman Pearlstine, made the decision on the grounds that no one is above the law after the Supreme Court refused to hear Cooper's appeal (Manly & Kirkpatrick, 2005). It was the first time that a news organization had complied with such an order against the wishes of the reporter. Pearlstine told the *Washington Post*: "Matt believed he'd granted confidence to his sources and ought to protect that. I respect his position, but as editor in chief, I have an institutional view of how a journalism organization ought to behave" in a case such as this (Leonnig, 2005, ¶7).

Time's action prevented Cooper from keeping his personal promise and from defending standards of excellence aimed at achieving the journalistic goods of knowledge, inquiry, and discovery. Time's decision hurt the credibility of both practitioner and practice. Cooper ultimately agreed to testify when his source, senior White House adviser Karl Rove, personally waived his anonymity a week before Cooper might have been jailed for contempt of court (Manly & Johnston, 2005). Cooper told the *Post*: "For almost two years, I've protected my confidential sources even under the threat of jail. So while I understand Time's decision to turn over papers that identify my sources, I'm obviously disappointed" (Leonnig, 2005, ¶8). Cooper's colleagues could have elected to put pressure on Time to stand fast through collective appeals to journalistic principles as well as through collective actions, such as walk-outs at the company's huge stable of publications. Instead, the practice deferred to Time's corporate hierarchy and responded after the fact in news stories quoting disapproving journalists. Cooper's case brings up the final reason why journalists might be responsible for resisting some business demands: Journalists are (most essentially) moral agents. As such, they must safeguard their personal integrity, apart from fulfilling their functions as practitioners or honoring promises they have made regarding their journalistic role (Elliott, 1986). When business constraints grieve a journalist's conscience to an insufferable extent, he is morally bound to resist as an expression of who he is.

Why Should Organizational Interests Count?

There are sound moral reasons for considering organizational interests when choosing whether and how to resist business constraints. First, most organizational goals do not pose moral problems in and of themselves. Therefore, they are worthy of respect, all things being equal, as a matter of justice. The mass communications literature, in fact, suggests that media organizations have some purely journalistic goals—even if they are subordinated to the overarching goal of making ever-increasing profits (Gallagher, 1982; McManus, 1994). Even when money is an issue, there are situations in which good business and good journalism coincide. For example, media organizations generally are willing to spend huge sums of money to cover a story of immense appeal such as the 2001 terrorist attacks on the Twin Towers. Failure to acknowledge the legitimacy of certain organizational goals may goad individual journalists into resisting when such resistance is neither desirable nor necessary. This is unfair and usually harmful to both parties.

Second, journalists make certain promises—at least implicitly—when they accept a job at a news organization. These promises include performing the job to the specifications set by the organization; that is, following newsroom policies, performing certain routine tasks, attending meetings, using professional judgment in the performance of their jobs, and so on. These tacit promises are part of a psychological contract between employer and employee (Maguire, 2002). Promises have moral force because they make the party to whom something is promised reliant on the one promising. Keeping one's promise demonstrates the virtue of fidelity.

Finally, journalists are responsible for exercising institutional stewardship. News organizations help sustain the practice by giving individual practitioners access to the privileges that come with being affiliated with a bona fide news organization (including such conveniences as press passes), as well as access to resources such as Internet connections, satellite dishes, and printing presses. Without this kind of support, the practice could not achieve excellence. To accomplish its mission, the practice must be willing to cooperate with business goals that do not threaten to corrupt the practice itself. This is desirable not only as a way to sustain the practice but also as a way to help individual journalists achieve integrity among the various aspects of the self.

Reasons for Preferring Open (Rather than Covert) Resistance

There is at least one other factor that should be considered when developing an ethical model of resistance: Should resistance strategies make obvious the journalists' preference for the practice's goals? Is there anything wrong with leaving this preference unspoken? Is this unspoken preference a problem only if journalists make it *appear* as if they prefer organizational goals? Bok (1989b) has pondered the complexities involved eloquently in her book *Secrets*. She says that there are both good reasons (such as preserving privacy) and bad ones (such as covering up wrong doing) for engaging in secrecy. In addition, secrecy may or may not cause harm to others. However, there are a number of factors that make secrecy suspect or even vicious. Secrecy can damage relationships because these depend on truthfulness.

Indeed, secret activities that undermine organizational directives would be perceived by most managers as violating the psychological contract mentioned earlier. Secrecy is easily abused precisely because its rationale cannot be inspected.

Certainly, any time a secret must be maintained at the cost of misleading others, it has an ethical strike against it, as Bok (1989b) argues. This would seem to be the case if journalists pretended to be looking out primarily (or even exclusively) for the organization's interests while surreptitiously acting with primary regard for the practice's goals. Finally, it should be noted that journalists themselves value and defend openness and disclosure in their own work. It would be inconsistent with journalism's tradition to opt first for cloaked resistance. On balance, an ethical model of resistance should prefer open strategies while giving journalists discretion to use covert ones.

A Model for Resisting Business Pressures

The proposed model reflects the ethical dimensions discussed earlier: whether organizational goals are given some weight (reflecting the virtues of justice, fidelity, and stewardship), and whether journalists openly privilege the practice's goals (reflecting the virtues of honesty and integrity). In keeping with the notion of shared responsibilities, the model allows broad discretion regarding how to embody the relevant virtues by providing examples of *types* of strategies that can be chosen. However, this typology speaks only to resistance strategies pursued internally. This partly reflects the desire to discuss practical solutions—those that are available to journalists with lots of options and those who may have to remain at their current place of work for whatever reason. This is not to say that externally oriented forms of resistance—such as whistle blowing or giving information to the competition—may never be morally desirable. However, based on the previous discussion, such strategies are not the most virtuous, all things being equal. The option of compliance with *no* consideration of the practice's goals is not either, as the model presumes that practitioners have shared responsibilities that cannot be ignored.

The resistance model proposes four types of approaches that can be described in terms analogous to those used to discuss political forms of resistance. Practical exemplars of these approaches are illustrated in the resistance strategies used by journalists at a Midwestern newspaper I will call *The Courier*, where I collected data in 1995 and 1996 as part of my dissertation research into how journalists managed potential ethical conflicts between journalism and business values.[5] The four types of resistance are presented in Table 6.1 in the form of a 2 × 2 matrix.

Type 1, *Declared Resistance*, is comparable to a country's declaration of war. Such options make it known very directly that the journalist objects to business requirements on the grounds of journalistic excellence and that there is no room for negotiation—or consideration of the organization's goals. It is the "take this job and shove it" stance of the professional-hero. Marin's resignation is an example, but quitting is only the most extreme response in this category. As Lambeth's (1992)

---

5   For methodological details, see Borden (2000).

Table 6.1   Ethical model of resistance within news organizations

	Professional goals overtly preferred	Professional goals covertly preferred
Organizational goals not given weight	Type 1: Declared Resistance Exemplar: Open protest	Type 3: Underground Resistance Exemplar: Sabotage (Least ethical)
Organizational goals given weight	Type 2a: Diplomatic Resistance Exemplar: Trump cards (Most ethical)	Type 2b: Diplomatic Resistance Exemplar: Principled compromises

Source: Borden (2000). Reprinted with permission from Lawrence Erlbaum Associates

examples of journalistic discretion illustrate, open resistance also can take the forms of refusing to write certain stories and negotiating conditions for reporting stories. Other options are refusing to put your byline on an objectionable story or candidly criticizing a supervisor's editorial decisions to his face. As can be seen in Table 6.1, however, this type of strategy turns out not to be the most virtuous form of resistance because it is deficient on the dimension of giving due consideration to organizational goals. Despite the exhortations of professional codes and the occupational lore of journalists, virtuous journalists would not pursue this as their first option.

The *least* virtuous kind of resistance is the repertoire of sabotage tactics at the other extreme, characterized by deficiency on both ethical dimensions identified by the model. Type 3, *Underground Resistance*, is so-called because this type of resistance occurs outside the establishment under the veil of secrecy. In this kind of resistance, journalists work exclusively in behalf of the practice's objectives, all the time giving the appearance of being good "patriots." This category would include the range of "covert writing techniques" (p. 163), including irony and "disdained news" (p. 159), described by McDevitt (2003). One way the journalists at *The Courier* resisted covertly was by bypassing higher levels of management. In one case, a copy-editor and photographer decided without consulting with anyone else to ditch an ethically questionable photograph. In another example, a photographer framed all the photographs in such a way that he could avoid including a business logo in the image. The photo editor was given no option containing the logo.

Sometimes the *Courier* journalists advocated strict adherence to orders, with the expectation of producing undesirable results that management would then not be in a position to criticize. An example is a story a reporter told about going to a grocery store to complete a "man on the street" assignment on a complicated issue. He gathered the quotes as required, even though he had to first explain the issue to respondents before they could answer the question. The reporter said he was never sent out on this type of assignment again. This is reminiscent of the "trickster stories" Fee (1997, p.19) has found in the occupational lore of journalists, and has many parallels to practices described in factories and other sites since the classic Hawthorne studies first documented the internal organization of the workplace (Roethlisberger & Dickson, 1939).

Even though such approaches are morally deficient, it may be necessary to at least tolerate instances of sabotage under conditions in which more open forms of resistance have proven ineffective—much as an underground resistance movement might be tolerated in a country under certain extenuating circumstances. An example of an intractable situation at *The Courier* was the economic development supplement the paper ran every year singing the praises of local businesses. This is something the newsroom had objected to for many years. Although *The Courier's* business office was not about to let the newsroom off the hook completely, several adjustments were made: The newsroom's involvement with so-called advertorials had been reduced; when it was involved with advertorials, its role often was limited to laying out wire or freelance copy; a part-time advertising photographer had been hired to take some of the load off the newsroom's photography department; and advertorials routinely were labeled "advertising supplements." At the individual level, journalists may have decided this was as good as it was going to get—and they may have been right. Subtle, "neglectful" resistance, such as minimizing effort on the articles that had to be written for this supplement, may have been the only available options—or at least the only options worth pursuing. The journalists minimized their contributions to the supplement by recycling old stories, spending as little time as possible on their assignments, and including some negative (but accurate) facts about businesses.

In keeping with Aristotle's Golden Mean, two moderate solutions that at first glance may seem wimpy actually fare better than the extremes. These are the Type 2a and Type 2b strategies labeled as *Diplomatic Resistance*. In keeping with the political analogy, these kinds of resistance seek to achieve primary interests through negotiation. The most virtuous kind of approach, in fact, is that of speaking up for the practice's goals within a framework that at least nods in the direction of organizational interests. This kind of moderate strategy is exemplified in "trump cards." I found that journalists at *The Courier* sometimes held some aces in reserve to use when the journalistic stakes were high enough that management could not ignore them without incurring flak or a loss of credibility. These "trump cards" were news criteria that could be used strategically—and openly—to override business constraints. That fact that these trump cards demonstrably were linked to organizational liabilities may have inoculated journalists from the typical costs of resistance. Notable among the trump cards was the potential of the story in question to affect a lot of people. If impact could be demonstrated, it could provide the means for challenging management policy and resource constraints. An example would be arguing that a story is so significant that its absence would be remarkable. With this Type 2a approach, the journalists were able to negotiate from a position of strength. This allowed them to pursue the practice's goals openly while still contextualizing them within the organization's own priorities.

Type 2b is exemplified in principled compromises, another moderate kind of strategy that fares well ethically. This type of resistance is akin to negotiating from a position of weakness. However, it should not be considered *morally* weak. The key to these principled compromises was to push the limits of business constraints while maximizing journalistic goals. For example, faced with a scenario in which budget cuts would preclude out-of-town travel to report on an important local story, the journalists put their minds to brainstorming ways in which they could get the story without actually driving out of town to personally attend a hearing and examine relevant government documents. The journalists suggested mainly technological alternatives, such as phone interviews and getting the documents by fax. Efficiency was emphasized, such that on the surface it is not readily apparent that the main aim was to achieve journalistic excellence (by writing a complete story). Nevertheless, these and other compromises advocated by *The Courier*'s journalists privileged the practice's goals by safeguarding its integrity as a condition of compromise, an orientation to conflict recommended by philosopher Martin Benjamin (1996). At the same time, these journalists did make some concessions to the institution.

This resistance model suggests a number of helpful lessons:

- The defiant stance of objecting to business constraints in the most confrontational and single-minded fashion possible is *not*, all things being equal, the best resistance mode for both practical *and* ethical reasons.
- There are resistance approaches that prioritize practitioner responsibilities but *still* give news organizations their moral due. These should be pursued first.
- There *are* open resistance approaches that journalists may use effectively even in newsrooms where the bottom line looms large in decision making. The key is to use organizational concerns as leverage to negotiate from a position of strength.
- Compromise does not have to be a bad word, as long as it safeguards the practice's goals. In fact, acknowledging the legitimacy of "the other side" is commendable as an expression of both moral and intellectual virtue.
- Underground resistance strategies are the least virtuous option for resistance within news organizations, but these may be morally tolerated in extenuating circumstances.

Finally, this analysis of resistance approaches suggests that news organizations themselves share some of the ethical burden for establishing a climate that encourages morally excellent kinds of resistance. The EVNL model shows that employees are more willing to resist openly and with due regard for the organization's interests when such responses are not punished and when those who resist can be reasonably sure that their efforts could result in positive organizational change. When this is not the case, journalists may adopt a stance characteristic of subordinates who feel relatively powerless to change organizational and social structures. "They operate on a thin line between the crushing reprisal of exposure and the torment of inaction. Risks are assumed because other forms of protest are expensive, intermittently effective, and delayed in their consequences. Thus, sabotage is usually a rational choice, but not without its regrets" (Jermier, 1988, p. 102). It is at least partly the fault of news organizations if this kind of fatalistic attitude is widespread within the journalism practice. The institution's responsibility for good journalism will be addressed in Chapter 8.

Practically Speaking

Janet Cooke, Moral Evaluation, and Journalism's Moral Community

Internet discourse produced in 1996 by journalists and journalism educators evaluating the Janet Cooke case 15 years later illustrates an important function of journalism as a moral community: providing an interpretive framework for practitioners to collectively understand and refine moral concepts important to their work.[1]

Cooke, a young *Washington Post* reporter, had to return her Pulitzer Prize in 1981 because it turned out she had made up the award-winning story of an 8-year-old cocaine addict. She re-emerged in 1996, telling her story in a *GQ* magazine story and seeking a second chance to work in journalism after living in France and selling cosmetics at a department store in Kalamazoo, Michigan. With word of the story came TV appearances on NBC's *The Today Show* and ABC's *Nightline*. Journalists around the country fumed at Cooke's gall. One place they vented was on the Internet, where a subscriber to an electronic discussion group sponsored by Investigative Reporters and Editors started a thread with a message containing the subject line "GAG!janet cooke."[2]

Zelizer (1993) notes that re-examination of such key events as the Janet Cooke case allows journalists to "consolidate authoritative evaluations of events that valorize them regardless of how problematic they might have been initially" (Watergate and McCarthyism, ¶18). In other words, the benefit of hindsight allows journalists talking to each other now to establish an authoritative interpretation of something that, at the time, might have been experienced by their younger selves or by their predecessors as a more befuddling event. As a result of such evaluative discourse, journalists "generate contemporary standards of action for other members of the interpretive community," that is, the "shared collectivity [of journalists], by which reporters engage in cultural discussion and argumentation across news organizations" (Zelizer, 1993, The Dominant Frame, ¶5).

Fabrication (or making up details and passing them off as verified "facts"), has long been part of the history of journalism, as Andie Tucher (1994) vividly demonstrates in her examination of the humbug in the early penny press. Nevertheless, the press eventually embraced the ideal of objectivity—the disinterested reporting of verified

---

1   This analysis was first published in Borden (2002). That article is reprinted here in condensed form with permission from Sage Publications.

2   The contributors to the IRE-L thread were one IRE officer, 14 journalists, five academics, and seven posters whose status could not be determined by either the content of their messages or their e-mail signatures. Nine posters posted more than one message regarding this thread, ranging from two to four messages.

facts. As Tucher noticed, "the enthronement of the objective voice survived" despite various challenges to it over the years (p. 201). The New Journalism of the 1960s and the investigative journalism of the 1970s posed challenges to objectivity, because, in Eason's (1988) words, their "claims to truth were often less dependent on verification than upon the reputation of the reporter" (p. 217). In New Journalism, journalists sought to convey a higher truth through imagined conversations, composite characters, and other literary techniques usually associated with literature. In investigative journalism, journalists claimed a more authoritative truth than that of the government by going around officials and relying instead on documents and whistleblowers, who were often shielded by promises of confidentiality. These new techniques had gained ground at the time of the Cooke scandal but had not completely taken hold. Commentary immediately after the Pulitzer was withdrawn pointed fingers at these unorthodox practices. Meg Greenfield (as cited in Friendly, 1981) wrote on the opinion page of the *Washington Post*: "The whole unfortunate progression has been toward a looser and looser and ever more self-indulgent and impressionistic conception of what is real and what is imagined" (p. A7).

Journalists at the time took special pains to praise Cooke's writing, and more than one commentator expressed the hope that she would continue to write. Indeed, much of the commentary drew attention to the moral sins of the *Post* and the press, discussing affirmative action and editorial supervision as major problems. In other words, there was some ambiguity over how the Cooke incident should be classified for purposes of moral evaluation. These alternative topics were ripe for discussion because of the relatively recent influx of minorities into newsrooms and because of the unprecedented public scrutiny of the press occasioned by the Cooke scandal.

By the time the subscribers to IRE-L revisited the Cooke scandal years later, several other cases of fabrication had been discovered and condemned, investigative journalism had embraced databases and hidden cameras, policies about anonymous sources had been tightened, and affirmative action had become a fact of life. The Cooke thread began on May 15, 1996, with a post to IRE-L containing the subject line "GAG!janet cooke":[3]

OK, did anyone out there read the GQ story about Janet Cooke speaking out after 15 years?

I am appalled. The piece was done by an ex-but-still-enamored lover who pleads that Janet "be given back her voice." Why? Well, it seems she did a very bad thing, lying and all, but, gee, she had a stern father and a mean editor and she is beautiful and makes cookies out of Godiva chocolate.

I kept thinking of IRE member Trudy Lieberman's piece in CJR about how easy we are on plagarists [sic]. I'd be happy if every plagarist [sic] suffered Janet's fate. Let 'em sell cosmetics at the local department store.

---

3   Despite the public nature of the messages, identifying information has been withheld out of respect for the discourse's peer context. The archives are available at http://www.ire. org/membership/listservs/ire-l.html.

In this message, the author indicates that Cooke's transgression is best classified as lying and that personal factors do not constitute an acceptable excuse for her behavior. The principle "lying in journalism is wrong" stands as an absolute moral prohibition at the outset of the discussion. The rest of the discussion fleshed out this principle and sometimes challenged its applicability. Each of the main competing principles—lying, stealing, and neglecting—was supported by reference to particular cases. Posters then would draw an analogy between the particular case and the Cooke incident, which functioned as proof that their classification was appropriate. To flesh out the no-lying principle, posters proposed analogies to other examples of lying, including Watergate reporting "excesses," and surreptitious taping in hidden-camera investigations. Posters also initiated substantial subthreads suggesting alternative principles for classifying the moral claims involved in this case.

IRE-L subscribers specified what kinds of actions constituted unacceptable forms of lying and discussed which actions were more repugnant than others. A poster who suggested that Cooke's offense was relatively minor if all she did was use a composite character was rebuked by the subscriber who initiated the thread:

> Cooke didn't do anything so benign as combine characters or use an interview given to someone else—she invented everything. She doesn't even know the neighborhood where "jimmy" [*sic*] supposedly lived. She made up the "jive" in which the boy and his family supposedly talked. Ugh. Then later she failed as a fiction writer.

Generally, fabrication (the wholesale invention of details) was deemed the "mortal sin of journalism," in the words of one contributor. The deceptive methods sometimes employed by investigative reporters and the use of composites were also deemed as lying offenses, but less serious than outright fabrication. In the end, the thrust of the IRE-L discussion honed fairly closely to objectivity's distinction between fact (the appropriate domain of journalism) and fiction (the appropriate domain of literature). One poster expressed this assumption succinctly: "Fiction writers write books, not news stories."

Investigative reporting and the New Journalism—the challenges to objectivity that journalists had at least partially accommodated at the time of the Cooke scandal—were still alive and kicking within the interpretive community enacted by IRE-L subscribers, but barely. It is possible that investigative techniques would have fared even worse among journalists who did not identify themselves with investigative reporting, and literary techniques were not admired in this group. One poster changed the subject line to: "I can't even type her name." Referring to Cooke as a "creature," the author inserted excerpts from a Reuters wire story regarding a deal Cooke had made to sell the rights to her story for a movie. The writer went on to proclaim Cooke "the anti-CHRIST [*sic*], she devil, and Satan of Journo-world ..." [*sic*; ellipses in original].

Posters recognized that Cooke had become iconic and advocated using her as a symbol of what *not* to do in journalism. Whether defined as fabrication, or investigative reporting excess, or playing around with fictional techniques—Cooke's action was a lying offense not to be tolerated. The public expected the unvarnished facts.

Chapter 7

Professionalism and the Practice[1]

When Garrett M. Graff decided to seek a daily White House pass to write for a blog about DC. media, White House Press Secretary Scott McClellan sought input from the White House Correspondents' Association. The group's president had interceded for Graff, who was having trouble getting a pass despite repeated phone calls. The correspondents association, formed in 1914 to represent the White House press corps on access and other issues affecting coverage of the president, gave the OK. McClellan explained: "It is the press corps' briefing room and if there are any new lines to be drawn, it should be done by their association" (Seelye, 2005a, ¶9). Graff, who writes about journalism on FishbowlDC (www.mediabistro.com//fishbowldc), was believed to be the first blogger to gain access to the briefing room (Seelye, 2005a; "Unverifiable leak," n.d.).

The Graff episode illustrates the potential for professional groups to control who gets to do their kind of work and who gets to define occupational standards. Meyer (2004b) considers this an urgent necessity as journalists take on more responsibilities requiring specialized skills. "If journalism is to survive," he writes, "it will need a professional apparatus as one of the tools in the fight" (p. 244). The purpose of this chapter is to critically analyze the potential of professionalism as a framework for formally organizing journalists. I suggested in Chapter 2 that some kind of formal organization may be necessary for *journalism as practice* to successfully withstand corruptive institutional pressures. It makes sense to start with professionalism as an option for meeting this requirement because professionalism already is part of journalism's tradition: As discussed in Chapter 3, journalists already have access to its language and at least partially identify with its fundamental principles. Professionalism also has anti-market elements (Larson, 1977; May, 2001; Ohmann, 2003) that can be useful in helping journalists to separate their role as practitioners from their role as employees. To begin, the history of professions in the United States will be briefly outlined and journalism's experience with professionalization will be discussed in more detail. Next, the two key functions of professional organization for journalists—ethical motivation and occupational power—are critically examined in terms of both their potential usefulness and their potential problems. A range of options for the formal organization of journalists is presented in light of this analysis.

---

1   A slightly different version of this chapter was presented in August 2005 at the annual convention of the Association for Education in Journalism and Mass Communication held in San Antonio, Texas.

Professionalism and American Journalism

What is a Profession?

For the purposes of my argument, there are at least two useful ways of thinking about a profession: as a source of ethical motivation (that is, a source of moral norms oriented to public service) and as a source of power (that is, a source of occupational privileges oriented to status). These are based on the dual foundations of modern professionalism itself: the traditional, communal wisdom that informed the ancient guilds of the Middle Ages and the Renaissance; and the specialized expertise that propelled the social status of the university-trained professional in the late 1860s and early 1900s (Krause, 1996; Larson, 1977; May, 2001). As argued in Chapter 4, journalist-practitioners are creators of a special kind of common civic knowledge needed for citizens to know well in the public sphere. However, when viewed as upwardly mobile entrepreneurs who attempt to control the market and other aspects of their working conditions, journalists may be described in a more class-based way as knowledge *workers* (Ohmann, 2003).[2] Larson notes that the service and status orientations, although analytically distinct, are fused together in professionals. However, the relative strength of each orientation may vary from profession to profession (and from professional to professional). In the case of journalists, the service aspect of professionalism seems to be more developed than the status side.

The service and status dimensions of professionalism are explored in different literatures. Professional ethics scholars define professions in terms that clarify the grounds for their special obligations to various stakeholders. William F. May (2001), for example, says there are three marks of a professional: intellectual, moral, and organizational. The intellectual mark includes mastery of rare knowledge related to a specific human need, including both theoretical and clinical knowledge. Through competent expertise, professions enhance human flourishing in complex societies that naturally require "a division of [epistemic] labour" (Brien, 1998, p. 397). Following May (2001), Chapter 4 suggested that the ultimate human need served by journalism is "to give citizens a sense of belonging" (p. 204). The intellectual mark establishes a power asymmetry between professionals and laypersons while it equalizes power among professionals themselves. This mark creates the collegial organization as the "natural mode" (p. 11) of professionalism (in contrast, for example, with the competitive mode of hierarchical business organization). The moral mark includes fidelity to clients and the common good. The moral mark requires that professionals act "in concert with others for the common good" (p. 10) in the areas of self-regulation, self-improvement, production of services, and distribution of services.

Sociologists, for their part, study professionals as a social class. The trait/functional approach developed in the 1950s and 1960s has been particularly influential in the media ethics literature (see Allison, 1986, for a review of approaches to studying journalistic professionalism). The criteria used to characterize professions

---

2   The organizations that employ journalists, interested in knowledge only as "a private property, not a public trust, to be sold for entirely personal advantage" (May, 1986, p. 23), play the role of knowledge *merchants*.

in the functional approach include specialization, advanced education, esoteric knowledge, self-regulation by a socially recognized group, autonomy, and a public-service orientation. Strict adherence to these criteria narrows the number of bona fide professions to just a handful. The paradigmatic professions are medicine and law; some scholars also include the professoriate, accounting, and engineering (see, e.g., Krause, 1996; Larson, 1977). The fit between journalism and traditional professional criteria is certainly imperfect. For example, journalists do not have proximate relationships with individual clients (Bivins, 2004). Journalists, rather, deal with a mass public as their clientele. Another departure regularly noted is the absence of any licensing in journalism equivalent to the credentials legally required for entrance into professions such as law. Professional ethicists downplay these discrepancies. May (2001) compares journalism to the church and the military, which have institutional relationships with society defined in terms of professional service, rather than relationships with individuals. Adam, Craft & Cohen (2004) accept the lack of credentials as a necessary concession to the First Amendment. Writers in the sociological tradition, on the other hand, would relegate journalism to the status of a semi-profession at best.

Professions in the United States

Krause (1996) and May (2001) trace the early roots of the professions to the Western European craft guilds of the Middle Ages and the Renaissance. Both medicine and law were well-established professions by the 1500s, along with the professoriate. The apprenticeship system of the guilds was codified in US laws creating elite monopolies of lawyers and doctors between the American Revolution and 1840. However, professionals in the United States conflicted with the ideal of "egalitarian democracy and economic liberalism" (Larson, 1977, p. 113). Public rejection of professional privilege was especially pronounced in the anti-intellectual Jacksonian era. From 1840 to the end of the nineteenth century, monopoly laws were repealed, and no state certification or formal apprenticeship was required to practice law or medicine. When examined as a class phenomenon, the modern re-professionalization movement from about 1880 to 1920 amounted to a push by middle-class professionals to gain entry to the higher professional echelons dominated until then by the learned elites who had come up through the class-based system of aristocratic patronage. The strategy of the "new" professionals was to beef up their credentials through university education and use expertise as a proxy for pedigree. For professionals, finding some basis outside of social status held out the promise that they could "assert (their) altruistic autonomy" (Larson, p. 144).

According to Larson (1977), professionals in America attained elite status and market control only after large corporations and the resulting market transformations of the late 1890s and early 1900s "provided a new context of ideological and organizational resources for diverse professional projects" (p. 135). Specifically, scientific management in the industrial sector and Progressivism in the political sector combined to produce the ideology of the expert as the impartial (classless) embodiment of science in the context of large-scale bureaucratization in industry, politics, and civil society. Journalism's adoption of objective procedures can be largely explained by these shifts. Although it seems counter-intuitive, Larson argues that modern professions would have been marginalized had it not been for large corporations. He rejects any strict demarcation between so-called classic or "free" professions (such as medicine and law) and so-called organizational or semi-professions (such as teaching and social work): "All professions are, today, bureaucratized to a greater or lesser extent. Organizational professions should not be seen, therefore, as sharply distinct from older and more independent professions, but as clearer manifestations of tendencies also contained within them" (p. 179).

Organizational professions—which would include journalism—are those that function in organizations guaranteeing demand for their professionals' services, providing their members' salaries, and providing a power structure that partially conditions professionals' authority over clients. For organizations, the benefit of employing professionals is their standardized judgment (Soloski, 1989). Organizational professions, meanwhile, use their expertise to create knowledge-based or "logocratic relations of production" in the workplace that increase their power relative to both management and unskilled labor (Derber & Schwartz, 1991, p. 76). Their actual degree of autonomy depends on their cognitive basis. The more esoteric this basis, the more discretion professionals are allowed over the means for achieving organizational goals.

Larson (1977) considers professionalism to be a distinctly modern phenomenon that developed hand-in-hand with capitalism. However, he acknowledges that the professions incorporated pre-industrial elements. Three traditional components in particular give professional ideology its anti-market cast: the professional "work ethic derived from ideals of craftsmanship, which finds *intrinsic* value in work and is expressed in the notion of vocation or *calling*" (p. 220); the "ideal of universal service" (p. 220) including pre-capitalist "ideals of community bonds and community responsibility" (p. 220); and the aristocratic "notion of noblesse oblige" (p. 220), which stressed the duties of those in higher stations and the dignity of those in lower stations.

Professionalization in American Journalism

At least as far back as press critic Will Irwin's famous 1911 series "The American newspaper" in *Collier's* magazine, people have proposed professionalism as a framework for understanding the moral responsibilities of journalists. Irwin asked in the first installment of his series:

> Is journalism a business or a profession? In other words, should we consider a newspaper publisher as a commercialist, aiming only to make money, bound only to pay his debts and obey the formal law of the land, or must we consider him a professional man, seeking other rewards before money and holding a tacit franchise from the public, for which he pays by observance of an ethical code? (p. 15)

The drive to professionalize journalism occurred in the context of the broader re-professionalization movement in the late nineteenth and early twentieth centuries

(Krause, 1996). Promising developments included the emergence of reporting as a new occupation with its own practices of interviewing and, later, verification. Prestige and authority became inhered partly in individuals, thanks to the byline and the semi-celebrity of some reporters during the Civil War. Reporters' income rose steadily in the 1880s and 1890s, as reporting came to be viewed more as a noble calling for professionals. However, working conditions were generally poor up to the beginning of the twentieth century. Even as reporters were becoming more "professional," they still were being paid by the column inch as late as 1900, though eventually news organizations found it practical to put them on salary (and thus control them), rather than continue to outsource the reporting function (Baldasty, 1992; Bussel, 1981; Dicken-Garcia, 1989; Smythe, 1980).

When compared with the traditional trajectory of professionalization, journalism's journey is rather incomplete, hampered by circumstances that make it less amenable to professionalization than other occupations. Ohmann (2003) describes the general process of becoming a profession:

> A group that is doing a particular kind of work organizes itself into a professional association; appropriates, shares, and develops a body of knowledge as its own; discredits other practitioners performing similar work; establishes definite routes of admission, including but not limited to academic study; controls access; and gets recognition as the only group allowed to perform that kind of work, ideally with state power backing its monopoly. The process doesn't end there. Every constituted profession must continue to defend its rights and its borders. (p. 66)

Despite the obstacles faced by journalism in its quest to become a profession, there are some indications that journalists increasingly identify themselves as professionals. For example, in a study of about 200 journalists at a metropolitan newspaper, Russo (1998) found that journalists identified primarily with the "profession," then with readers, and last with employing organization. Further, the extent of their organizational identification hinged on the degree to which their organization enacted what they perceived as professional practices and values. Meyer (2004b) points hopefully to signs of professionalization in journalism, including the quasi-certification provided by journalism degrees and cases in which professional groups have publicly criticized journalistic wrong-doing: "The nascent profession of journalism stands ready to emerge. The old culture of journalism that has resisted such change is already starting to yield" (p. 242). Nevertheless, journalists continue to lack common associations and a common literature; any professional identity they have at this point inheres in their individual attitudes and organizations rather than a collective body (Weaver, Bean, Brownlee, Voakes & Wilhoit, 2007).

The Ethical Motivation Function of Professionalism

The motivational model of professionalism relies on the original meanings of professionalism—before the term became so closely associated in the nineteenth century with technical expertise and individual, private gain (Sullivan, 1995). A "civic conception of professional ethics" (Jennings, 1991, p. 566) was founded on "internalized moral commitments" (p. 565), most prominently public service, community leadership, and love of knowledge. Sullivan calls this orientation *civic professionalism*. To satisfy the requirements of civic professionalism, professionals must accept somewhat more stringent responsibilities than non-professionals, do their best regardless of financial cost, curtail self-interested motives, and cultivate expertise of use to all. By taking on these commitments, professionals make themselves answerable to others—that is, morally accountable. Another benefit is providing journalists with an alternative identity that can foster excellence, collegiality, and critical distance from business goals.

Benefits of the Motivational Model

Accountability   Journalists have at least implicitly promised to observe the expectations of civic professionalism by accepting various privileges whose rationale rests on public service. The privileges journalists receive include special access (such as press passes and press pools), protections (such as state shield laws that protect journalists from revealing confidential sources), and autonomy (most notably in the form of broad protection from censorship under the First Amendment).[3] Like doctors and lawyers, journalists have given explicit assurances about their service orientation in various codes, legal testimony, and public documents. Accordingly, the public can reasonably expect journalists to serve the public interest, much as they expect that physicians will not open someone's chest unless it is a necessary or advisable medical treatment. The public, to be sure, is cynical about journalists' motivations, but it is precisely because they have normative expectations of journalists—different from the expectations they have of other public communicators—that they react angrily to press missteps (Project for Excellence in Journalism, 2005).

Although some writers shun accountability as a limitation on journalistic freedom (see, e.g., Merrill, 1989), other ethicists argue that accountability is the key to professional independence. Newton, Hodges & Keith (2004) suggest that professional accountability is especially complicated because professionals are answerable to so many different people, including clients/beneficiaries, certifiers who judge professional competence, employers, and society. They say that professionals are primarily accountable to what they know as a result of their expertise and secondarily to any code and/or association formed to protect that knowledge. Because professionals are the only ones in a position to evaluate expert knowledge, and because they cannot answer to all stakeholders at once, they are obligated—and free—to exercise their professional judgment according to their consciences. McDevitt (2003) similarly talks about journalists acting virtuously as an expression of professional autonomy. Nordenstreng (1998) characterizes professional ethics as a dialectic between accountability and autonomy. Brien (1998) puts the relationship between these concepts in contractual terms: Professionals will act in society's

---

3   Although some of these privileges are not accorded exclusively to journalists, journalists still are prioritized when it comes to questions such as access to military zones and publishing government information.

interests; in exchange, society will let professionals regulate themselves.[4] This formula, however, works best in the context of "free" professions; organizational professionals have circumscribed autonomy.

Professional identification   Becoming a professional involves taking on an additional personal and social identity (Larson, 1977) in the course of training and entry into the profession. Newcomers in journalism typically are indoctrinated into the professional ideology when they attend college. Even after they have been socialized to news organizations so that they know what sorts of actions will bring rewards (Breed, 1955), journalists with a professional identity can use these external professional standards to evaluate the standards of their employers, who may or may not be journalists themselves (Soloski, 1989).

Professional identification includes an expectation of collegiality premised on equality among members and a commitment to a common purpose. "Professions are essentially 'a privileged society of knowers' bound together by a sense of vocation, the prospect of stable careers, common training experiences, a roughly equal share in monopoly knowledge, and resulting authority" (Larson, 1977, p. 231). These conditions can promote the kind of moral solidarity discussed in Chapter 6. They also can promote self-improvement by providing local role models and collaborators who can work together to extend the practice's internal goods through experimentation and exchanges of ideas. Collegiality provides yet another corrective to the market orientation of news organization, as it "repudiates not simply the obsequies of hierarchy but also the ruthlessness of raw competition" (May, 1986, p. 22).

Finally, professional identification involves the construction of discourses or rhetorics to establish legitimacy (Demers, 1989; Winch, 1977). Legitimacy, in turn, safeguards professional discretion and inspires excellence. Of particular importance to the motivational function of professionalism are professional accountability discourse and professional rights discourse. The first, already mentioned, involves articulating the ethical standards of the profession in codes and such; explaining how these standards are (or are not) being followed in practice; and issuing explanations of wrong-doing and resulting disciplinary action. Even more pertinent to the commodification challenge is the language of rights that professionals have developed to protect their autonomy. The notion of professional rights gives professionals legitimate discretion to withdraw their skills if the organization that employs them plans to misuse or ignore these skills. This is based on the claim that professionals alone have the expertise and public-service orientation required to accomplish certain important social goals. If they do not safeguard their autonomy, they lose their professional authority and are of no use (Flores, 1983).

---

4   For an opposing view, see Davis (2004), who says media obligations can only be derived from convention, that is, actual promises journalists make. Only this gives others grounds to hold journalists accountable.

Problems with the Motivational Model

The downside of asserting professional authority is establishing a paternalistic relationship with clients and society, a situation that makes enforcement of ethical norms even more crucial to ensure accountability.

Paternalism   Some critics think professionalism is merely a way for certain intellectuals to establish domains of privilege. Indeed, professionalism inevitably poses the danger of paternalism—condescending to outsiders by making choices for them—because of its claim of exclusive expertise. This claim "is for professionalism both a foundation and a prison: for, indeed, even the purest and worthiest of professional behaviors cannot help legitimizing inequality and elitism by their factual demonstration that knowledge is beneficent power" (Larson, 1977, p. 243). Rosen (2005a) is skeptical about professionalism's effectiveness in journalism at a time when amateur journalists are making headlines. "During its 'trust us, we're the pros' era, journalism was not concerned very much with openness," he wrote in a post to his blog PRESSthink. "It was concerned with preventing interference in the news. It was concerned with professional autonomy—not transparency" (¶4).

Advocates of professionalism defend professional privilege as a call for a "responsible elite" (Sullivan, 1995, p. 214), who will receive the benefits of an extensive education, of access to scarce resources, of considerable autonomy and prestige, and of the public's trust—all in exchange for furthering important human goods, such as health, justice, and community membership. As long as professionals uphold their part of the bargain, there can be, if anything, great pride in being the recipient of the social benefits that come with professional status. Professionals become citizens who have earned distinction for taking on what are usually very demanding roles in society—for the good of all, not just for themselves. However, that is the key. Professionalism should not be an instrument for keeping the public out of the arena; professionalism should "stimulate, not supplant, popular involvement" (Sullivan, 1995, p. 232).

In short, professional journalists must take care not to become condescending and unresponsive toward the citizens that they purport to serve. At the least, they can communicate openly and regularly about how they select, construct, and play news stories and how they deal with difficult ethical choices and mistakes. It would be even better, as suggested in Chapter 5, if journalists engaged in a discipline of confirmation that involves non-journalists in a cooperative process to confirm and, if necessary, modify knowledge claims presented as news. Rosen (2004a) suggests that this kind of relationship with the public could establish "build-as-you-go trust" (¶8). However, journalists have been reluctant to radically change their relationships with citizens.

> Journalists' resistance to even moderate forms of community response, such as press councils, suggests that they would not welcome a more fully participatory model of journalism. A publication devoted to dialogue might empower its audience, but it would never be commercially profitable enough to sustain professional journalists' political privileges, social ambitions, or sense of moral grandeur. (Pauly, 1988, p. 257)

Lack of enforcement Newton, Hodges & Keith (2004) say that legal means seem to be the only effective way, ultimately, to protect people from professional violations of trust. However, they do not want to cancel out professional autonomy by imposing legal standards. The quintessential mode of professional accountability is, rather, the ethics code, which often includes some form of censure to give teeth to the standards it enumerates. In the case of journalism, however, not even this form of professional discipline has proved effective. Since the American Society of Newspaper Editors (ASNE) adopted the first national code for journalists in 1923, a number of other professional groups have followed suit (Rodgers, 2005). However, none of these codes has enforcement provisions. The Society of Professional Journalists debated whether its code should contain a censure clause, but the overwhelming response of the membership was that such a clause would amount to licensing and, therefore, would threaten the press's First Amendment freedom. The same reason has been cited by journalists who have opposed the establishment of news councils (unofficial bodies made up of citizens and journalists who hear complaints from people with grievances against specific journalists). Because of this quandary, news organizations, rather than professional associations, usually fire or otherwise discipline wayward journalists (sometimes for reasons having more to do with money than professional quality).

To sum up, the usefulness of the motivational model is that it can provide an aspirational ideal and a strong alternative identity within employing organizations. These resources can promote accountability, excellence, and critical distance from business goals, as long as professionals take care not to condescend to citizens and actually enforce their own ethical norms. However, "profession" only in the motivational sense has limited utility because it cannot overcome institutional constraints on the pursuit of journalistic goals. The power model also is needed.

The Power Function of Professionalism

Power in the workplace can be exercised by guilds, capitalism, the state, or some combination of these. The classic professions developed guild power, which is a system of control over association, workplace, market, and relation to the state. The system is dynamic in the sense that each element influences or confronts the power of the other (Krause, 1996). Organizational professions never developed much guild power because of the dominance of one of the classic professions (as in the case of nurses developing in the shadow of physicians), or because they were prevented by the state or capitalism (as in the case of engineers developing as part of management within commercial organizations). Professional journalists belong in the latter category. "Organizationally, journalists—as a guild—wield very limited power, hemmed in by the very Constitution that exalts them and by the marketplace that pays them" (May, 2001, p. 197). If professional journalists could boost their guild power, they could potentially increase control of their practice by enhancing their autonomy and by distinguishing themselves from others offering informational content in the marketplace.

Benefits of the Power Model

Autonomy   Discretion is essential to protecting the integrity of the practice from corruptive commercial influences. Editorial autonomy involves control over one's work (for example, freedom in choosing which stories to cover) and independence relative to competing journalists (for example, not following the pack or unwisely reporting something just to beat the competition). Although it is circumscribed, journalists do get to exercise some discretion at work, especially in smaller organizations where there are fewer layers of supervision (Weaver, Bean, Brownlee, Voakes & Wilhoit, 2007). Autonomy is a big draw for journalists, who gradually acquire an expectation of editorial autonomy through anticipatory socialization, education, and actual socialization (McDevitt, 2003). Perceived autonomy is a major prediction of job satisfaction and intention to continue working as a journalist. Without autonomy, professionalism as a source of power in journalism is a non-starter (Weaver, Bean, Brownlee, Voakes & Wilhoit, 2007).

Boundary marking   The kind of professional discourse most relevant to the power function of professionalism is boundary-work discourse. This discourse establishes professionals as the ones who know best—better than other occupations that might claim to know the territory and better than clients themselves. In effect, the professionalization of journalists amounts to "jurisdictional warfare" against look-alikes (Winch, 1997, p. 18). Without boundary work, professionals cannot consolidate control over their work, and they cannot count on clients to seek professional help. Hence, physicians take great pains to distinguish themselves from healers outside the medical establishment and to advise patients to seek medical attention when they experience unusual physical symptoms.[5] Professional journalists, for their part, have to reassure the public that they offer something substantially different from the musings of cable pundits or the late-night jokes of Jon Stewart. They also have to convince the public that people cannot rely solely on their preconceptions about the world, that they, in fact, need journalism. In essence, journalists have to retain "journalistic authority in relationship to the citizenry" (McDevitt, 2003, p. 162). Finally, professional journalists also must distinguish themselves from their employers. Demers (1989) notes the necessity of "both offensive and defensive" rhetorics distinct from those used by news organizations and others to "tame journalists for their own purposes" (p. 21).[6]

---

5   Alternatively, professionals may co-opt rivals by incorporating them in secondary roles. For example, some hospitals now offer acupuncture, chiropractic, and other holistic treatments as part of therapeutic plans supervised by licensed physicians. Similarly, some press watchers have suggested that Big Media will swallow up blogs as soon as they figure out how to make them profitable enough.

6   See this chapter's *Practically Speaking* feature for an example of boundary-marking discourse in action.

Problems with the Power Model of Professionalism

Despite the promise of the power model, several difficulties remain for professionalism in journalism. Key among these are the powerless discretion of journalists; the lack of a well-defined, esoteric knowledge base to anchor a market monopoly; lack of collective consciousness; and the decline of professionalism generally.

Powerless discretion   Journalists never acquired a level of autonomy comparable with widely recognized professions such as law and accounting. Besides the First Amendment barriers to control of association, this happened because the profession was organized mainly by the corporate institution as a way of rescuing its credibility and controlling employees, rather than by the journalistic occupation as a way to claim indispensability and, therefore, power (Birkhead, 1986; Dicken-Garcia, 1989). In fact, this is one of the strongest criticisms of professionalism in journalism: the fact that professional journalists have very limited influence on the policies and goals of their employers and that many of even their most cherished ideals (such as objectivity) can be shown to function in the interests of operating efficiently and making a profit (e.g. Breed, 1955; Gallagher, 1982; Schlesinger, 1977; Shoemaker and Reese, 1991; Soloski, 1989; Tuchman, 1977). As Pauly (1988) puts it, "No editorial independence exists if the publisher chooses to exercise the prerogatives of ownership" (p. 255). Journalism's predicament is an illustration of *powerless discretion* (Larson, 1977) in which professionalism "helps to conceal collective powerlessness, subordination, and complicity" (p. 243).

Lack of an esoteric knowledge base   Journalists' lack of autonomy is related to the absence of a well-defined, cognitive base for the profession. William May (2001) says that journalists differ most from the classic professions in this respect. It is crucial, however, for a profession's independence because it excludes rivals and amateurs, ensuring the profession's authority over a given field. However, journalism has no body of theory that must be mastered to practice journalism. Understanding what is and is not "news" is the closest thing to esoteric knowledge that journalism possesses—and traditional news values have long given way to market-oriented definitions and, increasingly, to overtly political ones. Because the work journalists do is largely public, moreover, there is no "mystery" to it—everyone feels competent to define, evaluate, and maybe even create, the news. Blurred genres, such as infomercials and talk shows, make it difficult to enforce clear boundaries between the market for journalism and markets for other kinds of information "content."

Journalists have tried to derive authority from the methods of objectivity (May, 2001), the safeguards of editorial gatekeeping, and the prestige of their news organizations. Whatever effectiveness these strategies might have had over the years, their persuasiveness is declining. University education has not translated into cognitive authority for journalists either. There are now more than 450 undergraduate programs in journalism and mass communication across the country, with nearly 191,000 students enrolled in fall 2003 (about two-thirds of them studying in majors with a journalism focus; Becker, Vlad, Hennink-Kaminski & Coffey, 2004). However, journalists cannot use degree requirements to control entry, as other professions do.

Lack of collective consciousness Sandel (1989) and others have written about the individualistic tendencies of American culture. American professions seem at first glance to provide an alternative to such tendencies because of their collective claims. However, Larson (1977) points out that professions, too, are individualistic at their core. Unlike bureaucratic roles that inhere in organizations:

> Typically, professions maintain indeterminate and untestable cognitive areas in order to assert, collectively, the uniqueness of *individual* capacities. Collectively, they solicit trust in *individual* professionals and *individual* freedom from external controls, except for the ritual entry examinations administered by peers. The fact that the safeguards offered to the public in exchange for its trust—knowledge and internalized ethical norms—are inalienable from the person of the producer emphasizes the producer's individuality and illuminates the essential individualism of the professional ideology. (p. 206)

The study of professional ethics has followed this individualistic take (Jennings, 1991). The journalism tradition, moreover, has additional individualistic tendencies that lionize individual uniqueness, creativity, and non-conformity, as seen in Chapter 3. These include beliefs in freedom premised on negative rights, the "voice" of authorship, and the rebellious stance inherent in adversarialism. These beliefs discourage collective action. For example, no one joined the president of the White House Correspondents Association when he walked out of a briefing during President George W. Bush's first term to protest anonymous sourcing. More recent efforts to organize a collective response to the president's aggressive efforts to expand the scope of government secrecy have failed due to an unwillingness of journalists and their news organizations to participate. This deficit also partly explains the failure of unions to take hold among rank-and-file journalists (Fedler, 2006). Concludes Eric Alterman (2005a), writing for *The Nation*, "Alas, reporters, like Democrats and cats, are maddeningly hard to organize" (Fake news, ¶10).

Decline of professions in general Just as industrial labor has been hard-pressed in recent decades, so has mental labor grounding the professional class:

> Capital seeks to bring all areas of human activity into the market, and in doing so increasingly commodifies "information," including the kinds that we proudly but perhaps quaintly call "knowledge," and that professionals have amassed as cultural capital, to ground their practices and justify their exclusiveness. (Ohmann, 2003, p. 130)

This demotion of professionals occurred as the state and capitalism first co-opted professions, then capitalism co-opted the state. Krause (1996) says this process has left professionals "as the middle-level employees of capitalism" (p. 281). Ohmann (2003) is equally pessimistic, predicting a "long decline and maybe ... permanent restructuring" (p. 95) of professions because of their inability to "combat public cynicism, ideological assault, and economic decline" (p. 122)

Professionalism's Prospects and Possible Alternatives

This analysis raises a number of important questions regarding the potential of professionalism to provide a formal organization for *journalism as practice*. Without a monopoly on an esoteric body of knowledge, do journalists have any realistic prospects for possessing the kind of professional authority needed to resist corruptive institutional influences? Would it be a good thing (normatively and strategically) to firm up boundaries between journalism and similar occupations, or would it be better to eliminate them? What about the relationship between journalists as "experts" and members of the public as "laypeople"? Has the age of the expert already passed journalists by? There are, unfortunately, no straightforward answers to these questions. Yet they do suggest a range of alternatives for journalists to consider:

- Identify with the "profession" only as a source of ethical motivation, with no aspirations to occupational power. Organization would be limited to professional associations without enforcement powers, and press clubs would serve mostly social purposes.
- Continue attempts to build up the profession in the classic mold, including gaining more market control, mystifying news judgment, engaging in aggressive boundary work contra similar occupations, and restoring the strict segregation between news and business.
- Build a formal alliance with the academic side of journalism, namely the professoriate, which is a higher-status profession than journalism (Krause, 1996).
- Set aside a professional orientation and instead form a national union that would organize journalists across the country to bargain for better working conditions and ensure contractual recognition of their rights in the workplace (including discretion about editorial choices).
- Form alliances with "lower status" knowledge-based occupations, such as schoolteachers; with non-profit organizations, such as the Pew Center or the Poynter Institute for Media Studies; and/or with citizens in news councils, grassroots groups, or lobbies.

Journalists in Australia and other countries have chosen the unionization option. Unionization has been relatively unsuccessful among journalists in the United States due largely to the efforts of the industry. These have included concentration of corporate power through economic consolidation, managerial use of workplace technologies to reshape news work, and negative news coverage of labor strikes in the information section and elsewhere (McKercher, 2002; Tracy, 2004). American journalists may find, like other professionals who work in commercial organizations, that negotiating as equal partners in the economic system is the only way to garner enough clout to counteract market pressures. This is the case, for example, with schoolteachers. They are similar to journalists in several respects: They require relatively low credentials for entry; they lack an extensive cognitive foundation for their practice (that is, pedagogical theory); they have an oversupply of recruits; they have relatively low social status; and they are hopelessly subordinated within their employing organizations. Given these conditions, Krause (1996) and Ohmann (2003) say it is only natural that schoolteachers have turned to union organization for collective advancement as an occupation.

The unionization solution has its own problems, most notably its focus on wages and benefits, rather than on public service. The situation in journalism is further complicated by the reluctance of news workers to engage in political activism. Andy Zipser, editor of *The (Newspaper) Guild Reporter*, noted in a 2004 commentary, "[I]t's not just the economic issues of the day that must be addressed. These days, that's a false distinction. With politics increasingly driven by economic values and considerations, failure to resolve questions of political legitimacy risks the loss of economic and journalistic rights, too" (p. 4). Further, unlike professions, unions have never managed to actually create markets that they controlled (Larson, 1977). In addition, although professions have been losing power, the decline of the labor movement arguably has been even more dramatic. Then there are the psychological impediments to making the switch. Those with professional aspirations traditionally see worker identification as a step down in status (Elsaka, 2005; Larson, 1977), which makes them reluctant to unionize. As we already have seen, the strong individualistic streak of most journalists hampers collective consciousness. The more collective focus of unions, however, could be useful in interrogating and shaping organizational goals. Professionals, after all, cooperate in their own co-optation:

> Flexibility, autonomy, and circumscribed responsibility are precisely the qualities expected from expert labor: as long as the protests of subordinate professional workers ask for more of these *individual* privileges, as long as that is the main purpose of their corporate associations, their potential disloyalty can easily be managed. (Larson, 1977, p. 237)

Three discursive practices are needed to increase union power and, by extension, the power of any group trying to assert its own interests as a collective entity: "agenda-setting capacity, internal solidarities, and external solidarities" (Johnston, 2004, p. 4). Through agenda-setting rhetoric, unions and other groups attempt to define matters they care about as issues of larger social concern; for example, unions need to persuade outsiders that labor actions are not just about salaries and job security. In the case of journalism, rhetorical-ethical strategies may include linking quality news to what is good for citizens; highlighting the limited self-interest of management when organizational policies interfere with the achievement of the practice's standards of excellence; and pointing out how certain media policies narrowly serve the interests of powerful corporations and interest groups while hurting the common good.

Internal-solidarity discourse refers to rhetoric that promotes identification of members with the group and provides assurances about expectations of moral support, issues discussed in Chapter 6. As an example, Newspaper Guild-Communications Workers of America (TNG-CWA) President Linda Foley noted in her plenary address to the 2005 sector conference that one of the Guild's purposes, as stated in its mission, is raising ethical standards. Because the Guild never adopted written standards of its own, however, she said newspaper owners stepped in and issued "codes of conduct that are really more about enhancing their property rights than about professional ethics or serving the public" ("We have to think big: Stressing leadership, sector conference adopts ambitious program," 2005, ¶6). During the conference, the TNG-CWA executive council passed a resolution to draft ethics codes for both the editorial and commercial sides of newspapers, drawing attention to the fact that the business of journalism has some responsibility for good journalism too. To further underscore its commitment to journalistic freedom and ethics, the Guild organized rallies around the country a couple of months later to support reporters Judith Miller and Matthew Cooper and advocate for a federal shield law. The rallies included silent vigils at the *Baltimore Sun, Denver Post, Rocky Mountain News* and the Reuters offices. In addition, Guild members protested at federal buildings in a number of cities, including Boston, Cleveland, Eugene, New York, and Washington, DC. In a show of international solidarity among journalists, the Guild received pledges of support from journalists' unions in France, Sweden, and the European Union ("Guild rallies nationally to protest jailing, push for federal shield law," 2005).

As for external-solidarity discourse, this concerns rhetoric promoting and sustaining alliances with sympathetic outsiders, including other occupational unions, professional associations, foundations, non-profit organizations, political interest groups, and grass-roots citizens groups. Such discourse in journalism could promote concrete actions such as "voting with your dollar" (that is, buying a particular newspaper) or participating in boycotts (for example, shunning a particular advertiser). In other words, allies may be persuaded to become political actors in behalf of journalism *itself*. Unions again are instructive, because of their experience forming alliances outside their immediate occupational specialties. In the United States, the Newspaper Guild for reporters and editors decided in 1993 to explore a merger to deal with the structural and technological changes that were making the industry focus on information across media, on electronic distribution, and on short-term returns:

> Neither the diagnosis of the Guild's situation nor the prescribed solution focused on traditional patterns, such as organizing newspaper units that had not yet been organized, or building solidarity among newspaper unions through things like joint bargaining or uniform contract expiry dates. Rather, it reflected an awareness that the Guild should be forging links with workers across the information sector. (McKercher, 2002, p. 93)

The Guild ultimately voted in 1997 to become a sector of the gigantic Communications Workers of America, which already counted telephone workers, broadcasting engineers, and technicians among its members. Canadian journalists similarly have adopted a strategy of labor convergence with other workers in the communications sector.

Such actions suggest that unionization has some potential for giving *journalism as practice* a formal organizational structure with both clout and reach. Indeed, Johnston (2004) suggests that labor unions—having lost workplace guarantees and facing a battle for their very survival—are emerging as broader social movements than those traditionally focused on wages and working conditions. As a result, labor movements have an affinity with "broader struggles for expanded citizenship" (p. 2). This is underscored by the Newspaper Guild-CWA's human-rights agenda, which includes a commitment to diversity and to journalists' political rights. Regardless of the formal organization ultimately adopted by journalists, it is crucial that the practice engage in the kinds of discourses emphasized in this section. It must redefine bad journalism as a social problem requiring political action; it must construct internal consensus around the practice's standards of excellence and demand accountability from news executives; and it must persuade citizens, officials, and non-profits to alter the political and economic conditions most hostile to journalism's best traditions. These provide the main themes for the final chapter.

Boundary Marking After "Memogate"

60 Minutes Wednesday's story about President George W. Bush's National Guard service prompted an outpouring of boundary-work rhetoric in journalism.

The piece, which suggested that Bush had not fulfilled his service commitment during the Vietnam War, was based partly on documents that CBS said were written by one of Bush's former commanders. The documents said Bush had been ordered to take a medical exam and suggested that one of his commanders felt pressured to take it easy on him. Before the piece had even finished airing, however, bloggers started questioning whether the fonts on the documents could have been made by typewriters typically used by the Texas Air National Guard at that time. Later, it turned out that the person who gave star producer Mary Mapes the documents was of questionable reliability and that the documents were not properly authenticated by experts, as claimed (Associated Press, 2005a). Dan Rather—who narrated the September 8, 2004 segment—apologized for the mistakes and announced his retirement from the anchor's desk of the *CBS Evening News* (though he did not directly link his decision to the controversy).

After an independent panel had completed its investigation of the incident, CBS CEO Leslie Moonves blamed Rather for not being skeptical enough to begin with and for going overboard defending the segment afterward. The network fired Mapes and asked four others involved in producing and supervising the segment to resign (Associated Press, 2005a). The investigating panel concluded that the failure to properly authenticate the documents was not the result of bias. Rather, the problem happened because of excessive deference to Mapes and Rather, along with a new management team, belief in the story's truthfulness, and eagerness to be first with the story (CBS, 2005). In response to the investigators' report, CBS News pledged to implement a number of changes to prevent similar problems in the future (Tompkins, 2005).

The incident provoked outcry in journalistic circles, with many writers and on-air commentators condemning CBS's performance—in effect, highlighting the boundaries of legitimate journalism that had been crossed. In addition, dozens of articles and commentaries speculated about the wider journalistic implications of blogging's role in this case. The following examples are illustrative.

Some journalists suspected a broad agenda to erode journalism's authority. For example, *Washington Post* columnist Dana Milbank (2005) wrote:

> Partisans on the left and right have formed cottage industries devoted to discrediting what they dismissively call the 'mainstream media'—the networks, daily newspapers

and newsmagazines. Their goal: to steer readers and viewers toward ideologically driven outlets that will confirm their own views and protect them from disagreeable facts. (¶5)

Several journalists took pains to show that bloggers are not real journalists (and, by implication, should not be accorded the same legitimacy). "Do bloggers have the credentials of real journalists? No," wrote Nick Coleman (2004) in a column for the Minneapolis–St. Paul *Star Tribune*. "Bloggers are hobby hacks, the Internet version of the sad loners who used to listen to police radios in their bachelor apartments and think they were involved in the world" (¶19). Later in the column, he was downright dismissive: "Most bloggers are not fit to carry a reporter's notebook" (¶24). Veteran *New York Times* columnist William Safire wrote that there was no substitute for "reporters on the scene to transmit facts" and "trustworthy editors to judge significance" (¶5). In one of the most talked-about swipes, the late *Los Angeles Times* media critic David Shaw (2005a) came down vehemently against giving "practitioners of what is at best pseudo-journalism" (¶20) the same legal right journalists enjoy in many states to protect the confidentiality of their sources. Unlike real journalists, he wrote, bloggers have no experience, no one looking over their shoulder, no accountability—making them a "solipsistic, self-aggrandizing journalist-wannabe genre" (¶26). He concluded:

> If the courts allow every Tom, Dick and Matt who wants to call himself a journalist to invoke the privilege to protect confidential sources, the public will become even less trusting than it already is of all journalists. That would ultimately damage society as much as it would the media. (¶29–30)

Some journalists writing about what has come to be known as Memogate compared the blogosphere to a mob, implying purposeful deviance and effectively degrading the status of the bloggers. Journalists use the status degradation strategy to "demonstrate the contours of the boundaries of journalism" (Winch, 1997, p. 98). An example is Pein's (2005) extensive *Columbia Journalism Review* critique of the scandal coverage headlined "Blog-gate." She prefaced her analysis by saying that "on close examination the scene looks less like a victory for democracy than a case of mob rule" (¶4). After criticizing the press for not giving enough attention to the highly speculative reasoning and questionable political motives exhibited by many bloggers, Pein concluded:

> While 2004 brought many stories of greater public import than how George W. Bush spent the Vietnam War, the year brought few of greater consequence for the media than the coverage of Memogate. When the smoke cleared, mainstream journalism's authority was weakened. But it didn't have to be that way. (The Double Standard, ¶17)

Some journalists rhetorically lowered the status of bloggers by categorizing blogging as a natural or passing phenomenon that does not threaten journalism. Coleman (2004) put it bluntly: "Blogs ... are to journalism what ticks are to elephants. Ticks may make the elephants nuts, but that doesn't mean they will replace them. You can't ride a tick" (¶10). William Powers (2005a), while calling bloggers "a fantastic addition to the media club" (¶12), saw them fulfilling a rather narrow set of roles in the shadow of the traditional press. Writing in the *National Journal*, he said:

> What independent bloggers don't have is the resources or, in most cases, the skills to do the heavy journalistic lifting that the big American outlets still do better than anyone, and will continue to do for a very long time. (¶14)

> Media consumers are not about to abandon their desire for solid, middle-of-the-road news from the old, largely trustworthy, still impressive establishment outlets. (¶16)

Whether this kind of boundary-work rhetoric will succeed in keeping bloggers at bay remains to be seen (see Bishop, 2004; and Winch, 1997, for other examples of boundary work by journalists).[1]

---

1   Not all journalistic commentary was negative toward bloggers. For example, *New York Times* Standards Editor Al Siegal, while still considering them outsiders, attributed a helpful role to bloggers as critics. Siegal, who headed the committee that investigated the Jayson Blair scandal, said bloggers seem to have created a new standard for journalism scrutiny by posting "real-time press criticism" (Scocca, 2005, ¶14). Some even took offense at the attacks on bloggers, as illustrated by two examples from the online magazine *Slate*. Media critic Jack Shafer (2005) rebuked Shaw's column, saying the Founders wrote the First Amendment "precisely to protect Tom, Dick, and Matt and the wide-eyed pamphleteers and the partisan press of the time" (¶21). Jacob Weisberg (2005) characterized concerns about bloggers as "self-interested whining" (¶5) and proclaimed bloggers good for the press.

Chapter 8

A Common Cause

Journalists have been criticized for being reactionary and impotent as they try to muddle through the current spate of challenges facing the practice. Their own discourse about the practice conveys a sense of internal distress. For example, Howard Goodman (2005), reflecting on the revelation of Deep Throat's identity, wrote in the *South Florida Sun-Sentinel*:

> The fearlessness and doggedness that drove *The Washington Post* to dig for the truth of the "third-rate burglary" of Democratic Party headquarters would nowadays be predictably denigrated as "liberal bias."
>
> Then, reporters were epitomized by Robert Redford and Dustin Hoffman. Now reporters must live down the fictions of Jayson Blair.
>
> Then, Dan Rather made his name by sparring with President Nixon. Now the Rather name is synonymous with shoddy documents on President George W. Bush's National Guard service.
>
> Then, Woodward and Bernstein used anonymous sources to expose a government's secrets. Now the White House excoriates *Newsweek* over the unreliability of an anonymous source. (¶9–12)

A group can suffer from a state of internal distress when its tradition is not widely shared or recognized, or when outside interests try to subsume the group (Faber, 2002). In the case of journalism, the discordance I have been describing results from both factors: On the one hand, journalists' self-conception as stewards of participatory democracy is not widely shared outside the practice. On the other hand, corporate owners, government officials, and partisan critics are trying to control and even marginalize the press.

The good news is that this state can be a precipitant for healthy change. Practices need to experience some hardship to continue being vital. Without any real challenges, practices stop questioning their role and become complacent, even arrogant (Code, 1987). Journalism's "misalignment" may have the beneficial effect of confirming the practice's mission and encouraging journalists to embrace high standards (Gardner, Csikszentmihalyi & Damon, 2001, p. 6). These perilous times may also constitute an opportunity for journalists to reach out to allies. A number of non-profit organizations already have joined the cause. The projects they have funded have had a positive impact on *journalism as practice* by backing the efforts of innovative master practitioners, experimenting with news coverage and business models, and engaging journalists around the country in serious reflection about the purpose of their work. The organizations involved include educational institutions, such as the Poynter Institute for Media Studies in St Petersburg, FL; charitable foundations, such as the Pew Charitable Trusts based in Philadelphia; and grass-roots media-reform groups, such as Free Press, based in Northampton, MA. This chapter discusses some of these efforts. It also considers the responsibilities of both news executives and citizens for sustaining *journalism as practice*. However, first I will discuss some things that journalists themselves must do to assert themselves as practitioners. As suggested in the previous chapter, the tasks involved are partly discursive. The practice must redefine bad journalism as a social problem requiring political action and managerial reform; it must construct internal consensus around the practice's standards of excellence; and it must persuade citizens to help it launch a successful social movement aimed at protecting journalism from the excesses of commodification.

What Do Journalists Need to do to Assert Themselves as Practitioners?

Faber's (2002) analysis of the relationship between a group's internal narratives and its external image highlights some lessons pertinent to journalism. First, journalists have to be aggressive about defining themselves, rather than letting others define them. In the past, journalists reluctant to "become the story" or to stoop to the level of their critics have allowed corporations to define journalism as just a business (a definition that has become widely accepted by the public). Alternatively, they have stood by while partisans have equated journalism with the one-sided (often intellectually dishonest) rhetoric produced in spin rooms. The outsiders are winning the image-power struggle to the detriment of *journalism as practice*. *Image power* is the power that "resides in people's ability to control the ways in which they, and others, are perceived across social structures and times" (p. 143).

To reverse this trend, journalists will need to engage in external and internal sense-making discourse that is political in the sense of being strategically aimed at restoring their legitimacy in the public sphere. However, traditional forms of storytelling and criticism may not suffice. Successfully re-articulating the practice's internal narratives and rebuilding its external image may require transgressing dominant forms of discourse (Faber, 2002). The Internet provides many opportunities for journalists to talk about their mission and their standards of excellence beyond the newspaper columns and trade review articles that have long characterized such public discourse. The potential of blogging already has been noted. Such discourse also does not have to exist solely in cyberspace. Online discourse also can promote face-to-face discourse about the practice's future. For example, the Internet was used to help organize the Restoring the Trust gathering held in conjunction with the 2005 convention of the Association for Education in Journalism and Mass Communication. Video streaming, transcripts, and blogs helped further disseminate the ideas discussed at this meeting.

However, journalists cannot talk just to each other about what it means to participate in *journalism as practice*. Although peer discourse is important for maintaining the collegial relationships that promote the practice's internal goods, it is not enough to keep the practice strong. Finally, journalists have to educate the public about its philosophy and about the contributions the practice has made to American history and democracy. This kind of discourse could take a number of forms, including telling the stories of great journalists and their achievements. Kovach (2005) suggests that news organizations encourage "civic literacy" curricula that "help create an informed demand for their work" (¶19). Wyatt (2006) likewise suggests that media literacy efforts should emphasize "sympathetic tools to understand the press" as well as "adversarial tools to critique the press" (p. 18). In short, citizens need to be reminded of why America has a journalistic tradition and what it means to civic participation and human flourishing. Such discourse about the history and purpose of the practice also can help create role models for future practitioners. As Johnston (2004) notes, groups must frame their interests as issues of larger social concern to succeed in a match against a dominant power such as Big Media. There is, of course, a danger that such discourse will come across as hypocritical and self-serving as long as journalism consistently fails to reach its highest aspirations. It will take real improvement in journalistic performance to align the practice's internal narratives with its external image.

Partnerships with Non-profits

As journalists and others concerned about civic life began to appreciate the dangers of the press's increasing commodification, foundations and other non-profits began to sponsor efforts to improve the performance of newspapers and local television stations. These efforts have been crucial to preserving and strengthening public broadcasting and alternative news media. For example, the Ford Foundation, which has been an important supporter of public broadcasting from the beginning, announced a $50 million initiative in 2005 to help public broadcasters and independent media develop and distribute public affairs programs on a larger scale. The announcement came at a time when Congress was considering large cuts to public broadcasting (Manly & Jensen, 2005). Foundations also have pumped some money into commercial outlets through civic journalism projects and other civic-minded programs, including Best Practices 2000 (BP2K). BP2K, funded by the Pew Center for Civic Journalism and the Corporation of Public Broadcasting, stimulated short-term collaborations between local commercial and public TV stations in 11 markets to improve public affairs programming.[1]

In addition to the Pew Center for Civic Journalism, the Pew Charitable Trusts also underwrite the Project for Excellence in Journalism (PEJ), a journalist-run think tank that started at the Columbia University Graduate School of Journalism and is now affiliated with the Pew Research Center in Washington, DC. PEJ has been particularly effective in drawing on the journalistic tradition of research and open

---

1   Although BP2K had limited success in boosting issues programming, Kurpius (2003) concluded that these changes were unsustainable without continued outside funding. "Large foundations can and do make a difference in improving democratic media performance of local television stations but when the foundations leave, the stations revert back to traditional norms and routines of coverage" (p. 90).

exchange of ideas to advocate for quality journalism. PEJ (www.journalism.org) conducts research, including the influential State of the News Media reports. Among its first projects was the Committee of Concerned Journalists (CCJ), a consortium of journalists, owners, and educators who advocate for quality journalism. CCJ has separated from PEJ and now has its own website (www.concernedjournalists.org/) and nearly 2000 members (including me). Its biggest achievement to date has been publication of *The Elements of Journalism: What Newspeople Should Know and the Public Should Expect*. Written by PEJ director Tom Rosenstiel and CCJ Chair Bill Kovach, it deduces the core ideas of journalism based on years of surveys, forums, content analyses, and interviews. These ideas have been incorporated into workshops conducted at newsrooms across the country. In addition, CCJ (which also receives funding from the Knight Foundation) provides a number of journalism-related resources for use in communities, classrooms, and newsrooms. The Poynter Institute has performed a similar role over the years. It provides continuing education opportunities for journalists and journalism educators and convenes special symposia whenever an urgent issue arises within the practice, such as the Jayson Blair scandal of 2003. Through its web presence (www.poynter.org), Poynter also has made research and other tools available to journalists striving for excellence and hosts the influential Romenesko weblog.

What all these groups have in common is credibility among journalists: They are run by journalists and speak to journalists in their own language. Richard Reeves, a faculty member at the University of Southern California, writes in Pew's quarterly magazine, *Trust*:

> PEJ is essentially reporting to reporters—with attitude. That attitude is: We all know journalism is changing with the times and technology, and a lot of people think we're not doing a very good job. Well, let's take a look and see what we can do before bad guys come in and throw us out with the bath water! (Reeves, 1999, pp. 13-14)

Other internal and external actors have contributed to the conversation about the practice's goals over the years, including journalism reviews, professional societies, ombuds, and media critics on programs such as National Public Radio's *On the Media* and in newspaper columns such as those written by *Washington Post* media reporter Howard Kurtz (Newton, Hodges & Keith, 2004). The Society of Professional Journalists has long been active in promoting journalism ethics through its code, an online ethics hotline, and its magazine, *The Quill*. It also recognizes exemplary performance by journalists and started an annual Ethics Week to encourage discussion of journalism ethics with the public. *Columbia Journalism Review* (*CJR*), for its part, started a web site during the 2004 election to criticize press coverage of the presidential contest, then continued it afterward under the name *CJR Daily*. *CJR Daily* (www.cjrdaily.org) engages in real-time press criticism in a tongue-in-cheek style similar to the tone of web logs, which themselves have become increasingly influential vehicles of press criticism. Ombuds, meanwhile, gained prestige with the successful tenure of *The New York Times*'s first person in that role, Daniel Okrent.

A number of media-reform groups have also sprung up, especially since the 1996 Telecommunications Act. Among them is Free Press, a non-partisan organization founded in 2002 by critical media scholar Robert McChesney. According to the group's web site (www.freepress.net), its aim is to generate and promote public support for "policies that will produce a more competitive and public interest-oriented media system with a strong nonprofit and noncommercial sector" (www.freepress. net; About us, ¶1). Free Press works with other groups to influence Congress on specific issues such as protection of federal funding for public broadcasting, broad community access to the Internet, advertising regulations, and the establishment of non-commercial low-power FM radio stations. Free Press was involved in channeling public outcry against proposed Federal Communications Commission (FCC) rules loosening media ownership rules in 2003. Some of these rules were sent back to the agency for review by a federal appeals court in 2004; the Supreme Court refused in 2005 to hear appeals filed by the media industry (Associated Press, 2005d). Free Press has organized three national conferences on media reform and distributes free education kits on media activism through its web site. It also helps produce, along with the University of Illinois Institute for Policy Research, a brief weekly radio program called "Media Minutes" that is distributed by 25 broadcast stations and seven online stations.

Although for-profit corporations distribute the vast majority of news, charitable foundations, educational institutions, and non-profit companies have had good results with alternative ownership models. At least one local radio station and one national magazine in the United States are owned by non-commercial entities, along with several newspapers that passed into the hands of non-profits upon the deaths of their publishers. A non-profit holding company owns Independent Newspapers Inc., which publishes several weeklies and a daily in Dover, DE; a charitable trust owns the 42,000-circulation *Day* in New London, CT; the Poynter Institute for Media Studies owns the venerable *St. Petersburg* (FL) *Times*; and universities own newspapers in Manchester, New Hampshire, and Columbia, MO. Family owners started a non-profit foundation to run *The Anniston* (AL) *Star*. The profits are being used to fund a graduate program in journalism at the University of Alabama. Students will work in the newsroom to learn the ropes of journalistic practice (Shepard, 2006). Non-profit newspapers sometimes accept single-digit profit margins (compared with the industry standards of 20 percent or more) so that they can put money into more local news, bigger newsholes, and larger staffs than papers of similar size. PBS NewsHour senior correspondent Ray Suarez told the *American Journalism Review*: "I could be making more money working elsewhere, but I wouldn't be a happy guy, and I wouldn't work out of the conviction that I would be allowed to do the best work I am capable of" (Sessions Stepp, 2004, ¶105).

Ownership, Management, and Journalism Ethics

The reason that alternative ownership models are so attractive to journalists and press reformers is that publicly held corporations are structurally predisposed to emphasize short-term profits rather than long-term stability and community service

(Cranberg, Bezanson & Soloski, 2001). Editorial employees have even taken a stab at buying the companies that employ them. Thanks to various arrangements allowing employees to buy and own stock as long as they remain with the company—ranging from a trust to an Employee Stock Ownership Plan (ESOP)—employees have a controlling interest at four daily newspapers. These papers, including the Milwaukee *Journal Sentinel* and the *Omaha World-Herald*, have done "an exceptional job of serving their communities," maintaining higher levels of staffing, coverage, and penetration than their peers (Fedler & Pennington, 2003, p. 271). However, at least nine other employee-owned dailies failed between 1926 and 2000, plagued by poor management, inadequate capital for expansion, and other problems. Further, such arrangements are difficult to construct because they require complex bylaws and financing to ensure that employees can afford to buy stock and that they will not sell to outsiders. The advantages for owners of selling to chains, in any case, are hard to surmount with idealistic calls for quality and local control (Fedler & Pennington, 2003). The obstacles were illustrated most recently by the ultimately unsuccessful attempt by six *St. Louis Post-Dispatch* employees to buy the newspaper before Pulitzer sold it to Lee Enterprises in 2005. Nevertheless, the attempt inspired The Newspaper Guild to pass a resolution later in the year pledging to produce a guidebook and research other resources to help such efforts have a better shot at success in the future ("Employee ownership of media outlets," 2005).

Meyer (2004b) writes about a "golden age" when newspapers were run by the "philosopher-kings of publishing" (p. 202), who were focused on the long-term goals of dominating their respective markets and producing influential newspapers that would promote their personal or family pride:

> The reason newspapers were as good as they were in the golden age was not because of the wall between church and state. It was because the decision making needed to resolve the profit-service conflict was made by a public-spirited individual who had control of both sides of the wall and who was rich and confident enough to do what he or she pleased. In today's world, most leaders of the press do not have that kind of functional autonomy. (pp. 206–207)

However, the future of the publicly held newspaper corporation is in doubt as the Internet eats into advertising revenue and executives find that there is not much more left to cut from their news operations. Wall Street, with its short-term outlook, has opted to cut its losses. Knight Ridder, then the second-largest newspaper company in the United States, put itself up for sale in 2006 under pressure from investors. The McClatchy newspaper chain acquired most of Knight Ridder's properties, then promptly auctioned off 12 of the newspapers it had just bought, including the Pulitzer Prize-winning *Philadelphia Inquirer*. Chicago-based Tribune, the largest U.S. newspaper publisher, also went on the market after several years of managerial decisions that not only irked the Chandler family and other shareholders, but also editorial staffs, unions, community leaders, government officials, activists, and readers in Los Angeles, Boston, Hartford, Baltimore, and other cities with venerable newspaper traditions (Rainey & Mulligan, 2007). Ultimately, it was local multimillionaire Sam Zell of Chicago who struck a deal in 2007 to take Tribune private through a series of complex transactions built on an ESOP trust. Eventually,

Zell will end up with 40% of the company's common stock to the employees' 60% (Oneal, 2007).

Tribune's tribulations illustrate how money has the potential to corrupt the business sphere, as well as the journalism sphere, by pushing boards and executives to extremes of greed and callousness. CEOs used to see themselves as stewards and weighed shareholder interests against those of other stakeholders. Now shareholders expect CEOs such as Tribune's Dennis J. FitzSimons to act as their agents, motivated by self-interest rather than moral obligation:

> The cultural pressures of traditional society pushed people into moral behaviour even when this went against their perceived self-interest, but at least they were praised for it. The cultural pressures of a market society push people into self-interested behaviour even when it goes against their altruistic instincts, but there is no blame and they get rewarded economically. (Hendry, 2004, p. 24)

Hendry (2004) says we are transitioning from hierarchical organizations with morality built into their rules to network organizations in which morality is being replaced by raw power. "If network organizations are to thrive, however, they must act as traditionally moral as well as economic communities, and they must be managed as such" (p. 30); that is, they must be characterized by mutual trust and accountability. However, this is difficult to achieve in the absence of long-term commitments from either employers or employees.

Alternative ownership arrangements can only accomplish so much. Private owners still have bank loans to pay and may not understand the spirit of journalistic practice any better than the FitzSimonses of this world. In Philadelphia, the local businessmen who bought the *Inquirer* with promises of "the next great era of Philadelphia journalism" (Smolkin, 2006, p. 30) were announcing job cuts just a few months later (Fabrikant & Waxman, 2006); and in Santa Barbara, California, all the top editors and a long-time columnist quit the award-winning *News-Press* in the summer of 2006 to protest what they saw as unethical editorial interference from co-publishers Wendy McCaw and her fiancé, Arthur von Wiesenberger. Nearly two dozen other newsroom employees (about one-third of the editorial staff) eventually resigned as well. Many of those who remained encouraged readers to cancel their subscriptions (several hundred did), organized a 500-strong demonstration outside the paper's landmark building, and eventually voted to join the Teamsters. Community leaders and prominent journalists joined the fray, writing open letters to the owners with no immediate success (Pomfret, 2006; Rainey, 2006b).

Journalists are primarily responsible for the integrity of their practice, but they are not solely responsible. After all, they do not ultimately control the conditions of their work (Adam, Craft & Cohen, 2004; Borden, 2000; McManus, 1997). Media executives, acting in behalf of owners, control the purse strings of newspapers, magazines, and television stations. Therefore, they are indirectly responsible for good journalism. They may even have a role in monitoring and correcting the practices that they house (Moore, 2002). At the least, they should wield their power well, rather than causing harm by interfering with news judgments, putting out poor-quality news, or curtailing access to the news. At best, they can be proactive in exercising stewardship over *journalism as practice*. An example was the decision by management at ABC affiliate KSTP-TV in the Twin Cities to reject an ad proffered in early 2007 by the conservative Progress for America, which claimed that "the media" have only reported bad news about the Iraq war. KSTP General Manager Rob Hubbard thought the specific claims in the ad were not true about his news operation or about ABC News. As commentators noted at the time, such "push back" is all too rare by news organizations (Mosedale, 2006).

Such actions could conceivably become more common if business could re-imagine management as "an explicitly value-oriented activity" (Hendry, 2004, p. 30):

> In flexible organizations, managers are no longer needed to make economically objective decisions, the routine resource selection and allocation decisions that were the staple of the old managerial role. That can now be done perfectly well by market mechanisms, and the whole point of flexible organizations is to enable these mechanisms to operate. What managers are needed for now is precisely to call the moral shots, and in so doing to maintain the environment of mutual trust, mutual respect, sympathy, awareness, and compassion within which teams can function effectively and the interests of their members can be productively engaged. (p. 221)

If commercial organizations could be organized around moral virtues, rather than money, we might end up with "a condition where individuals and organizations can both exist in a mutually satisfying, harmonious condition of virtue" (Scott & Mitchell, 1988, p. 48). To build a virtuous corporation, argues Moore (2002), news organizations would have to recognize that they house *business as practice*:

> The virtuous corporation will be one which has a corporate character that acknowledges that it houses a practice, that encourages pursuit of excellence in the practice, aware that this is an entirely moral pursuit, *and* one which pursues the external goods in so far as they are necessary to and support the development of the practice. But it will not be so focused on the external goods that it fails to support the practice on which it is founded. (p. 30)

It is not clear exactly what Moore (2002) has in mind as the defining characteristics of *business as practice*. To conform to MacIntyre's (2007) conception, *business as practice* would have to be based on the pursuit of goods external to journalism in a way that does not emphasize them as individual possessions but, rather, as contributions to the common good. Moore alludes to this, saying that *business as practice* would consider the effects of business on society (although this does not seem to go far enough). At a minimum, *business as practice* would emphasize the common good of the "business community" (as opposed to individual managers, or single organizations). Ideally, it would stress the role of business in creating opportunity and meeting real needs that could not otherwise be met (with profit-making as an instrumental goal, rather than as an end in itself). Nor does Moore acknowledge that the claims of one practice may conflict with the claims of another. MacIntyre suggests that such conflicts can be resolved only by appealing to the whole of a human life. In the context of news coverage, such conflicts may be resolved by focusing on how good business and good journalism intersect to promote human flourishing. Meyer (2004b), for example, notes that the "concept of market is inseparable from the concept of community" (p. 206) because communities consist of both social and economic links "to build and maintain a public sphere" (p. 206). Likewise, institutions such as newspapers combine commercial and journalistic strands in ways that may not be separable. For example, newspapers need to think about ways to compete with new technologies as a matter of economic success, but also as a matter of promoting "trust associated with the brand, regardless of platform" (p. 222).

In short, it is not a matter of *either* shareholders' interests *or* the community's interests, of *either* quality *or* profit. It is a matter of emphasis, of keeping both spheres—or practices—in proper perspective, and of thinking through needed trade-offs so that both can maintain their legitimacy. At the corporate level, for example, it is probably too restrictive to preclude executives from participating in lobbying and incentives, such as stock options, that are standard operating procedure in most publicly held companies. At the same time, non-financial objectives can be added to the managers' agenda and rewarded so that short-term profit orientation is not pursued at the expense of all other considerations (Cranberg, Bezanson & Soloski, 2001). These could include objectives tied to the moral management role (Hendry, 2004):

- "Supporting and enhancing the moral leadership of the firm" by effectively communicating the value judgments of leaders with respect to balancing the interests of stakeholders and honoring commitments made to them (p. 221).
- "Maintaining ethical standards" (p. 221) by responding to any "potential disasters of ethical malpractice" and by legitimating "moral discussion and debate within their teams and work groups and so create a climate in which engagement is at least possible" (p. 222).
- "Creating and maintaining a moral community within the manager's own areas of responsibility" (p. 221) by giving proper consideration to the "specific circumstances, needs, and commitments" of individual employees (p. 222), promoting honesty and personal growth, providing support, "enhancing … capacity for moral judgement" (p. 222), and honoring trusting relationships.

Openness also is needed in terms of disclosing details about financial incentives awarded to media executives. Many parties have interests at stake. Shareholders have their investments at stake. Employees have their livelihoods and careers on the line. Readers and viewers invest their time and money and make day-to-day decisions using the news. The public sphere depends heavily on journalistic quality to promote well-reasoned choices about civic life. The practice needs the cultural legitimacy it gets from doing journalism well. Advertisers, of course, rely on the media to put them in touch with consumers and to compete successfully in the marketplace. All these parties have a right to know about corporate and operating decisions that may affect their interests. News executives should do more than merely inform these parties of decisions that will affect them, of course. They should give their needs thoughtful consideration, taking care to balance the competing interests of various stakeholders while acting to protect the company's viability in the long run (Stern, 2006).

Figure 8.1 illustrates how various agents in news organizations should orient themselves relative to the goals of profit and journalistic quality. I suggest that news executives try to approach a virtuous mean when balancing journalism and business against each other. The closer their role is to the heart of the journalistic enterprise, the more the focus should shift from financial objectives to journalistic objectives, and the more force journalistic considerations should have. For example, editors should not get bonuses for cutting newshole; their primary concern should be quality. The primary concern of executives higher up in the corporation may be to ensure profitability. However, corporate executives should limit their pursuit of profit at the point at which the business sphere threatens to corrupt the journalism sphere. That is the ethically necessary trade-off, given the need to compensate for the general tendency in the industry and society as a whole for economic rationales to dominate thinking in all spheres. Ideally, corporate executives strive for profits that are enough to give a fair return to investors but not so much as to endanger the news organization's long-term prospects or unnecessarily weaken journalistic performance. Publishers, as the executives who mediate between the parent company and the local newsroom, should strive for something approaching balance between profits and quality.

Profit_____**Quality**
     Corporate officers   Publishers   Editors

Figure 8.1   Managers' ideal orientations to profit and quality

The structural incentives in the media market should be changed to create better conditions for the exercise of virtuous management. As Cranberg, Bezanson & Soloski (2001) note, different legal structures need to be put in place for investors (and their corporate agents) to expand their visions beyond short-term returns. "Journalists will not likely perform their tasks of prophetic criticism unwaveringly without some institutional protection of their independence, not only from the government but from the conglomerates that increasingly own the newspapers" (May, 2001, p. 271). Corporations, their boards, and their compensation systems also need reforms to eliminate organizational obstacles to ethical behavior. It is not easy being ethical when everything from the regulatory environment and market dynamics to bureaucratic systems and workplace cultures preclude or at least downplay ethics as a consideration in day-to-day decision-making. Without structural, hierarchical, and legal reforms, even managers who want to do right by journalism will have a hard time of it.

What Can Citizens do to Support *Journalism as Practice*?

Citizens are the natural allies of journalists in pressing for these types of reform. They rely on journalism to deal responsibly with the complexities of the modern world and to participate meaningfully in public life. They have a strong interest in quality journalism. Newton, Hodges & Keith (2004) suggest that citizens may be effective as external mechanisms of press accountability by holding public forums on press performance, developing their own media-criticism programs on cable-access television, and posting media criticism on citizen-produced journalism reviews online, and on other kinds of web sites. Some have even suggested that citizens be allowed to buy shares in private news companies, make donations to fund reporting on particular stories that interest them, and even to accept reporting and fact-checking assignments (Glaser, 2006; Rosen, 2006).

Croteau & Hoynes (2001) recommend a sustained social movement focused on media reform, alternative media, and media literacy similar to that advocated by Free Press. Specific proposals include: content regulation (including mandated educational and public affairs programming and free airtime to political candidates), access-oriented policies (including low-power radio and public funding of Internet access in schools and libraries), more funding and restructuring of public media (see specifics on pp. 228–232), new limits on ownership concentration, and more media analysis in the press. To get this kind of social movement going, however, journalists and their allies will have to successfully define press reform as a social problem. This is particularly true for changes that depend on government policy, including content regulation and the industry's ownership structure. Nelson (1984) has examined how child abuse—considered until the 1870s to be a private child-rearing choice by parents—became a bona fide political issue with legislative support. She notes:

> A social problem is a social construct. Its "creation" requires not only that a number of individuals feel a conflict of value over what is and what ought to be, but also that individuals organize to change the condition, and achieve at least a modicum of recognition for their efforts from the wider public. (p. 5)

Nelson (1984) suggests that social problems have a natural history proceeding in stages: *issue recognition* (an official notices a concern and thinks it might be addressed through government action), *issue adoption* (an official decides whether it is legitimate for the government to act on the problem and whether there is an appropriate governmental response available), *setting priorities among issues* (officials find a place for the problem on their agenda, sometimes displacing older issues), and *initial issue maintenance* (the official gets the issue to the point of actual government action; for example, introduction of a bill). *Recurring maintenance* is the "process by which established issues are periodically examined" or not (p. 23). Fortunately for advocates of child welfare, child abuse is a *valence issue*, that is, one on which there is widespread consensus (nobody is *for* child abuse, though people may disagree on the causes and characteristics of child abuse). Press reform, on the other hand, is a *position issue*, that is, one that tends to "engender alternative and sometimes highly conflictual responses" (p. 277). Valence issues are more likely to find official advocates than position issues. Other factors affecting rapid diffusion or adoption of issues include low cost (financial and political) and "narrow definition of the problem and a simple solution" (p. 132). Unfortunately, these tendencies mean that some problems lose support once their complexity becomes fully appreciated.

What is needed to get a social problem on the radar of government officials?

- *Catalysts for change*: one or more dramatic instances to arouse concern, or "technological and demographic changes and dissatisfaction with the existing distribution of resources" (Nelson, 1984, p. 24). Although most citizens do not understand the inner workings of the press, they probably could rattle off Jayson Blair, Memogate, and several other journalistic scandals from the last few years with little difficulty. Such incidents arguably contribute to growing dissatisfaction with press performance. In short, as Free Press puts it, "Media *is* the issue."
- *The right frame*: leadership by concerned individuals to frame these examples or circumstances as instances of a larger problem and to create groups that will organize a solution (some of these individuals and groups have already been mentioned in the journalistic context). Initial frames for constructing the problem are often decisive. A difficulty for press reform is that the US government is less likely to accept issues constructed in terms that threaten the status quo, such as attacks on the ownership structure that has allowed huge corporations to control the vast majority of US media with the FCC's blessing. In this regard, it is noteworthy that Free Press (as one example) has stated that its first goal is public participation in media policy.
- *Readiness for change*: As much as the public may be willing to accept that media corporations are largely to blame for the worst journalistic excesses and deficiencies, survey data suggest that a sizable proportion of citizens think that the biggest ethical problem in journalism is bias and already questions whether journalists have too much freedom, rather than too little.

Mueller, Page & Kuerbis (2004) trace political advocacy for communication-information policy (CIP)—including the press, but also telephones, broadcasting and the Internet—to a 1969 case in which the United Church of Christ Office of Communication successfully challenged the broadcast license of a racist broadcaster in Mississippi. The case gave citizens the legal right to weigh in on broadcast license renewals by the FCC. Although deregulation subsequently reduced the influence of citizen groups regarding government broadcast policy, various groups have managed to influence network programming decisions since the 1970s by becoming part of the routine process of enforcing network standards. This kind of content-oriented activism characterized CIP advocacy from the late 1960s into the 1980s; examples are campaigns against cigarette ads, news bias, and racial stereotypes. The 1990s saw growth in movements organized around individual rights associated with the Internet (for example, privacy and access), and also an increase in advocacy combining these two concerns with economic ones, such as those associated with infrastructure regulation. This trend peaked with interest group lobbying on the 1996 Telecommunications Act, which prompted the formation of the Telecommunications Policy Roundtable (TPR), an informal group formed by 40 interest groups pursuing CIP advocacy in Washington, DC.

The way a movement mobilizes is dependent on the political opportunities that exist at any given time. In more favorable conditions, movements may take on a more activist stance; in less favorable times, they may opt to simply stay on politicians' radar screens (Mueller, Page & Kuerbis, 2004). Further, the circumstances that give rise to social movements also restrict the effective repertoire for collective action (Staggenborg, 1991). For example, a proactive and successful counter-movement has forced pro-choice activists to be reactive and adopt single-issue tactics. In the case of media reform, the fact of entrenched business interests may demand a rhetorical strategy that emphasizes public participation and the social impact of policies benefiting Big Media's bottom line. In fact, this line of argument won over congressional members who actively fought proposed FCC regulations loosening ownership rules for media corporations in 2003. Activists also found elite support in 2005 for restoring proposed federal cuts to public broadcasting.

These successes can be traced at least partly to an increase in political advocacy for media reform. Congressional activity on CIP, in terms of hearings anyway, has become a prominent part of the federal policy agenda, probably in response to the growth in the number of CIP advocacy groups (Mueller, Page & Kuerbis, 2004). However, the Big Media lobbies are long-time political insiders with institutional advantages, while those pressing for media reform have only recently begun to have any political influence on official bodies, such as government agencies, Congress, and state legislatures. Further, successful social movements need elite access and support as well as mass mobilization—both "direct-action tactics" and "conventional methods of influence," such as lobbying (Staggenborg, 1991, p. 153) and filing formal complaints with the FCC. Allies are indispensable, especially those with money to give to the cause and those from previous (successful) movements who can provide "experienced activists, organizational and ideological bases, and tactical models" (p. 148). Foundations, grass-roots organizations, labor unions, and established advocacy groups such as the American Civil Liberties Union and Common Cause are needed to organize citizen efforts to protect *journalism as practice*:

> We are on the cusp of a major structural change in the organizational form and the program of CIP advocacy, something analogous to what occurred between the 1960s and 1970s, but involving transnational collective action and the use of the Internet for organization and mobilization. All that is missing is the spark of an opportunity created by change in the political structure. (Mueller, Page & Kuerbis, 2004, p. 183)

The 2004 presidential campaign clearly demonstrated the potential of the Internet for grass-roots organizing. Over time, we may see a more formal press reform movement develop as part of a larger effort directed at the "media" that can withstand challenges from those opposing change and that would sustain political pressure over the long term.

Summary and Conclusion

This book presents an argument for providing journalists with a robust group identity that could distinguish them from others in the media marketplace and reinvigorate the occupation with a new sense of purpose. I ground my argument in MacIntyre's (2007) notion of a practice. Briefly, a practice is an established human cooperative activity in which one participates for the purpose of achieving excellence in the realization of certain goods whose point and meaning are internal to the practice. In Chapter 2, I discussed MacIntyre's ideas in the context of virtue theory and argued that journalism meets the basic requirements for being considered a practice, including an institutional context, an overriding purpose, an effective moral community, and internal goods that can only be realized and extended through the practice. Chapter 3 provided a brief "MacIntyrean history" (Lambeth, 1992, p. 79) of journalism focusing on ideas related to the development of reporting as an occupation and as a distinct identity: storytelling and authorship, truth and objectivity, professionalism and social responsibility, power of the press and the people's right to know, participatory citizenship and the press. These ideas—the reporter's inheritance—are embodied in what MacIntyre would call key *characters*, or models of virtue in journalism, including the muckrakers, Edward R. Murrow, and Watergate reporters Bob Woodward and Jim Bernstein.

Journalism's tradition was used to derive a theory of journalism in Chapter 4 that sets out the distinguishing marks of *journalism as practice*, as well as its *telos*, or ultimate purpose. My theory proposes that *journalism as practice* is distinguished by being a way to make a living and effect political reform that is linked to human flourishing and committed to the common good. Its defining activity is reporting. Like all practices, journalism relies for excellence on a set of skills, a vocational aspect, and certain institutional resources. Journalism's immediate goal is to create a special type of common civic knowledge necessary for citizens to know well in the public sphere; journalists produce and disseminate this knowledge in the form of "news." News is defined in terms of a communitarian account of participatory citizenship and Code's (1987) notion of epistemic responsibility, emphasizing the functions of surveillance, interpretation, and reckoning. The theory, finally, offers a preliminary account of the practice's internal goods—those that are oriented toward the realization of the *telos* and that can only be realized as a journalist.

I argue that journalism's internal goods can be deduced from an analysis of science as an exemplary intellectual practice. Like journalists, scientists cooperatively determine what counts as a particular kind of knowledge, what is worthy of investigation, what is worthy of dissemination, and in what form. Journalism, like all intellectual practices, pursues *knowledge* and *inquiry* as goods in themselves (not mainly as means to other ends such as career advancement); *discovery* (in the senses of both finding out and making known), *originality* (in the sense of doing your own investigation and thinking), and *newness* (in the sense of being the first to find out, think, or experience something). In addition, journalism shares some internal goods with other kinds of practices that have intersecting traditions, including politics and literature.

In Chapter 5, I discussed five functions of virtues in sustaining *journalism as practice*. Corrective virtues protect the practice from the corruptive influence of external goods by compensating for the detrimental effects of efficiency, competition, and other goals oriented toward achieving business's overriding goal of maximizing profits. The virtue of stewardship was discussed in relation to sustaining the institutions that house *journalism as practice*, including the First Amendment and the news organizations that employ most journalists. This chapter also looked at honesty, justice, and courage as virtues needed in collegial relationships to support a cooperative discipline of verification marked by intersubjectivity, redundancy, and skepticism. Trustworthiness was critically examined as a virtue characterizing the relationship between practitioners and citizens.

Chapter 5 also looked at appreciating one's legacy as a special virtue needed to preserve continuity with the practice's tradition. Another function of virtues is supporting the practice's regenerative capacities. Here, I focused on intellectual accountability and intellectual modesty as the virtues needed to support a discipline of confirmation characterized by accessibility, transparency, and tentativeness. Conducted in cooperation with non-journalists, this discipline can provide a system for the practice to continually improve itself and extend its conceptions of ends and means.

Next, my argument focused on the practice's function as a source of moral identity for journalists, with special attention to the role played by peer discourse in shaping shared understandings of excellent journalism. Relying on Larry May's (1986) analysis of the concepts of shame and solidarity, I argued in Chapter 6 that a strong moral community could successfully support individual members who resist ethically questionable business requirements. The chapter concluded with a discussion of individual resistance in the absence of a true willingness among journalists to sanction each other and to go to each other's aid. This discussion included an ethical model illustrating resistance approaches varying along the ethical dimensions of: (a) consideration of both the organization's goals and the practice's goals; and (b) openness with regard to journalists' preference for the practice's goals. Part of my argument is that journalists are not solely responsible for the health of their practice.

Chapter 7 critically analyzed the potential of professionalism as a possible formal organization for *journalism as practice*. I concluded that the motivational model of professionalism provides journalism with an aspirational ideal and a strong alternative identity within employing organizations. These resources can promote accountability, excellence, and critical distance from business goals. However, "profession" only in the motivational sense has limited utility because it cannot overcome institutional barriers to the pursuit of journalistic goals. Unfortunately, the occupational power function of professionalism is severely curtailed by journalism's lack of monopoly over an esoteric body of knowledge, minimal collective consciousness, and powerless discretion within news organizations. Nevertheless, I suggested that there are a range of options that journalists should explore to counter market forces increasingly hostile to the traditions of *journalism as practice*. These included a closer look at union organization and a variety of potential alliances with non-journalists. Future research should examine the literatures on labor and social movements in more depth to investigate potential partnerships between journalists and other workers and between journalists and other segments of the community.

Fortunately, the same developments that have caused alarm about journalism's integrity may also have created the conditions for a genuine breakthrough—within and without journalism—that could make *journalism as practice* a full-fledged reality. Journalists are thinking seriously about their purpose and their future, and a number of efforts led by citizen groups and non-profit organizations in the last few years have resulted in a fledgling media reform movement. The problems afflicting journalism are not amenable to easy political solutions, especially at a time when resources are scarce. However, these developments, as well as the grass-roots organizing potential of the Internet, are encouraging. Code's (1987) notion of epistemic responsibility provides a basis for holding citizens partly responsible for supporting good journalism, too. We also cannot leave out media owners and executives. Because of the way journalism is produced in the United States, they also have some responsibility for seeing that journalism turns out well for the community. More analysis of the basis, scope, and limits of these responsibilities is needed.

Developments related to the Valerie Plame CIA leak case are suggestive of the prospects for *journalism as practice*. Tom Shelby, a well-known anchor and investigative reporter for a local television station in Minneapolis, offered in a 2005 column to serve some jail time for *New York Times* reporter Judith Miller, who was incarcerated for refusing to testify about her confidential sources. He suggested all journalists should do the same. Many other journalists did, in fact, offer their support for Miller and lambasted Time Inc. for turning over *Time* magazine Matthew Cooper's notes against his wishes. As noted in the previous chapter, the Newspaper Guild also successfully organized protests across the country in support of Miller and Cooper. However, after Miller agreed to testify and was released from jail, her fellow journalists soon began to direct their disapproval at her. Miller refused to cooperate with colleagues assigned to reconstructing her part in the Plame investigation for *Times* readers and revealed a number of ethically questionable decisions in her own accounts of what happened. As a result, her editor apologized for backing her, and the paper's public editor suggested that it would be best if she did not return after her leave of absence. If she did, wrote *Times* columnist Maureen Dowd (2005) in a scathing critique, "the institution most in danger would be the newspaper in your hands" (¶17). The editor of *Editor & Publisher* went further, calling for Miller to be fired "for crimes against journalism, and her own newspaper" (Mitchell, 2005, ¶1).

In these actions, we begin to see the outlines of a substantive collective identity for journalists based on a willingness to go to each other's aid when appropriate—and to sanction each other when that is called for. The dogged pursuit of Miller and Cooper by Special Prosecutor James Fitzgerald, meanwhile, prompted a bipartisan bill in Congress to establish a federal shield law protecting journalists from disclosing confidential sources except in extreme circumstances. This bill was supported not only by a number of professional groups and the Newspaper Guild, but also by several citizens groups and the American Bar Association. This coalition gives reason to hope for future alliances united behind the common cause of a flourishing *journalism as practice*, as do the protests that have united practitioners, community leaders, union leaders, business executives, and elected officials against unwise managerial decisions by Tribune and other press owners. A healthy practice would have fewer "lone guns" like Carol Marin, who ended up taking action alone and was in a better position than most to land on her feet following such a grand gesture. Instead, we would have a situation more closely resembling the vision articulated by Bill Egbert (personal communication, November 23, 1997) in a message posted to an online journalism ethics discussion group a few years ago:

The goal would be to create a culture of muscular opposition to the commodification of news (which is the root of most of our ethical and reputational worries), in which media companies would be afraid not to cover the next Telecommunications Act, because if they tried not to, the staff of every major news organ in the country would walk out. When the papers didn't come out the next day, and the network screens went blank at 6:30, and attention-getting luminaries like Ted Koppel went on the News Hour to explain the action, the fallout could reverse the tide.

Bibliography

Adam, G.S., Craft, S., & Cohen, E.D. (2004). Three essays on journalism and virtue. *Journal of Mass Media Ethics*, *19*(3–4), 247–275.

Allison, M. (1986). A literature review of approaches to the professionalism of journalists. *Journal of Mass Media Ethics*, *1*(2), 5–19.

Alterman, E. (2005a). Bush's war on the press. *The Nation*, May 9. Retrieved April 26, 2005, from http://www.thenation.com

Alterman, E. (2005b). Found in the flood. *The Nation*, September 26. Retrieved September 9, 2005, from http://www.thenation.com

Altschull, H. (1990). *From Milton to McLuhan: The Ideas Behind American Journalism*. New York: Longman.

American Historical Association. (2005). Statement on standards of professional conduct. Retrieved May 24, 2005, from http://www.historians.org/pubs/Free/ProfessionalStandards.cfm

Andersen, K. (2005). Premodern America, *NewYorkmetro.com*, March 14. Retrieved March 7, 2005, from http://www.newyorkmetro.com

Anderson, R., Dardenne, R., & Killenberg, G.M. (1997). The American newspaper as the public conversational commons. In J. Black (Ed.), *Mixed News: The Public/Civic/Communitarian Journalism Debate* (pp. 96–115). Mahwah, NJ: Lawrence Erlbaum.

Applbaum, A.I. (1999). *Ethics for Adversaries: The Morality of Roles in Public and Professional Life*. Princeton, NJ: Princeton University Press.

Aristotle (1984). *The Nicomachean Ethics* (W.D. Ross, Trans. with an Introduction). Oxford: Oxford University Press. (Originally published by Oxford in 1925.)

Arjoon, S. (2000). Virtue theory as a dynamic theory of business. *Journal of Business Ethics*, *28*, 159–178.

Arrow, K. (1963). Uncertainty and the welfare economics of medical care. *The American Economic Review*, *53*, 941–973.

Associated Press. (2005a). CBS ousts four in wake of National Guard story flap. *USA TODAY*, January 10. Retrieved January 10, 2005, from http://www.usatoday.com

Associated Press (2005b). Mankato editor resigns rather than cut staff. *Star Tribune*, March 15. Retrieved March 17, 2005, from http://www.startribune.com

Associated Press (2005c). "Newsweek" revamps source policies following Koran story. *USA TODAY*, May 22. Retrieved May 22, 2005, from http://www.usatoday.com

Associated Press. (2005d). High court declines FCC ownership rules case: Media groups want restrictions relaxed to adapt to growing market. *MSNBC.com*, June 17. Retrieved August 1, 2005, from www.msnbc.msn.com

Baldasty, G.J. (1992). The rise of news as a commodity: Business imperatives and the press in the nineteenth century. In W.S. Solomon & R.W. McChesney (Eds),

Ruthless Criticism: New Perspectives on U.S. Communication History (pp. 98–121). Minneapolis, MN: University of Minnesota Press.

Baltimore Sun Newspaper Guild Unit. (2006). Baltimore Sun staffers letter to Tribune CEO. *Romenesko* blog, September 26. Retrieved October 3, 2006, from http://www.poyter.org/forum

Barger, W. & Barney, R.D. (2004). Media-citizen reciprocity as a moral mandate. *Journal of Mass Media Ethics*, 19(3–4), 191–206.

Bauder, D. (2004). Does backlash loom against opinion news? *Boston.com*, November 14. Retrieved November 15, 2004, from www.boston.com

Bauder, D. (2005). NBC anchor says Katrina legacy is reporters taking gloves off again. *Kalamazoo Gazette*, September 12, p. D5.

Becker, L., Vlad, T., Hennink-Kaminski, H., & Coffey, A.J. (2004). 2003–2004 enrollment report: Growth in field keeps up with trend. *Journalism & Mass Communication Educator*, 59(3), 278–308.

Benjamin, M. (1996). Compromise and integrity in ethics. In Kent, T. & Gentry, M.B.(Eds), *The Theory and Practice of Ethics* (pp. 21–36). Indianapolis, IN: University of Indianapolis Press.

Birkhead, D. (1986). News media ethics and the management of professionals. *Journal of Mass Media Ethics*, 1(2), 37–46.

Bishop, R. (2004). The accidental journalist: Shifting professional boundaries in the wake of Leonardo DiCaprio's interview with former President Clinton. *Journalism Studies*, 5(1), 31–43.

Bivins, T. (2004). *Mixed Media: Moral Distinctions in Advertising, Public Relations, and Journalism*. Mahwah, NJ: Lawrence Erlbaum.

Blanks Hindman, E. (2003). The princess and the paparazzi: Blame, responsibility, and the media's role in the death of Diana. *Journalism & Mass Communication Quarterly*, 80(3), 666–688.

Blondheim, M. (1989). The news frontier: Control and management of American news in the age of the telegraph (Doctoral dissertation, Harvard University, 1989).

Blood, R. (2004). A few thoughts on journalism and what can weblogs do about it. *Rebecca's Pocket*, April 15. Retrieved May 28, 2005, from http://www.rebeccablood.net/essays/what_is_journalism.html

Blood, R. (2005). Weblogs and journalism in an age of participatory media. *Rebecca's Pocket*, January 7. Retrieved May 28, 2005, from http://www.rebeccablood.net/essays/weblogs_journalism.html

Bok, S. (1989a). *Lying: Moral Choice in Public and Private Life*. New York: Vintage.

Bok, S. (1989b). *Secrets: On the Ethics of Concealment and Revelation*. New York: Vintage.

Bondi, R. (1984). The elements of character. *The Journal of Religious Ethics*, 12, 201–218.

Borden, S.L. (1997). *Value Judgments: How Journalists Think About the Ethics of Good Business*. (Doctoral dissertation, Indiana University, 1997).

Borden, S.L. (1999). Character as a safeguard for journalists using case-based ethical reasoning. *International Journal of Applied Philosophy*, 13(1), 93–104.

Borden, S.L. (2000). A model for evaluating journalist resistance to business constraints. *Journal of Mass Media Ethics, 15*, 149–166.

Borden, S.L. (2002). Janet Cooke in hindsight: Reclassifying a paradigmatic case in journalism ethics. *Journal of Communication Inquiry, 26*(2), 155–170.

Borden, S.L. (2003). Deviance mitigation in the ethical discourse of journalists. *Southern Communication Journal, 68*(3), 231–249.

Borden, S.L. (2005). Communitarian journalism and flag displays after September 11: An ethical critique. *Journal of Communication Inquiry, 29*(1), 30–46.

Borden, S.L. & Pritchard, M.S. (2001). Conflict of interest in journalism. In M. Davis & A. Stark (Eds), *Conflict of Interest in the Professions* (pp. 73–91). Oxford: Oxford University Press.

Bovens, M. (2002). Information rights: Citizenship in the information society. *The Journal of Political Philosophy, 10*(3), 317–341.

Breed, W. (1955). Social control in the newsroom: A functional analysis. *Social Forces, 33*, 326–335.

Brien, A. (1998). Professional ethics and the culture of trust. *Journal of Business Ethics, 17*, 391–409.

Buck, R. (2006). A letter from a writer to his publisher. *Romenesko*, September 18. Retrieved September 19, 2006, from http://www.poynter.org/forum

Bumiller, E. (2005). White House presses Newsweek in wake of Koran report. *The New York Times*, May 18. Retrieved May 18, 2005, from http://www.nytimes.com

Bussel, A. (1981). *Bohemians & Professionals: Essays on Nineteenth-century American journalism.* Atlanta, GA: Emory University.

Buttry, S. (2006). *Training Tracks: When does Sloppy Attribution Become Plagiarism?* American Press Institute, September 20. Retrieved September 20, 2006, from www.americanpressinstitute.org

Cable News Network (2005). *Larry King Live* [Cable program, June 2]. Transcript retrieved June 6, 2005, from http://www.cnn.com

Carey, J.W. (1995). *The Struggle against Forgetting.* Speech delivered at Columbia University, New York, September. Retrieved May 25, 2005, from http://www.jrn.columbia.edu/admissions/struggle/

Carr, D. (2005). An appreciation: The Thompson style: A sense of self, and outrage. *The New York Times*, February 22. Retrieved May 31, 2005, from http://www.nytimes.com

CBS. (2005). CBS ousts 4 for Bush Guard story. *CBSNEWS.com*, January 10. Retrieved January 10, 2005, from http://www.cbsnews.com

Christians, C.G., Ferre, J.P., & Fackler, P.M. (1993). *Good News: Social Ethics & the Press.* New York: Oxford University Press.

Code, L. (1987). *Epistemic Responsibility.* Hanover, NH: Brown University Press.

Coleman, N. (2004). Nick Coleman: Blogged down in web fantasy. *Star Tribune*, September 29. Retrieved September 29, 2004, from http://www.startribune.com

Cooper, T. (1993). Lorraine Code's "epistemic responsibility," journalism, and the Charles Stuart case. *Business and Professional Ethics Journal*, 12(3), 83–106.

Cranberg, G., Bezanson, R., & Soloski, J. (2001). *Taking Stock: Journalism and the Publicly Traded Newspaper Company.* Ames, IA: Iowa State University Press.

Cronkite, W. (2004). March 9, 2004: McCarthy on "See It Now." National Public Radio. Retrieved May 31, 2005, from the LexisNexis Academic database.

Croteau, D. & Hoynes, W. (2001*). The Business of Media: Corporate Media and the Public Interest.* Thousand Oaks, CA: Pine Forge Press.

Cunningham, B. (2005). Working the fringes. *Columbia Journalism Review.* Retrieved November 29, 2005, from http://www.cjr.org

Cunningham, R.P. (1995). APME's move helps separate trash from "serious" journalists. *The Quill*, March, p. 12.

Davis, M. (1987). The moral authority of a professional code. In J.R. Pennock & J.W. Chapman (Eds). *Authority Revisited* (pp. 302–337). New York: New York University Press.

Davis, M. (1999). Professional responsibility: Just following the rules? *Business and Professional Ethics Journal*, *18*(1), 65–87.

Davis, M. (2004). The one-sided obligations of journalism. *Journal of Mass Media Ethics*, *19*(3–4), 207–222.

Davis, C. & Craft, S. (2000). New media synergy: Emergence of institutional conflicts of interest. *Journal of Mass Media Ethics*, *15*(4), 219–231.

Demers, F. (1989). Journalistic ethics: The rise of the "good employee's model": A threat for professionalism? *Canadian Journal of Communication*, *14*(2), 15–27.

Derber, C. & Schwartz, W.A. (1991). New mandarins or new proletariat? Professional power at work. *Research in the Sociology of Organizations*, *8*, 71–96.

DiCarlo, L. (2005). Can you tell blogs from "real" news? *Forbes.com*, October 11. Retrieved October 12, 2005, from http://www.forbes.com

Dicken-Garcia, H. (1989). *Journalistic Standards in Nineteenth-century America.* Madison, WI: The University of Wisconsin Press.

Donahue, J.A. (1990). The use of virtue and character in applied ethics. *Horizons*, *17*(2), 228–243.

Dowd, M. (2005). Woman of mass destruction. *The New York Times*, October 22. Retrieved October 24, 2005, from http://www.nytimes.com

Eason, D.L. (1988). On journalistic authority: The Janet Cooke scandal. In J.W. Carey (Ed.), *Media, Myths, and Narratives: Television and the Press* (pp. 205–227*).* Newbury Park, CA: Sage.

Edgerton, G. (n.d.) Edward R. Murrow (Egbert Roscoe Murrow). The Museum of Broadcast Communications. Retrieved August 29, 2005, from http://www.museum.tv/archives/etv/M/htmlM/murrowedwar/murrowedwar.htm

Ekström, M. (2002). Epistemologies of TV journalism: A theoretical framework. *Journalism*, *3*(3), 259–282.

Elliott, D. (1986). Foundations for news media responsibility. In D. Elliott (Ed.), *Responsible Journalism* (pp. 32–44). Beverly Hills, CA: Sage.

Elsaka, N. (2005). New Zealand journalists and the appeal of "professionalism" as a model of organization: An historical analysis. *Journalism Studies*, *6*(1), 73–86.

Employee ownership of media outlets [Resolution passed by The Newspaper Guild-Communications Workers of America]. *The Guild Reporter*, *72*(4), 5.

Ettema, J.S. & Glasser, T.L. (1998). *Custodians of Conscience: Investigative Journalism and Public Virtue.* New York: Columbia University Press.

Ettema, J., Whitney, D.C., & Wackman, D. (1987). Professional mass communicators. In C.R. Berger & S.H. Chaffee (Eds), *Handbook of Communication Science* (pp. 747–780). Newbury Park, CA: Sage.

Faber, B.D. (2002). *Community Action and Organizational Change: Image, Narrative, Identity*. Carbondale, IL: Southern Illinois University Press.

Fabrikant, G. & Waxman, S. (2006). Billionaires fight to buy the Los Angeles Times. *The New York Times*, November 9. Retrieved November 9, 2006, from www.nytimes.com

Fathi, N. (2005). Yesterday, an Oscar; today, covering Tehran. *The New York Times*, June 13. Retrieved June 13, 2005, from http://nytimes.com

Fedler, F. (2006). *Reporters' conflicting attitudes and struggle to unionize.* Paper presented to the Association for Education in Journalism and Mass Communication, San Francisco, August.

Fedler, F. & Pennington, R. (2003). Employee-owned dailies: The triumph of economic self-interest over journalistic ideals. *The International Journal on Media Management*, 5(4), 262–274.

Fee, F.E. (1997). *Heroes, Villains & Twice-told Tales: The Normative Power of Journalism's Worklore.* Paper presented at the annual convention of the Association for Education in Journalism and Mass Communication, Chicago, IL, August.

Fishman, M. (1980). *Manufacturing the News*. Austin, TX: University of Texas Press.

Flores, A. (1983). On the rights of professionals. In W.L. Robison, M.S. Pritchard & J. Ellin (Eds), *Profits and Professions: Essays in Business and Professional Ethics* (pp. 305–315). Clifton, NJ: Humana Press.

Folkenflik, D. (2005). Major US newspapers announce staff cuts. *All Things Considered* [National Public Radio broadcast, September 21]. Transcript retrieved September 25, 2005, from LexisNexis Academic database.

Foot, P. (1978). *Virtues and Vices and Other Essays in Moral Philosophy*. Berkeley, CA: University of California Press.

Friedland, L.A. & Nichols, S. (2002). *Measuring Civic Journalism's Progress: A Report Across a Decade of Activity.* Retrieved July 14, 2004, from http://www.pewcenter.org/doingcj/research/r_measuringcj.html

Friendly, F. (1981). Disclosure of two fabricated articles causes papers to re-examine their rules. *The New York Times*, May 25, p. A7.

Futrelle, D. (1997). Anchors away. *Salon Magazine*, May 5. Retrieved September 29, 1998, from http://www.salonmagazine.com

Gallagher, M. (1982). Negotiation of control in media organizations and occupations. In M. Gurevitch & M. Levy (Eds), *Culture, Society and the Media* (pp. 151–173). London: Methuen.

Gans, H.J. (1980). *Deciding what's News: A Study of CBS Evening News, NBC Nightly News, Newsweek and Time*. New York: Vintage.

Gardner, H., Csikszentmihalyi, M., & Damon, W. (2001*). Good Work: When Excellence and Ethics Meet*. New York: Basic.

Gewirth, A. (1985). Rights and virtues. *Review of metaphysics, 38*, 739–762.

Gieryn, T.F. (1983). Boundary-work and the demarcation of science from non-science: Strains and interests in professional ideologies of scientists. *American Sociological Review, 48*, 781–795.

Glaser, M. (2006). The case for citizen ownership of the *Los Angeles Times*. Media Shift, September 21. Retrieved September 24, 2006, from www.pbs.org.

Glasser, T.L. & Ettema, J.S. (1991). Investigative journalism and the moral order. In R.K. Avery & D. Eason (Eds), *Critical Perspectives on Media and Society* (pp. 203–225). New York: Guilford.

Golden, T. (2005). In U.S. report, brutal details of 2 Afghan inmates' deaths. *The New York Times*, May 20. Retrieved September 4, 2005, from http://www.nytimes.com

Goodman, H. (2005). Journalism's shining moment is long gone. *South Florida Sun-Sentinel*, June 2. Retrieved June 6, 2005, from http://www.sun-sentinel.com

Gough, P.J. (2005). Emotional Rather blasts "new journalism order." Reuters, September 19. Retrieved September 21, 2005, from http://news.yahoo.com

Graber, D. (2003). The media and democracy: Beyond myths and stereotypes. *Annual Review of Political Science*, 6, 139–160.

Guersney, L. (2005). Hurricane forces New Orleans newspaper to face a daunting set of obstacles. *The New York Times*, September 5. Retrieved September 5, 2005, from http://www.nytimes.com

"Guild rallies nationally to protest jailing, push for federal shield law" (2005). *The Guild Reporter*, July 15. Retrieved July 22, 2005, from http://www.newsguild. org/gr/index_archive.php?volume=72&number=7

Gurnett, K. (2005). No shelter from storm of issues: Observers say Katrina disaster could be time to reflect on societal values. Albany (NY) *Times Union*, September 9. Retrieved November 12, 2005, from http://www.timesunion.com

Haas, T. & Steiner, L. (2001). Public journalism as a journalism of publics: Implications of the Habermas-Fraser debate for public journalism. *Journalism*, 2(2), 123–147.

Habermas, J. (1989). *The Structural Transformation of the Public Sphere: An Inquiry into a Category of Bourgeois Society* (T. Burger & F. Lawrence, Trans.). Cambridge, MA: MIT Press.

Hallin, D. (1992). The passing of the "high modernism" of American journalism. *Journal of Communication*, 42(3), 14–25.

Hanson, C. (2005). The "scoop" heard 'round the world. Sadly. *Washington Post*, May 22. Retrieved September 4, 2005, from http://www.washingtonpost.com

Hendry, J. (2004). *Between Enterprise and Ethics: Business and Management in a Bimoral Society*. Oxford: Oxford University Press.

Henry, M. (2005). The age of byline counts and corporate loyalty. Letter posted on *Romenesko*, February 23. Retrieved February 25, 2005, from http://poynter.org/ forum/view_post.asp?id=8931

Hodges, L.W. (1986). Defining press responsibility: A functional approach. In D. Elliott (Ed.), *Responsible Journalism* (pp. 13–31). Beverly Hills, CA: Sage.

Hodges, L.W. (Ed.) (2004). Tearing down the walls. [Cases and commentaries]. *Journal of Mass Media Ethics*, 19(3–4), 293–306.

Hursthouse, R. (2001). *On Virtue Ethics*. Oxford: Oxford University Press.

Irwin, W. (1911). The American newspaper I: The power of the press. *Collier's: The National Weekly*, January 21, 46(18), 15, 18.

Isikoff, M. & Barry, J. (2005). Guantanamo: A scandal spreads. *Newsweek*, May 9.

Retrieved September 8, 2005, from LexisNexis Academic database.

Jackson, R. (1998). *Searching for a Voice of Authority: Journalism between the Modern and Postmodern.* Paper presented to the Association for Education in Journalism and Mass Communication, Baltimore, MD, August.

Jacobs, J. (1992). *Systems of Survival: A Dialogue on the Moral Foundations of Commerce and Politics.* New York: Vintage.

Janis, I.L. & Mann, L. (1977). *Decision Making: A Psychological Analysis of Conflict, Choice, and Commitment.* New York: Free Press.

Jennings, B. (1991). The regulation of virtue: Cross-currents in professional ethics. *Journal of Business Ethics, 10,* 561–568.

Jermier, J.M. (1988). Sabotage at work: The rational view. *Research in the Sociology of Organizations, 6,* 101–134.

Johnson, P. (2005). "Even a few sentences can have a huge effect." *USA TODAY,* May 17. Retrieved September 4, 2005, from http://www.usatoday.com

Johnston, P. (2004). Outflanking power, reframing unionism: The Basic strike of 1999–2001. *Labor Studies Journal, 28*(4), 1–24.

Jurkowitz, M. (2005). The Romenesko effect: How a media web site is changing the face—and pace—of media culture. *The Boston Phoenix,* August 26–September 1. Retrieved August 25, 2005, from http://www.bostonphoenix.com

Kassing, J.W. (1997). Articulating, antagonizing, and displacing: A model of employee dissent. *Communication Studies, 48,* 311–332.

Kelley, R.E. (1992). *The Power of Followership: How to Create Leaders People Want to Follow and Followers who Lead Themselves.* New York: Doubleday.

Kelly, K.J. (2007). Time drops bomb. *New York Post,* January 19. Retrieved January 22, 2007, from www.nypost.com

Kendrick, A. (1969). *Prime Time: The Life of Edward R. Murrow.* Boston, MA: Little, Brown.

Keough, C. & Lake, R.A. (1993). Values as structuring properties of contract negotiations. In C. Conrad (Ed.), *The Ethical Nexus* (pp. 171–189). Norwood, NJ: Ablex.

Klaidman, S. & Beauchamp, T.L. (1987). *The Virtuous Journalist.* New York: Oxford University Press.

Kovach, B. (2005). Guest essay: Three keys to newspaper survival. In Project for Excellence in Journalism, *The State of the News Media 2005: An Annual Report on American Journalism.* Retrieved December 5, 2005, from http://www.stateofthemedia.org/2005/narrative_newspapers_guest.asp

Kovach, B. & Rosenstiel, T. (2001). *The Elements of Journalism: What Newspeople Should Know and the Public Should Expect.* New York: Three Rivers Press.

Krause, E.A. (1996). *The Death of the Guilds: Professions, States, and the Advance of Capitalism, 1930 To The Present.* New Haven, CT: Yale University Press.

Kurpius, D.D. (2003). Bucking a trend in local television news: Combating market-driven journalism. *Journalism, 4*(1), 76–94.

Kurtz, H. (2005). At last, reporters' feelings rise to the surface. *Washington Post,* September 5. Retrieved September 10, 2005, from http://www.washingtonpost.com

Lambeth, E.B. (1992). *Committed Journalism: An Ethic for the Profession* (2nd edn). Bloomington, IN: Indiana University Press.

Larson, M.S. (1977). *The Rise of Professionalism: A Sociological Analysis*. Berkeley, CA: University of California Press.

"LA Times" cuts 160 jobs, shuts 2 papers, in round of cutbacks. (2004). *Editor & Publisher*, June 21. Retrieved July 30, 2004, from http://www.editorandpublisher.com

Leonnig, C.D. (2005). Time will surrender reporter's notes. *Washington Post*, July 1. Retrieved July 1, 2005, from http://www.washingtonpost.com

Louis, T. (2004). Thoughts before BloggerCon 2—blogs and journalism. *TNL.NET*, April 16. Retrieved May 25, 2005, from http://www.tnl.net/blog/entry/Thoughts_before_BloggerCon_2_-_Blogs_and_Journalism

Lucas, G.R. (1988). Agency after virtue. *International Philosophical Quarterly*, *28*(3), 293–311.

MacIntyre, A. (1979). Corporate modernity and moral judgment: Are they mutually exclusive? In K.E. Goodpaster & K.M. Sayre (Eds), *Ethics and Problems of the 21st Century* (pp. 122–135). Notre Dame, IN: University of Notre Dame Press.

MacIntyre, A. (2007). *After Virtue* (3rd edn). Notre Dame, IN: University of Notre Dame Press.

Madigan, N. (2005). TV reporter files lawsuit against Sinclair over his dismissal. *Baltimore Sun*, December 9. Retrieved December 27, 2005, from www.baltimoresun.com

Madore, J.T. (2004). Newsday to cut staff by 100. *Newsday*, November 11. Retrieved November 11, 2004, from http://www.newsday.com

Maguire, H. (2002). Psychological contracts: Are they still relevant? *Career Development International*, *7*(3), 167–180.

Mail call: Furor and fallout. (2005). *Newsweek*, June 6. Retrieved September 8, 2005, from LexisNexis Academic database.

Manly, L. & Jensen, E. (2005). Public TV and radio to receive big grants. *The New York Times*, May 10. Retrieved May 10, 2005, from http://www.nytimes.com

Manly, L. & Johnston, D. (2005). Reporter says he first learned of C.I.A. operative from Rove. *The New York Times*, July 18. Retrieved July 18, 2005, from http://www.nytimes.com

Manly, L. & Kirkpatrick, D.D (2005). Top editor at Time Inc. made a difficult decision his own. *The New York Times*, July 1. Retrieved July 1, 2005, from http://www.nytimes.com

Matheson, D. (2004). Weblogs and the epistemology of news: Some trends in online journalism. *New Media & Society*, *6*(4), 443–468.

Matoesian, G.M. (1999). The grammaticalization of participant roles in the constitution of expert identity. *Language in Society*, *2*, 491–521.

May, L. (1996). *The Socially Responsive Self: Social Theory and Professional Ethics*. Chicago, IL: University of Chicago Press.

May, W.F. (1986). Professional ethics, the university, and the journalist. *Journal of Mass Media Ethics*, *1*(2), 20–31.

May, W. (2001). *Beleaguered Rulers: The Public Obligation of the Professional*. Louisville, KY: Westminster John Knox Press.

McCollam, D. (2005a). Attack at the source. *Columbia Journalism Review*, March/

April. Retrieved October 19, 2005, from http://www.cjr.org

McCollam, D. (2005b). Uncharted waters. *Columbia Journalism Review*, November/ December. Retrieved November 17, 2005, from http://www.cjr.org

McDevitt, M. (2003). In defense of autonomy: A critique of the public journalism critique. *Journal of Communication, 53*(1), 155–164.

McKercher, C. (2002). *Newsworkers Unite: Labor, Convergence, and North American Newspapers.* Lanham, MD: Rowman & Littlefield.

McManus, J.H. (1994). *Market-driven Journalism: Let the Citizen Beware?* Thousand Oaks, CA: Sage.

McManus, J.H. (1997). Who's responsible for journalism? *Journal of Mass Media Ethics, 12*(1), 5–17.

McNair, R. (1998). *The Sociology of Journalism.* London: Arnold.

Merrill, J.C. (1989). *The Dialectic in Journalism.* Baton Rouge, LA: LSU Press.

Meyer, P. (2004a). Journalism must evolve—and quickly: Science provides a model, with objectivity at its heart. *USA TODAY*, September 23. Retrieved September 23, 2004, from http://www.usatoday.com

Meyer, P. (2004b). *The Vanishing Newspaper: Saving Journalism in the Information Age.* Columbia, MO: University of Missouri Press.

Milbank, D. (2005). My bias for mainstream news. *Washington Post*, March 20. Retrieved March 21, 2005, from http://www.washingtonpost.com

Miller, R. (2005). *Moral Courage: Definition and Development*, March. Retrieved June 26, 2005, from http://www.ethics.org/pdfs/erc_moralcourage_rmiller.pdf

Miller, W.L. (1997). *Journalism as a High Profession in Spite of Itself.* Paper presented at the Freedom and Responsibility in a New Media Age conference, Dallas, TX, February 18.

Mitchard, J. (1997). Jerry Springer debacle illustrates TV's spiraling bad taste. *Houston Chronicle*, May 21. Retrieved September 29, 1998, from http://www.chron.com

Mitchell, G. (2004). Reporters trail badly (again) in annual poll on honesty and ethics. *Editor & Publisher*, December 7. Retrieved December 7, 2004, from http://www.editorandpublisher.com

Mitchell, G. (2005). After "NY Times" probe: Keller should fire Miller—and apologize to readers. *Editor & Publisher*, October 15. Retrieved October 17, 2005, from http://www.editorandpublisher.com

Montopoli, B. (2005). The story of the story isn't the story at all. *CJR Daily*, May 17. Retrieved May 18, 2005, from http://www.cjrdaily.org

Moore, G. (2002). On the implications of the practice-institution distinction: MacIntyre and the application of modern virtue ethics to business. *Business Ethics Quarterly, 12*(1), 19–32.

Moriarty, G. (1995). Ethics, *ethos* and the professions: Some lessons from engineering. *Professional Ethics, 4*(1), 75–93.

Morrissey, B. (2004). Forbes.com removes paid links from news stories. *DMNews: The online newspaper of record for direct marketers*, December 3. Retrieved December 3, 2004, from http://www.dmnews.com

Mosedale, M. (2006). Hell no, we don't blow: KSTP refuses ad that criticizes the media for reporting bad news about Iraq. *City Pages*, February 22. Retrieved January 22, 2007, from http://www.citypages.com

Mueller, M., Page, C., & Kuerbis, B. (2004). Civil society and the shaping of communication-information policy: Four decades of advocacy. *The Information Society, 20*, 169–185.

Murrow, E.R. (2004). Ed Murrow's speech at the 1958 RTNDA convention, Chicago, IL, October 15, 1958. *Media Ethics, 16*(1), 4, 18–22.

Murrow, E.R. (2005). Report from Buchenwald. Jewish Virtual Library. Retrieved August 29, 2005, from http://www.jewishvirtuallibrary.org/jsource/Holocaust/murrow.html

Nelson, B.J. (1984). *Making an Issue of Child Abuse: Political Agenda Setting For Social Problems.* Chicago, IL: University of Chicago Press.

Nerone, J. & Barnhurst, K.G. (2003). US newspaper types, the newsroom, and the division of labor, 1750–2000. *Journalism Studies, 4*(4), 435–449.

Newton, L.H., Hodges, L., & Keith, S. (2004). Accountability in the professions: Accountability in journalism. *Journal of Mass Media Ethics, 19*(3–4), 166–190.

Nichols, B. (2005). "Newsweek" retracts Koran desecration story. *USA TODAY*, May 16. Retrieved May 17, 2005, from http://www.usatoday.com

Nord, D.P. (1985). The ideology of the press: Why press bias isn't always what it appears to be. *The Cresset*, December, *49*, 14–17.

Nord, D.P. (2001). *Communities of Journalism: A History of American Newspapers and their Readers.* Urbana, IL: University of Illinois Press.

Nordenstreng, K. (1998). Professional ethics: Between fortress journalism and cosmopolitan democracy. In *The Media in Question: Popular Cultures and Public Interests* (pp. 124–134). London: Sage.

Oakley, J. & Cocking, D. (2001). *Virtue Ethics and Professional Roles.* Cambridge: Cambridge University Press.

Ohmann, R. (2003). *Politics of Knowledge: The Commercialization of the University, The Professions, and Print Culture.* Middletown, CT: Wesleyan University Press.

O'Keefe, K. (2005). Ethical firestorm: A month after one of the greatest natural disasters in American history, experts grade the media on their coverage of Hurricane Katrina. *Quill Online*, December 1. Retrieved December 1, 2005, from http://www.spj.org/quill_list.asp

Oneal, M. (2007). Zell lands Tribune: Employees to get majority stake in debt-heavy company. *Chicago Tribune*, April 3. Retrieved July 11, 2007, from www.chicagotribune.com

Pauly, J.J. (1988). Rupert Murdoch and the demonology of professional journalism. In J.W. Carey (Ed.), *Media, Myths, and Narratives: Television and the Press* (pp. 246–261). Newbury Park, CA: Sage.

Pein, C. (2005). Blog-gate: Yes, CBS screwed up badly in "Memogate"—but so did those who covered the affair. *Columbia Journalism Review*, January/February. Retrieved January 4, 2005, from http://www.cjr.org

Pellegrino, E.D. (1995). Toward a virtue-based normative ethics for the health professions. *Kennedy Institute of Ethics Journal, 5*(3), 253–277.

Pew Research Center for the People and the Press, in association with *Columbia Journalism Review* (2000). Self-censorship: How often and why; journalists avoiding the news, April 30. Report retrieved November 15, 2005, from http://people-press.org/reports/display.php3?ReportID=39

Pew Research Center for the People and the Press (2004a). *Voters Liked Campaign 2004, but too Much "Mud-slinging,"* November 11 Report retrieved November 17, 2004, from http://people-press.org/reports/display.php3?ReportID=233

Pew Research Center for the People and the Press (2004b). *Press Going too Easy on Bush: Bottom-line Pressures now Hurting Coverage, say Journalists,* May 23. Report retrieved July 30, 2004, from http://www.stateofthenewsmedia.org/journalist_survey_prc.asp

Pitts, R. (2004). Online columns viewed cautiously, but are a vital new medium. *APME Roundtables: Readers Speak (Second of Three Parts).* Retrieved November 18, 2004, from http://www.apme-credibility.org/readersspeak2004electionOct2a.html

Pomfret, J. (2006). Calif. newspaper battles ex-editors. *Washington Post,* July 20. Retrieved July 20, 2006, from www.washingtonpost.com

Potter, N.N. (2002). *How can I be Trusted? A Virtue Theory of Trustworthiness.* Lanham, MD: Rowman & Littlefield.

Powers, W. (2005a). Off message: Why blogs are like tulips. *National Journal,* February 18. Retrieved February 18, 2005, from http://www.nationaljournal.com

Powers, W. (2005b). Off message: The human touch. *National Journal,* April 1. Retrieved April 1, 2005, from http://www.nationaljournal.com

Press briefing by Scott McClellan (2005). Office of the White House Press Secretary, May 17. Transcript retrieved May 18, 2005, from http://www.whitehouse.gov/news/releases/2005/05/20050517-2.html

Prior, W.J. (2001). *Eudaimonism* and virtue. *The Journal of Value Inquiry, 35,* 325–342.

Project for Excellence in Journalism (2004). *The State of the News Media 2004: An Annual Report on American Journalism* [Executive summary]. Washington, DC: The Project for Excellence in Journalism.

Project for Excellence in Journalism (2005). *The State of the News Media 2005: An Annual Report on American Journalism.* Retrieved April 29, 2005, from http://www.stateofthemedia.org/2005/index.asp

Project for Excellence in Journalism (2006). *The State of the News Media 2006: An Annual Report on American Journalism.* Retrieved December 22, 2006, from http://www.stateofthenewsmedia.com/2006/

Putman, D. (1997). The intellectual bias of virtue ethics. *Philosophy, 72,* 303–311.

Rainey, J. (2006a). Local leaders urge owner of *The Times* to avoid cuts. *Los Angeles Times,* September 14. Retrieved September 19, 2006; from www.latimes.com.

Rainey, J. (2006b). Santa Barbara's summer of discontent sizzles toward fall. *Los Angeles Times,* September 9. Retrieved September 19, 2006, from www.latimes.com.

Rainey, J. & Mulligan, T.S. (2007). Chandlers, moguls in battle for Tribune. *Los Angeles Times,* January 18. Retrieved January 22, 2007, from www.latimes.com

Reeves, R. (1999). Rends or mends. *Trust* magazine, *2*(2), 8–14.

Rich, F. (2004). Bono's new casualty: 'Private Ryan.' *The New York Times,* November 21. Retrieved November 18, 2004, from http://www.nytimes.com.

Rich, F. (2005a). All the president's newsmen. *The New York Times*, January 16. Retrieved January 13, 2005, from http://www.newyorktimes.com

Rich, F. (2005b). We're not in Watergate anymore. *The New York Times*, July 10. Retrieved July 10, 2005, from http://www.nytimes.com

Roberts, E.L. (2004). Once impregnable, the walls are crumbling [Case commentary]. *Journal of Mass Media Ethics*, *19*(3–4), 299–302.

Robison, W.L. (1991). Subordinates and moral dilemmas. *Business and Professional Ethics Journal*, *10*(4), 3–21.

Rodgers, R.R. (2005). *"Journalism is a loose-jointed thing": A content analysis of* Editor & Publisher's *discussion of journalistic conduct prior to the* Canons of Journalism, *1901–1922*. Paper presented at the Association for Education in Journalism and Mass Communication, San Antonio, TX, August.

Roethlisberger, F.J. & Dickson, W.J. (1939). *Management and the Worker: An Account of a Research Program Conducted by the Western Electric Company, Hawthorne Works, Chicago* (with the assistance and collaboration of H.A. Wright). Cambridge, MA: Harvard University Press.

Romano, A. (2005). Sinclair critic denied unemployment pay. *Broadcasting & Cable*, April 12. Retrieved April 13, 2005, from http://www.broadcastingcable.com

Rosen, B. (1990). *Ethics Companion*. Englewood Cliffs, NJ: Prentice-Hall.

Rosen, J. (2003). PRESSthink: An introduction. *PRESSthink*, August 18. Retrieved November 16, 2004, from http://journalism.nyu.edu/pubzone/weblogs/Pressthink/2003/08/18/introduction_ghost.html

Rosen, J. (2004a). Journalism is itself a religion: Special essay on launch of The Revealer. *PRESSthink*, January 7. Retrieved January 27, 2005, from http://journalism.nyu.edu/pubzone/Weblogs/pressthink/2004/01/07/press_religion.html

Rosen, J. (2004b). BloggerCon: Discussion notes for, "What is journalism? And what can weblogs do about it? *PRESSthink*, March 25. Retrieved May 20, 2005, from http://journalism.nyu.edu/pubzone/weblogs/pressthink/2004/03/25/con_prep.html

Rosen, J. (2004c). Brain food for BloggerCon. *PRESSthink*, April 16. Retrieved May 20, 2005, from http://journalism.nyu.edu/pubzone/weblogs/pressthink/2004/04/16/con_prelude.html

Rosen, J. (2004d). Are we headed for an opposition press? *PRESSthink*, November 3. Retrieved November 15, 2004, from http://journalism.nyu.edu/pubzone/weblogs/pressthink/2004/11/03/op_press.html

Rosen, J. (2005a). After trust me journalism comes openness: Rather report released. *PRESSthink*, January 10. Retrieved January 27, 2005, from http://journalism.nyu.edu/pubzone/Weblogs/pressthink/2005/01/10cbs_rept05.html

Rosen, J. (2005b). Trust-me journalism and the Newsweek retraction. *PRESSthink*, May 22. Retrieved June 8, 2005, from http://journalism.nyu.edu/pubzone/weblogs/pressthink/2005/05/22/trst_nwsk.html

Rosen, J. (2006). Editing horizontally: Thanks to Reuters, NewAssignment.Net can hire someone. *PRESSthink*, September 20. Retrieved September 20, 2006, from http://journalism.nyu.edu/pubzone/weblogs/pressthink/2006/09/20/rts_gft.html

Rosenthal, P. (2005). Ways being found to get news out. *Chicago Tribune*, August 31. Retrieved August 31, 2005, from http://www.chicagotribune.com

Rosenstiel, T. (2003). *Snob Journalism: Elitism versus Ethics for a Profession in Crisis*. Speech delivered at Ruhl Symposium in Eugene, OR, May 22. Retrieved April 23, 2004, from http://www.journalism.org/resources/publications/articles/oregon.asp

Russo, T.C. (1998). Organizational and professional identification: A case of newspaper journalists. *Management Communication Quarterly*, *12*(1), 72–111.

Rutten, T. (2006). Regarding media: Effects of cost-cutting are felt in Reuters flap, *Los Angeles Times*, August 19. Retrieved September 19, 2006, from http://www.latimes.com

Rymes, B. (1995). The construction of moral agency in the narratives of high-school drop-outs. *Discourse & Society*, *6*, 495–516.

Safire, W. (2005). The depressed press. *The New York Times*, January 17. Retrieved January 17, 2005, from http://www.nytimes.com

Salcetti, M. (1995). The emergence of the reporter: Mechanization and the devaluation of editorial workers. In H. Hardt & B. Brennen (Eds), *Newsworkers: Toward a History of the Rank and File* (pp. 48–74). Minneapolis, MN: University of Minnesota Press.

Samuels, R. (1998). The end of an era at WMAQ-TV … Broadcasting in Chicago: 1921–1989 (and thereafter), with special emphasis on the NBC Studios in the Merchandise Mart, an on-line Museum of Broadcast History, October 8. Retrieved, 2007, from http://www.richsamuels.com/nbcmm/era.html

Sandel, M.J. (1989). *Liberalism and the Limits of Justice*. Cambridge: Cambridge University Press.

Schlesinger, P. (1977). Newsmen and their time-machine. *British Journal of Sociology*, *28*(3), 336–350.

Schudson, M. (1978). *Discovering the News: A Social History of American Newspapers*. New York: Basic.

Schudson, M. (1988). What is a reporter? The private face of public journalism. In J.W. Carey (Ed.), *Media, Myths, and Narratives*. Newbury Park, CA: Sage.

Schudson, M. (1998). *The Good Citizen: A History of American Civic Life*. New York: The Free Press.

Schudson, M. (2001). The objectivity norm in American journalism. *Journalism: Theory, Practice and Criticism*, *2*(2),149–170.

Scocca, T. (2005). CBS News report a prototype for journo-purges. *The New York Observer*, January 17. Retrieved January 12, 2005, from http://www.observer.com

Scott, W.G. & Mitchell, T.R. (1988). The problem or mystery of evil and virtue in organizations. In Kolenda, K. (Ed.), *Organizations and Ethical Individualism* (pp. 47–72). New York: Praeger.

Seeger, M.W. (1997). *Ethics and Organizational Communication*. Cresskill, NJ: Hampton.

Seelye, K.Q. (2005a). Bloggers as news media trophy hunters. *New York Times*, February 14. Retrieved February 14, 2005, from http://www.nytimes.com

Seelye, K.Q. (2005b). Newsweek apologizes for report of Koran insult. *New York Times*, May 16. Retrieved May 16, 2005, from http://www.nytimes.com

Seelye, K.Q. (2005c). At newspapers, some clipping. *New York Times*, October 10. Retrieved October 10, 2005, from http://www.nytimes.com

Seelye, K.Q. (2005d). Snared in the web of a Wikipedia liar. *New York Times*, December 4. Retrieved December 12, 2005, from http://www.nytimes.com

Seelye, K.Q. (2006). Times to reduce page size and close a plant in 2008. *New York Times*, July 18. Retrieved July 20, 2006, from http://www.nytimes.com

Seelye, K.Q. & Lewis, N.A. (2005). Newsweek says it is retracting Koran report. The *New York Times*, May 17. Retrieved May 17, 2005, from http://www.nytimes.com

Seelye, K.Q. & Steinhauer, J. (2006). At Los Angeles Times, a civil executive rebellion. *New York Times*, September 21. Retrieved September 21, 2006, from http://www.nytimes.com

Sessions Stepp, C. (2004). Journalism without profit margins. *American Journalism Review*, October/November. Retrieved October 5, 2004, from http://www.ajr.org

Shafer, J. (2005). Don't fear the blogger: Will somebody please help the *Los Angeles Times'* David Shaw get a grip? *Slate*, March 28. Retrieved March 29, 2005, from http://www.slate.com

Shaw, D. (2005a). Do bloggers deserve basic journalistic protections? *Los Angeles Times*, March 27. Retrieved March 28, 2005, from http://www.latimes.com

Shaw, D. (2005b). There are reasons for the breakout of duplicity. *Los Angeles Times*, May 8. Retrieved May 10, 2005, from http://www.latimes.com

Shepard, A.C. (2006). Newspapers: Profits versus public trust. *Chicago Tribune*, July 2. Retrieved July 7, 2006, from www.chicagotribune.com

Shoemaker, P.J. & Reese, S.D. (1991). *Mediating the Message: Theories of Influence on Mass Media Content.* New York: Longman.

Siebert, F.S., Peterson, T., & Schramm, W. (Eds). (1956). The social responsibility of the press. In *Four Theories of the Press: The Authoritarian, Libertarian, Social Responsibility and Soviet Communist Concepts of what the Press Should be and do.* Urbana, IL: University of Illinois Press.

Silverman, D. (1993). *Interpreting Qualitative Data: Methods for Analyzing Talk, Text and Interaction.* London: Sage.

Simpson, J. (2005). One of the best. *BBC News*, August 8. Retrieved December 13, 2005, from http://news.bbc.co.uk/go/pr/fr/-/2/hi/americas/4131186.stm

Smolkin, R. (2005). A source of encouragement. *American Journalism Review*, June/July. Retrieved July 19, 2005, from http://www.ajr.org

Smolkin, R. (2006). Life with Brian. *American Journalism Review*, August/September, pp. 29–39.

Smythe, T.C. (1980). The reporter, 1880–1900: Working conditions and their influence on the news. *Journalism History*, *7*(1), 1–10.

Socolow, M. (2005). Can newspapers reverse their decline? *Baltimore Sun*, August 14. Retrieved August 19, 2005, from http://www.baltimore.com

Soloski, J. (1989). News reporting and professionalism: Some constraints on the reporting of the news. *Media, Culture and Society*, *11*, 207–228.

Staggenborg, S. (1991). *The Pro-choice Movement: Organization and Activism in the Abortion Conflict.* New York: Oxford University Press.

Stern, R.J. (2006). *Stakeholder Theory and Media Management: An Ethical Framework for News Company Executives.* Paper presented to the Association for Education in Journalism and Mass Communication, San Francisco, CA, August.

Strupp, J. (2005). 'Gannon' fodder: Real White House reporters weigh in. *Editor & Publisher*, February 10. Retrieved February 11, 2005, from http://www.editorandpublisher.com

Sullivan, W.M. (1995). *Work and Integrity: The Crisis and Promise of Professionalism in America.* New York: HarperBusiness.

Thomas, E. (with Yousafzai, S., Moreau, R., Hussain, Z., Conant, E., & Hores H, A.). (2005). How a fire broke out. *Newsweek*, May 23. Retrieved September 8, 2005, from LexisNexis Academic database.

Thomas, E. & Isikoff, M. (with Hirsh, M.) (2005). The Qur'an question. *Newsweek*, May 30. Retrieved September 8, 2005, from the LexisNexis Academic database.

Thompson, J.D. (1967). *Organizations in Action: Social Science Bases of Administrative Theory.* New York: McGraw-Hill.

Thornton, B. (2000). The moon hoax: Debates about ethics in 1835 New York newspapers. *Journal of Mass Media Ethics*, *15*(2), 89–100.

Thornton, B. (2002). *Murrow Squares off Against McCarthy: Not many Brickbats or Bouquets from the Audience.* Paper presented to the Association for Education in Journalism and Mass Communication, Miami Beach, FL, August.

Tompkins, A. (2005). Mapes: Decision to air National Guard story was made by CBS superiors, including Heyward: Heyward stays, five others leave CBS "60 Minutes Wednesday" after report released. *Poynteronline*, January 10. Retrieved January 11, 2005, from http://www.poynter.org

Toppo, G. (2005). Education dept. paid commentator to promote law. *USA TODAY*, January 6. Retrieved October 10, 2005, from http://www.usatoday.com

Tracy, J.F. (2004). The news about the newsworkers: Press coverage of the 1965 American Newspaper Guild strike against *The New York Times. Journalism Studies*, *5*(4), 451–467.

Tucher, A. (1994). *Froth & Scum: Truth, Beauty, Goodness and the Ax Murder in America's First Mass Medium.* Chapel Hill, NC: University of North Carolina Press.

Tuchman, G. (1972). Objectivity as strategic ritual: An examination of newsmen's notion of objectivity. *American Journal of Sociology*, 77, 660–679.

Tuchman, G. (1977). The exception proves the rule: The study of routine news practices. In P.M. Hirsch, P.V. Miller, & F.G. Kline (Eds), *Strategies for Communication Research* (pp. 43–62). Beverly Hills, CA: Sage.

Tuchman, G. (1978). Objectivity as strategic ritual: An examination of newsmen's notions of objectivity. *American Journal of Sociology*, 77, 660–679.

Underwood, D. (1993). *When MBAs Rule the Newsroom: How the Marketers and Managers are Reshaping Today's Media.* New York: Columbia University Press.

Unverifiable Leak Leads to Modern WHCA. (n.d.). Retrieved May 6, 2005, from http://www.whca.net/history.html

Von Drehle, D. (2005). FBI's No. 2 was "Deep Throat." *Washington Post*, June 1. Retrieved June 1, 2005, from http://www.washingtonpost.com

Ward, S.J.A. (2005). *The Invention of Journalism Ethics: The Path to Objectivity and Beyond*. Montreal: McGill-Queen's University Press.

Watson, J.C. (2005). *Civic Responsibility: A Casualty of Ethical Principle*. Paper presented the Association for Education in Journalism and Mass Communication, San Antonio, TX, August.

Weaver, D.H., Bean, R.A., Brownlee, B.J., Voakes, P.S., & Wilhoit, G.C. (2007). *The American Journalist in the 21st Century: U.S. News People at the Dawn of a New Millennium*. Mahwah, NJ: Lawrence Erlbaum.

"We have to think big": Stressing leadership, sector conference adopts ambitious program (2005). *The Guild Reporter*, May 20, *72*(5), 1–2.

Weick, K. E. (1995). *Sensemaking in Organizations*. (D. Whetten, Series Ed., Foundations for Organizational Science). Thousand Oaks, CA: Sage.

Weisberg, J. (2005). Who is a journalist? Anybody who wants to be. *Slate*, March 9. Retrieved March 15, 2005, from http://www.slate.com

Wells, M. (2005). Viewpoint: Has Katrina saved US media? *BBC News*, September 5. Retrieved September 10, 2005, from http://news.bbc.co.uk/go/pr/fr/-/1/hi/world/americas/4214516.stm

Wershba, J. (n.d.) Edward R. Murrow and the time of his time. *Eve's Magazine*. Retrieved August 29, 2005, from www.evesmag.com

Whitaker, M. (2005). The editor's desk. *Newsweek*, May 23. Retrieved September 8, 2005, from the LexisNexis Academic database.

Williams, J. (2005). Virginia state officials begin making amends for the closing of schools in 1954 after Supreme Court ended school segregation. *National Public Radio*, June 24. Retrieved June 26, 2005, from the Lexis Nexis Academic database.

Winch, S. P. (1997). *Mapping the Cultural Space of Journalism: How Journalists Distinguish News from Entertainment*. Westport, CT: Praeger.

Withey, M.J. & Cooper, W.H. (1989). Predicting exit, voice, loyalty, and neglect. *Administrative Science Quarterly*, *34*, 521–539.

Woestendiek, J. & West, P. (2005). When reporters were heroes: The scandal that brought down a president marked the heyday of print journalism. *Baltimore Sun*, June 5. Retrieved June 7, 2005, from http://www.baltimoresun.com

Woodward, K. (2002). In the beginning, there were the holy books. *Newsweek*, February 11. Retrieved September 8, 2005, from the Lexis Nexis Academic database.

Wyatt, W.N. (2006). *Media Literacy as Trust Builder: How Media Education Can Foster Critical and Sympathetic News Audiences*. Paper presented to the Association for Education in Journalism and Mass Communication, San Francisco, CA, August.

Zagzebski, L.T. (1996). *Virtues of the Mind: An Inquiry into the Nature of Virtue and the Ethical Foundations of Knowledge*. New York: Cambridge University Press.

Zelizer, B. (1993). Journalists as interpretive communities. *Critical Studies in Mass Communication*, *10*, 219–237.

Zipser, A. (2004). Journalists under fire as never before. *The Guild Reporter*, *71*(12), 1, 4.

Index